# Waterside Walks

## 70 Walks Along the
## Canals and Rivers of Britain

### Edited by Euan Corrie

**Waterways World**
Burton-on-Trent

Published by Waterways World Ltd
The Well House, High Street, Burton-on-Trent,
Staffordshire DE14 1JQ, England

British Library Cataloguing In Publication Data
A catalogue record for this book is available from the British Library.

ISBN 1 187002 01 6

Cover design by Grant Rose, photograph of the Llangollen Canal by Peter
Ivermee
Maps by Janet Hoult
Typeset by M-J-P, Doveridge, Derbyshire
Printed and bound in the United Kingdom by Page Bros, Norwich

# Contents

Introduction   7

Key Map   11

A Brief History of the Inland Waterways   12

Key to Map Symbols   15

1   **Caledonian Canal**   Loch Oich to Loch Ness
*Colin Tucker*   16

2   **Caledonian Canal**   Banavie & Corpach – Circular
*Carol Lawrence*   18

3   **Forth & Clyde Canal**   Clydebank to Bowling
*Colin Tucker*   20

4   **Forth & Clyde Canal**   Maryhill to Kirkintilloch
*Guthrie Hutton*   22

5   **Edinburgh & Glasgow Union Canal**   Linlithgow to Falkirk   *Guthrie Hutton*   24

6   **Lancaster Canal**   Lancaster to Glasson Dock
*Colin Tucker*   26

7   **The Pocklington Canal**   Canal Head to Melbourne
*David Slater, revised by John Lower*   28

8   **Leeds & Liverpool Canal**   Shipley to Bingley
*Tony Pierce, revised by Tim Young*   30

9   **Leeds & Liverpool Canal**   Appley Bridge to Wigan
*Dennis Needham*   32

10   **Rochdale Canal**   Sowerby Bridge to Hebden Bridge
*John Lower*   34

11   **Rochdale Canal**   Mills Hill to Rochdale
*Frank Shackleton*   36

12   **Rochdale Canal**   In Manchester
*Joseph Boughey*   38

13   **Huddersfield Narrow Canal**   Huddersfield to Marsden
*Tony Pierce, revised by Dennis Needham*   40

14   **Huddersfield Narrow Canal**   Greenfield to Diggle
*David Slater, revised by John Lower*   42

15   **Huddersfield Narrow Canal**   Ashton to Stalybridge
*Joseph Boughey*   44

16 **Barnsley Canal** Walton to Notton
*David Slater, revised by John Lower* 46

17 **Manchester, Bolton & Bury Canal** Pendleton to Clifton
*Joseph Boughey, revised by Frank Shackleton* 48

18 **Peak Forest Canal** Marple Flight
*Stephen Barrett, revised by Rodney Corrie* 52

19 **Sheffield Canal** Sheffield to Rotherham
*Dave Dawson* 54

20 **Chesterfield Canal** Staveley to Chesterfield
*John Lower* 56

21 **Chesterfield Canal** Shireoaks to Worksop
*Louise Mathurin, revised by John Lower* 58

22 **St Helens Canal** Earlstown to Bank Quay, Warrington
*Joseph Boughey* 60

23 **Shropshire Union Canal** Ellesmere Port to Chester
*Dennis Needham* 62

24 **Shropshire Union Canal** Acton to Hurleston
*Joseph Boughey* 64

25 **Trent & Mersey Canal** Kidsgrove to Sandbach
*Tom Foxon* 66

26 **Trent & Mersey and Macclesfield Canals** Kidsgrove to
Congleton *Dennis Needham* 68

27 **Trent & Mersey Canal** Stoke to Barlaston
*Dennis Needham* 70

28 **Trent & Mersey and Staffs & Worcs Canals** Colwich to
Stafford *Dennis Needham* 72

29 **Trent & Mersey Canal** Shardlow Circular
*John Roddis* 74

30 **Caldon Canal** Etruria to Stockton Brook
*Dennis Needham* 76

31 **Caldon Canal** Cheddleton to Froghall
*Ann Lee* 78

32 **Cromford Canal** Bullbridge to Langley Mill
*David Slater, revised by Mike Harrison* 80

33 **Llangollen Canal** Chirk to Llangollen
*Dennis Needham* 82

34 **Llangollen Canal** Ellesmere to Hampton Bank
*Joseph Boughey* 84

35 **Montgomery Canal** Frankton to Maesbury Marsh
*Ann Lee* 86

36 **Montgomery Canal** Four Crosses to Welshpool
*Ann Lee* 88

37 **Montgomery Canal** Aberbechan to Garthmyl
*Ann Lee* 90

38 **Shrewsbury & Newport Canal** Newport – Out and Back
*Joseph Boughey* 92

39 **Grantham Canal** Gamston to Cropwell Bishop
*David Slater, revised by Jack Lynam* 94

40 **BCN**  Cannock and Anglesey Circular
   *David Sewell*                                                96
41 **BCN**  Tame Valley Locks
   *Joseph Boughey, revised by John Lower*                       98
42 **BCN**  Dudley No2 Canal
   *John Lower*                                                 100
43 **BCN**  Birmingham to Smethwick
   *Patrick Thorn*                                              104
44 **Stourbridge and Staffs & Worcs Canals**  Stourbridge to
   Kinver   *Chris Dyche*                                       106
45 **Ashby Canal**  Shackerstone to Shenton
   *John Cormack*                                               108
46 **Coventry Canal**  Foleshill Road to Bedworth
   *David Sewell*                                               110
47 **Worcester & Birmingham Canal**  Tardebigge to Stoke
   Works  *'Walshy'*                                            112
48 **Stratford and Grand Union Canals**  Lapworth Circular
   *Carol Lawrence*                                             114
49 **Stratford Canal**  Lapworth to Wilmcote
   *David Sewell*                                               116
50 **Norfolk Broads: River Waveney**  Beccles to Geldeston
   *Barry Green*                                                118
51 **Well Creek**  Upwell and Outwell Circular
   *Barry Green*                                                120
52 **Little Ouse**  Thetford to Brandon
   *Barry Green*                                                122
53 **River Lark**  Bury St Edmunds to Lackford
   *Barry Green*                                                124
54 **River Avon**  Stratford-upon-Avon to Marlcliff
   *David Bolton*                                               126
55 **Grand Union Canal**  Blisworth to Northampton
   *Dennis Needham*                                             128
56 **Grand Union Canal**  Tring Summit
   *David Cragg*                                                130
57 **Swansea Canal**  Clydach to Ynysmeudwy
   *Patrick Moss and Julia Edwards*                             132
58 **Thames & Severn Canal**  Thames Head and the Golden
   Valley   *Tony Davis*                                        134
59 **River Thames and Oxford Canal**  Oxford Circular
   *Colin Ward*                                                 136
60 **River Thames**  Molesey to Walton
   *Louise Mathurin*                                            138
61 **Kennet & Avon Navigation**  Limpley Stoke to Bath
   *John Cormack*                                               140
62 **Kennet & Avon Navigation**  Seend to Devizes
   *Dennis Needham*                                             142
63 **Kennet & Avon Navigation**  Kintbury to Great Bedwyn
   *Ruth Parry*                                                 144

64 **Basingstoke Canal**  Odiham to The Hatch
   *Dennis Needham*                                    146

65 **River Wey**  Guildford to Godalming
   *Louise Mathurin*                                   148

66 **Bude Canal**  Out and Back or Circular
   *Gerry Hollington*                                  150

67 **Bridgwater & Taunton Canal**  Bridgwater Circular
   *Gerry Hollington*                                  152

68 **Tavistock Canal**  Tavistock to Lumburn
   *Gerry Hollington*                                  154

69 **Exeter Ship Canal**  Exeter to Starcross
   *Tony Davis*                                        156

70 **Itchen Navigation**  Winchester to Eastleigh
   *David Foster*                                      158

# INTRODUCTION

This is the first collected volume of Waterside Walks, all of which have been published in *Waterways World*. All the walks have been fully revised and updated using the collected expertise of many well-known contributors to the magazine. In a few cases the original authors were unable to undertake this task and we are grateful to them for allowing their work to be critically examined by others as well as to the present authors for stepping in so ably.

We hope that this volume is not too heavy to travel comfortably in your rucksack or anorak pocket, but that it will at the same time provide a choice of inland waterway exploration in all parts of the country. We hope too, that you will enjoy the variety of writing and interests of the different authors and may be able to travel further afield to walk all the routes explored by your favourite author.

## SO ... WHAT IS A 'WATERSIDE WALK'?

These suggested routes follow the remit of *Waterways World* magazine (see page 160). They feature inland navigations, avoiding tidal water or our major lakes and reservoirs. Some of the waterways you will see are man made, some are rivers whose surroundings range from the lush meadows and orchards of Shakespeare's Avon to the manicured lawns of the Thames. There is peace and quiet for those with an interest in the plentiful wildlife on Scotland's Caledonian Canal or city centre industrial archaeology in Manchester or Birmingham. If you want to see boats, the Llangollen Canal is one of our busiest holiday routes; if you prefer to relive the commercial past other routes, such as the Barnsley, are only just beginning to display the influence of the restoration movement and will not be navigable until the twenty first century.

## HOW TO USE THIS BOOK

The key map on page 11 will help you to locate walks in your chosen area. There is a good spread throughout the waterway system but you can also make your choice between the rural and built up, or busy and un-navigable, waterways as you read the detailed descriptions before setting out.

Each description starts with notes which will allow you to see at a glance the distance involved. Few of these walks require any serious gradients to be tackled since they are generally on towpaths alongside canal water which is flat! Only at locks will a slight rise or fall, occasionally a few steps, be encountered. Where the walks leave the water's edge and encounter less regulated paths the fact is clearly pointed out in the description.

Every walk is provided with a map (not always to scale) which we have tried to keep as clear and uncluttered as possible. With this in mind, the route of the walk is not shown where it is almost entirely along a clearly defined towpath. (The key to these is on page 15) Should you crave greater detail or the names of distant hills we have listed the appropriate Ordnance Survey Landranger Maps which you may also find useful if driving to the start point. For this reason too, we include the grid reference of this spot. We have also provided suggestions for parking your car.

Almost all these Waterside Walks are designed to connect with suitable public transport to return you to the start; of the rest, most are circular but just a few have lost their train or bus services. We have felt that these were sufficiently attractive and interesting routes to justify their retention in this book although they may require some lateral thinking and the use of two cars. For details of rail services we recommend the use of the 24-hour national rail enquiries link line on 0345 48 49 50. Other transport information is detailed alongside each walk but do check before setting out as services are constantly changing.

## MORE WALKS

Please let us know if you find any changes or have any suggestions for improvements to the descriptions in this book. We are also interested in hearing from potential authors of walks which are not included here, both for future books and for publication in *Waterways World*. Notes which will help those thinking of contributing to either can be obtained from Notes For Walk Contributors, Waterways World Ltd, The Well House, High Street, Burton-on-Trent, Staffordshire DE14 1JQ in return for a stamped addressed envelope.

## WHAT TO TAKE

None of these walks are in particularly remote countryside as the construction of canals tended to introduce a corridor of civilisation to even the most rural of the areas through which they pass. However, it is always a good idea to be properly equipped for walking with suitable outdoor clothing and strong foot wear. Heavy walking boots will not be essential for the walks in this book but towpaths are laid over the puddled clay lining which keeps the water in many canals and therefore the paths do not drain in wet weather. Mud is bound to be encountered. Some of the walks involve passing through tunnels for which a torch is an essential aid. The writers have suggested routes over the top of these where any exist but naturally no special road was constructed for the boat horses when these were expected to be at work on the subterranean path.

## FINDING OUT MORE

Cross references to our canal guide books have been included in those of the walks which are on canals covered by the Waterways World Cruising Guides. These give full details of the navigational features and boating facilities of the whole of each waterway involved as well as much more of help to those undertaking longer walks than those featured in this book. Waterways World are also distributors of the Pearson's Canal Companions series of waterway route guides.

We intend that the maps included here are sufficient to follow the routes described without the need for more detailed maps but have included a note of the Ordnance Survey 1:50,000 scale Landranger Sheet numbers for any reader interested in a wider coverage. Stockists of these should also be able to provide a copy of the Ordnance Survey's free Mapping Index sheet which will allow the larger scale (1:25,000) Pathfinder series Explorer or Outdoor Leisure sheets covering any of the walks to be identified.

## FURTHER READING

Those wishing to know more about the waterway system in general and its craft, history and maintenance could do no better than obtain a copy of Edward Paget-Tomlinson's *The Illustrated History of Canal and River Navigations* (Sheffield Academic Press, 1993) from their local book shop or library. This covers all aspects of the waterways including giving a historical sketch of each waterway but full histories may be found in the learned David & Charles 'Canals of the British Isles' series.

## CONTACTS

Many of the waterways in this volume are managed by British Waterways, Willow Grange, Church Road, Watford, Hertfordshire WD1 3QA (01923 226422) who also have details of long distance walks which incorporate canal towpaths, including the Grand Union Canal Walk from London to Birmingham and the Oxford Canal Walk from Oxford to Coventry. A number of the river navigations are managed by the Environment Agency who may be contacted at Kings Meadow House, Kings Meadow Road, Reading RG1 8DQ (0118 9535000) with regard to the Thames or at Kingfisher House, Goldhay Way, Orton Goldhay, Peterborough PE2 5ZR (01733 371811) for information about their waterways in eastern England.

Hopefully there is no need to remind readers not to litter or pollute the waterways and always to observe the Country Code:

Guard against fire risks * Fasten all gates * Keep dogs under proper control * Keep to the paths across farmland * Avoid damaging fences, hedges and walls * Protect wildlife, wild plants and trees * Go carefully on country roads.

*Inclusion of the names and addresses of companies and other organisations, their services or facilities does not imply recommendation by the authors, editor or publishers. Whilst doing their best to ensure accuracy, the publishers cannot accept responsibility for any errors or omissions, or the consequences thereof.*

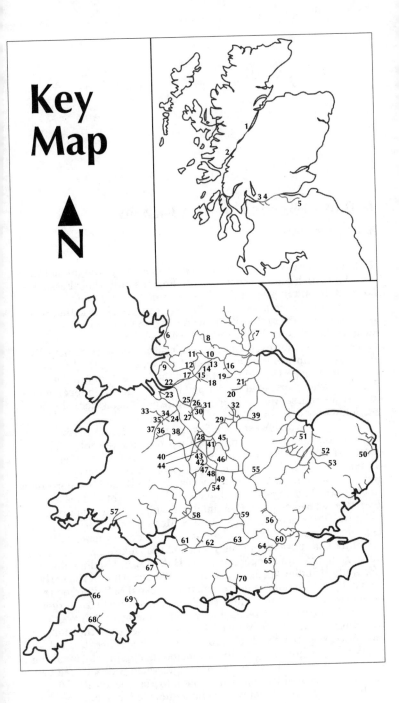

# A BRIEF HISTORY OF THE INLAND WATERWAYS

Inland waterway transport has been important to the inhabitants of the British Isles since before the Romans built their Fossdyke Navigation and improved the river Witham to serve their settlement at Lincoln. In the Middle Ages material for cathedrals was often brought to the site by water and there is evidence to suggest that this mode of transport was well known to the builders of Stonehenge. However the first 'modern' canals were principally schemes to improve the navigation of rivers, such as the Exeter Ship Canal (page 156) which parallels the Exe Estuary, in Devon. The first wholly artificial navigation in this country, independent of any river's course, was built by the Duke of Bridgewater. The first section was opened in 1761.

The Duke's Worsley estate, a few miles from the small town of Manchester, included coal pits but their product was only sold locally since transport costs ruled out much use further afield. It seems that the Duke conceived the idea of a canal to carry his coal to the growing population of Manchester. The Duke's brother-in-law Lord Gower had engaged an ill-educated millwright, James Brindley, who came from Pennine Derbyshire, to survey part of what was later to become the Trent & Mersey Canal. Brindley has been described as a 'schemer' and it is not clear how much of the credit for the subsequent construction of the Duke's canal should be apportioned to him as opposed to the Duke's Agent, John Gilbert. Certainly Brindley spent much time at Worsley Hall in the early 1760s. It had been intended to construct a canal to Salford on the river Irwell's west bank and cart coal over the river to the larger town of Manchester. It seems likely that Brindley first suggested diverting the canal into Manchester itself rather than the more easily accessed Salford. It also seems that John Gilbert tackled many of the engineering problems, including making the resulting aqueduct over the river Irwell water-tight when it threatened to collapse. The canal was opened through to Manchester in 1763.

The Bridgewater Canal was an immediate success, halving the

price of coal to Manchester's poor, as well as its industries, overnight. Plans were already in hand for the canal's extension through Cheshire to the Mersey near Runcorn where it would give access to the estuary and so to the port of Liverpool. Brindley was collaborating with the potter Josiah Wedgwood and others in projecting a canal from the Mersey to the river Trent and was soon to be involved in more projects throughout the country than he could possibly supervise personally. He eventually died before the majority were complete at only 55 years of age as a result of overwork compounded by a chill caught whilst surveying. He had meanwhile suggested a grand cross scheme of waterways to link the Mersey, Severn, Trent and Thames.

Few, however, had Brindley's breadth of vision. Whilst the waterways with which he was involved were generally built to accommodate what became known as narrowboats (71ft by 7ft), which were intended to pass from end to end of the country, most waterways were devised for purely local purposes. As a result locks and bridges were generally built to accommodate craft already in use on the nearest estuary or river navigation. Thus, even to this day, broad canals radiate from the Thames, Mersey and Humber but they are interconnected by narrow canals which accommodate boats of only 7ft beam. This situation reaches heights of incomprehensible confusion in the north where local Mersey barges (known as 'Flats') up to 74ft by 14ft 6in can enter the Bridgewater or Leeds & Liverpool canals (pages 30–33) from the Mersey. These can pass into the Rochdale Canal (pages 34–39) at Manchester but not out of it into the Ashton and Huddersfield Narrow (pages 40–45) canals which are narrow (7ft) beamed. Continuing on the wide canal over the Pennines these flats could reach the Huddersfield Broad Canal which is wide enough for them but whose locks are only 57ft long, matching the Humber barge (or 'keel'). An alternative trans-Pennine route appears on the map as the Leeds & Liverpool Canal but whereas this accommodates the long boats at its western extremity these cannot pass through the 62ft locks east of Wigan (page 32). At Leeds this canal discharges into the Aire & Calder Navigation whose locks have been, by stages, lengthened to over 450ft and can accommodate 650 ton barges!

The system gradually expanded until there were over 4,250 miles of non-tidal inland navigation on the British mainland. Much of this had a short heyday before the spread of railways. As the new-comers gained power their owners also acquired controlling interests in many navigations. Those which remained outside railway control were often paralleled by competing lines and all were affected by the fact that the ownership of through routes was often fragmented in such a way as to allow railway owners much leverage with which to divert cargoes to the new form of transport. It should not be thought, however, that canal transport was abruptly extinguished in the first half of the nineteenth century. Tonnages continued to increase in many areas as railways employed the waterways as feeders to their trains, and other navigations were modernised, or even new ones, such as the Manchester Ship Canal, built to meet the challenge. Despite this the percentage of the total goods moved on the British mainland which was carried on the waterways was dropping.

Although many independent waterway companies paid their shareholders a dividend until the majority of the system was nationalised in 1948 the wholesale destruction of the carrying industry can be traced to the sale of surplus army lorries after the First World War. Like the railways the waterways were badly hit by the speed and door-to-door convenience of artificially cheap road transport. By the late 1940s it was apparent to all concerned that the days of the carrying trade, especially on Brindley's narrow canals, were numbered and the decline was hastened by departure of many good boat crews to more secure employment 'on the land'. This was recognised by author, and boat dweller, L.T.C. Rolt whose book *Narrow Boat*, published in 1944 and in print ever since, sparked the formation of the Inland Waterways Association.

This pressure group campaigns for authorities to recognise the value of our waterways for both transport and recreational purposes. Whilst many waterways suffered from extreme neglect and even destruction in the 1950s and '60s the IWA and locally formed societies have been able to persuade all but the road transport industry and its associated government departments of the value of our waterways. Even the former Department of Transport has been soundly defeated at several Public Inquiries into proposals to further obstruct canals by cutting their channels with new roads and so destroy their potential for reopening. Roughly three quarters of the original mileage remains available to pleasure craft and enthusiasts have restoration schemes in hand for a high proportion of the remainder, although some of these are very long term. The walks in this book provide opportunities to visit active commercial and pleasure boat waterways and restoration schemes as well as to visit some that lie dormant awaiting the restorers.

# KEY TO MAP SYMBOLS

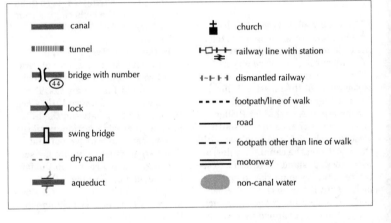

| | |
|---|---|
| canal | church |
| tunnel | railway line with station |
| bridge with number (44) | dismantled railway |
| lock | footpath/line of walk |
| swing bridge | road |
| dry canal | footpath other than line of walk |
| aqueduct | motorway |
| | non-canal water |

15

# 1 CALEDONIAN CANAL

## Loch Oich to Loch Ness

*by Colin Tucker*

**WALK TALK**

**Distance** – Aberchalder Bridge to Fort Augustus, 5½ miles.

**Start at** – Aberchalder Bridge; Grid Ref: NH 337035.

**OS Landranger Map** – 34, Fort Augustus.

**Public Transport** – Highland and Skyeways run about 5 buses per day. Times from tourist office at Fort Augustus, or bus stop.

**Car Parking** – near Fort Augustus Locks.

This is a walk between two lochs, Oich and Ness, along a stretch of the Caledonian Canal. Amidst magnificent highland scenery it offers peace and quiet, and a chance to see many of the massive Telford-designed features of the canal.

Starting at Aberchalder Bridge gives you the chance to look south west to Loch Oich, the smallest of the three lochs on the canal. It is narrow with wooded islands, and you can see the red and green marker buoys picking out the deep channel. Also notice the weir where the river Oich leaves the loch, spanned by a stone bridge. The canal bridge swings for yachts and the larger commercial craft using the canal, while headroom is sufficient for most cruisers.

Follow the western towpath and about ½ mile brings you to the well-kept Cullochy Lock. Before then is a glimpse of the river Oich as you cross a spillway from the canal – watch for puddles! The lock, like all on the canal, is electrically worked by a friendly lock keeper, but there is still evidence here of the manual equipment used until the 1960s.

Below the lock the route continues through birch and rowan woodland, with conifer plantations spreading up the hillside. At a couple of places the canal widens on the far side into shallow lagoons, not recommended for boaters. The towpath here is wide enough for a car – indeed it is the only road access for the next lock at Kytra. This is a beautiful isolated spot – a well kept lock, lock keeper's house and a couple of cottages. Add on colourful gardens beside the lock and the magnificent highland trees and hills and you have some idea of the magic of this spot. No wonder a lock keeper stayed here for nearly twenty years, saying it was so quiet he could hear the bells ringing from the Abbey at Fort Augustus two miles away.

In the early days of regular MacBraynes steamers, passengers could walk from Kytra to join their boat again at Fort Augustus. The views will have changed little since then, continuing between the hills, past another wide section, until the valley begins to broaden out and there are glimpses of white houses ahead, and a golf course on the far bank, evidence of nearing Fort Augustus. A sign stating 'Locks 600 metres' also indicates a change in the nature of the walk.

Round a bend and the locks are in sight and also plenty of boats. On the south bank cruisers may be tied up, while others may be waiting to enter the locks. The locks are a flight of five – a magnificent sight dropping down between the village shops and houses, with a tantalising glimpse of Loch Ness in the background.

It is worth following a lock full of boats down (or up) the locks. You will be in the company of plenty of gongoozlers of all nationalities (even the odd Scot!) for this is a big tourist attraction. The boats – maybe over ten at a time – are marshalled by the lock keeper and rope hauled from lock to lock by the crews. As an 'expert' it can be fun listening to the comments of the tourists – "can the boats go up as well as down?" – being a not atypical question asked by a Canadian lady!

It takes about an hour to work through the locks, giving you time to shop – food, souvenir, chandlery – or to eat and drink at the Lock Inn. By then the boats may be leaving the bottom lock and through another swing bridge. If this has to be opened then queues of road traffic quickly build up. Below the bridge the canal is in a small cutting. To the south is the Abbey, source of those bells which chime every quarter of an hour in a rather minor key, and the mooring of the *Royal Scot*, providing regular trips onto Loch Ness – a chance for some monster hunting perhaps! On the other bank, moorings are provided, well used by cruisers and yachts. At the end of this stretch are moorings for larger craft – I have seen a huge yacht from Denver USA and navy vessels tied up here, next to British Waterways' barge *Muriel* and tug.

The view now changes completely. Beyond you is Loch Ness – 24 miles long, about a mile wide and about 900ft deep. Depending on the weather you may see anything from sunlit blue glassy water to what resembles the North Sea in a gale – even in summer the wind can whip up plenty of white horses on the loch, and Thomas Telford's little lighthouse at the canal entrance must have been a welcoming sight to many a boater.

Thus in 5½ miles you will have seen the many facets of the Caledonian Canal – the use of lochs, rivers, large stone-built locks, single and staircase, swing bridges, cruisers, yachts, larger commercial shipping and magnificent highland scenery. A walk to enjoy and remember.

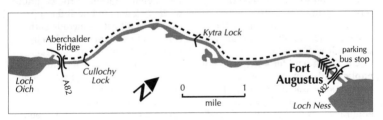

17

# 2 CALEDONIAN CANAL

## Banavie & Corpach – Circular

*by Carol Lawrence*

**WALK TALK**
**Distance** – 3¼ miles.
**Start at** – Banavie Staircase Locks; Grid Ref: NN 115771.
**OS Landranger Map** – 41, Ben Nevis & Fort William.
**Public Transport** – Alight at Banavie or Corpach stations on the Fort William–Mallaig Railway.
**Car Parking** – Signposted 'Neptune's Staircase' from the A830 Fort William–Mallaig road.

From the car park at Banavie Staircase Locks go up the path and steps to the towpath, arriving at about the centre of the staircase of locks. A board gives brief historical details and the fact that the construction workers coined the term 'Neptune's Staircase'.

The canal was proposed by the government – unlike other canals in Britain it was a national undertaking paid for entirely out of public funds. One motive for construction was to alleviate unemployment and discourage emigration following the Highland clearances. Another was the threat of the Napoleonic navy; it would be a strategic route for our navy. Work started in 1803 and the canal opened in 1822. It is 60 miles long: 38 miles of natural lochs and 22 manmade.

Turn right, and go down the track towards the two swing bridges. Taking due care, cross the road and then the railway. The towpath continues beyond the railway between gorse and blackberry bushes, well surfaced and wide, curving to the right, with moorings near two water points.

The next locks are a little way beyond the moorings – Corpach Double Lock, a staircase of two. For securing boats there is a variety of swivelling hooks and hefty bollards. Locks are a standard 150ft by 35ft; the size and proportions were dictated by the shape of contemporary sailing vessels, wide in relation to length.

The area between the locks and Corpach Sea Lock is Corpach Basin. The wharf no longer has cranes – visiting craft are equipped with derricks for self operation. Corpach railway station is alongside the wharf area. The Sea Lock gives access to Loch Eil (a dead end to the right) and Lock Linnhe to the left, and thence to the Atlantic Ocean.

At the Sea Lock is a canal office where entering craft pay their dues. Nearby, a pair of flagpoles for the Canadian and Scottish flags flank a panel giving details of the twinning of the Caledonian and Rideau canals. Similarities include both connecting a number of lakes by artificial channels, and military reasons for their construction.

The Sea Lock was lengthened to 203ft in the 1960s to allow larger craft to enter the basin – the original gate position can be seen. When I walked this route the coaster *Danica Four* from Nakskov in Denmark arrived with only 3ft to spare for length. She delivers 1,100 tonnes of wood pulp in 100-tonne bales three times per month for the nearby Corpach paper mill.

Note the lighthouse on the pier end, cross over the Sea Lock by the top gates, and return by the other towpath. The town on the far side of the loch is Fort William. Ben Nevis rises above it directly ahead. Mature trees screen a housing estate called Caol below the slight embankment.

At the foot of the major staircase Banavie station is just beyond the signal box, from which railway staff control the rail bridge. Carefully cross the railway and the road again to regain the towpath by the road-bridge control office, occupied by BW personnel. The climb begins. Eight locks, each with a rise of 8ft, lift the canal 64ft in about ½ mile. This must rank as the most magnificent staircase of locks in Britain, but the scale of its surroundings demeans its grandeur.

Robert Southey, the poet laureate, described the Banavie staircase in 1819: 'The greatest piece of such masonry in the world and the greatest work of its kind beyond all comparison'.

At the third lock chamber are the footings of a long-dismantled swing bridge – indicating the original alignment of the main road.

Mechanisation of the locks was completed in 1969 – nowadays gates and sluices are operated from control panels. The gates were moved by capstans, four of which remain (disconnected) in situ at the next set of gates – one capstan would open a gate, the other one would close it. When a lock chamber is empty the hole from which the chain connecting gate to capstan emerged can be seen. Long poles were put in each of the capstan's four apertures and the lock keepers pushed them round.

Near the top of the staircase is a cluster of canal buildings including an exhibition occupying the original sawpit and a yacht chandlery shop, emphasising that this is primarily a waterway for sea-going craft. The hire cruisers that frequent Loch Ness and the northern stretches of the canal are not permitted to traverse the Banavie staircase.

The Glasgow to Fort William railway opened in 1894 and the branch to Banavie a year later. At the foot of the embankment, adjacent to the top lock, is the old station building, now a private house. Passengers would walk up to the canal and embark on one of the express paddle steamers to reach Inverness.

At the top of the locks just beyond the existing wooden landing stage the route of the track is visible where the railway came up to the level of the canal. The wagons that struggled up this steep slope only carried cargo, a service that ceased in 1919.

Cross over the top gates and proceed downhill to the car park – the imposing bow-fronted lock keepers' houses on the right were designed by Thomas Telford, the canal's engineer.

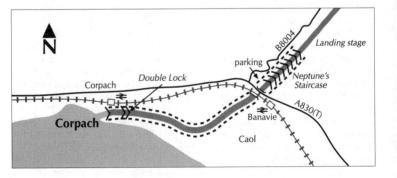

# 3 FORTH & CLYDE CANAL

## Clydebank to Bowling

*by Colin Tucker*

**WALK TALK**

**Distance** – Clydebank to Bowling, 4 miles (plus ½ mile to Bowling Station).

**Start at** – Kilbowie Road, Clydebank; Grid Ref: NS 497704.

**OS Landranger Maps** – 63, Firth of Clyde and 64, Glasgow.

**Guide** – *Forth & Clyde Canal Guidebook*, revised edition 1991, with updates; from East Dunbartonshire Cultural Services, William Patrick Library, 2 West High Street, Kirkintilloch, Glasgow G66 1AD.

**Public Transport** – Rail: Bowling to Singer, served every ½ hour (not Sundays) by trains from Glasgow Queen Street. Bus: Regular service – Bowling to Clydebank.

The western end of the Forth & Clyde Canal provides the route for this walk. It starts in Clydebank, where a low-level bridge crosses the canal at Kilbowie Road. The view to the left here is of traditional Clydebank – the big cranes of the former John Brown's shipyard and the tenement houses – while the right shows the new, with the modern industries of Clydebank Business Park (on the site of the old Singer factory) and, beyond, high rise flats. Ahead, however, are the Kilpatrick Hills, layered outpourings of lava, promising more pleasant views.

The canal here is reedy, especially where the railway dives under it – perhaps this had encouraged the moorhens I saw to settle here. Unsightly post-war housing now flanks the left, kept back by spiky railings, but then newer housing takes its place on both sides, linked by a new footbridge built to resemble an old one. A sharp turn left and you are faced with a sad sight – Dumbarton Road crossing at ground level. Pause here if you wish, for 100 yards on your right is the Horse & Barge, with interesting painted sign. (You could start the walk here, returning to Dalmuir Park Station.)

Over the road the canal turns west and the views become kinder with trees on either side. Soon the first bascule bridge is reached. Bridges of various kinds feature on this walk, for ahead can be seen the graceful and fragile looking Erskine Bridge opened in 1971 to replace a chain ferry across the Clyde. But before we pass under its 180ft clearance we reach a steel swing bridge with cottage alongside. This bridge provides access to the main road, and also the Lussa Glen Steakhouse.

Then past a lock, with derelict top gates showing evidence of paddle gear, and on past Old Kilpatrick, where a second lift bridge, with attendant cottage and family of swans, provides a feature of interest. Beyond here the Clyde is immediately to your left, glimpsed through trees and bushes, while the Kilpatrick Hills now loom immediately to the right.

The canal and towpath bend round left to reveal a scene contrasting with the disused section. For now Bowling is reached, where the canal links with the river Clyde. The canal broadens out and on the right is a new landing stage next to the Custom House, a pointer to the canal's former importance. The lock gates are smartly painted and one could almost believe traffic still plied up to Maryhill and beyond.

Below the lock are the canal basins, separated by a railway embankment with huge girder

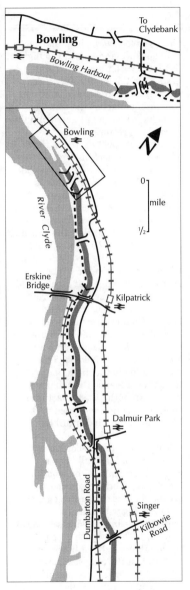

swing bridge and another bascule bridge. The upper basin is now almost empty; gone are the craft in various states of repair and disrepair, some ready to put to sea while others used to suggest a reluctance to move at all judging from mossy mooring ropes and attempts to become submarines! In the lower basin a variety of boats are moored, ranging from small cruisers and yachts to larger definitely sea-going vessels. Two sets of locks lead out from the canal into the Clyde. The original one is now derelict, but the newer one is in working order, with huge balance beams about thirty feet in length. It is a pleasant landscape spot, with views looking over Bowling Harbour down the Clyde beyond the former Scott's shipyard, birthplace of some 'puffers', to the widening Firth of Clyde.

Return under the railway bridge and signs point you in the direction of the main road and public transport for your return journey. These signs also tell you that your walk has been along part of the Glasgow to Loch Lomond Cycleway, a scheme set up by the Scottish Development Department in 1984 to make use of disused railways, riverbanks and towpaths for walkers and cyclists. So you will not be alone on this walk, but the cyclists do not 'intrude' into your walk which through the scheme is also suitable for those with prams and those in a wheelchair.

# 4 FORTH & CLYDE CANAL

## Maryhill to Kirkintilloch

*by Guthrie Hutton*

**WALK TALK**

**Distance** – Maryhill Top Lock to Kirkintilloch Townhead, 7½ miles.

**Start at** – Maryhill Top Lock; Grid Ref: NS 565690.

**OS Landranger Map** – 64, Glasgow.

**Guide** – *Forth & Clyde Canal Guidebook*, revised edition 1991, with updates; from East Dunbartonshire Cultural Services, William Patrick Library, 2 West High Street, Kirkintilloch, Glasgow G66 1AD.

**Public Transport** – Glasgow City Centre to Maryhill: Strathclyde Buses No 61 from Argyle St; No 60 & 1 from George St. Kirkintilloch to Glasgow: Strathclyde No 33; Kelvin Central buses various to Buchanan St Bus Station.

**Trip Boat** – Restaurant boats *Lady Margaret* and *Caledonian* operate all year, *Caledonian* doubles as trip boat in the summer season.

(*Ferry Queen* has done her job and may not operate next season – the Society will probably not replace her and concentrate on more needy areas with smaller boats!)

The Forth & Clyde Canal was closed in 1963, yet despite some major obstructions to navigation it is still largely intact. The towpath however is ideal for a walk into the country.

So, take a bus to the top of Maryhill Road. Get off beside the (disappointing) White House pub and follow the sign pointing to the canal along a path to the west of the pub. Within a few strides you will find yourself crossing the tail of the Maryhill Top Lock and looking to left and right at one of the finest legacies of Glasgow's industrial past.

It seems an odd thing to do at the start of a walk to go the wrong way, but if you feel compelled (and you will) go down and look at the flight of five locks with the slipway and drydock of the former Kelvin dock halfway down and the magnificent Kelvin Aqueduct at the foot. The locks have all been re-gated and the water level restored to the intermediate pounds giving the flight an operational look in contrast to the shallowed, weedy water above the top lock. From here the walk to Kirkintilloch is all on one level beside a canal restricted in headroom halfway along by a low bridge.

The first landmark is the aqueduct over Maryhill Road. It was built in 1881 to replace the smaller original which was identical to the aqueduct over Lochburn Road at Stockinfield Junction. Here the towpath from Maryhill goes along the Glasgow Branch Canal to Port Dundas, so to continue out along the main line you have to go down a side ramp and cross under the aqueduct. This interruption to the main line towpath is because the canal was first cut from the East Coast into Glasgow and not continued past Maryhill to the Clyde until ten years later.

The old run down soot-blackened tenements of Maryhill have now mostly been replaced by modern housing. At Ruchill, golf course greenery offers a pleasant change before giving way to an unprepossessing housing scheme at Lambhill. The towpath goes under the old Balmore Road lifting bridge to reveal, at the almost majestic elevation of street level, a splendid stables built in the 1820s for the 'swifts'.

After Lambhill the town quickly, almost magically, changes to countryside. The Campsie Hills lie ahead and, all around, trees, small plants and even the weeds in the canal, seem to have a fresher, more natural look. The change is quickly emphasised at Possil Loch and its associated marshland which serves as a canal feeder, but it is perhaps more significant as a Site of Special Scientific Interest for its unique plant and insect life, a remarkable oasis on the edge of a great city.

The canal is now broad and fringed with water lilies, attractions once spoiled by the aptly named Wilderness refuse tip, now thankfully closed. Ahead is Bishopbriggs.

The road over the low bridge here interrupts the towpath (take care crossing it) beyond the canal is relatively busy.

This is a very attractive section of canal that steadily improves the closer you get to Cadder, where the canal cottages, an old mill and a historic church combine with graceful mature trees to create a picturesque, private and tranquil world. It was not always so, for here the Roman Empire built its most northerly frontier, the Antonine Wall, and an overgrown remnant of it can be seen on the offside rising high out of the canal. The canal banks are lined with stones quarried from the Roman fort behind the wall.

At Glasgow Road Bridge is another of the 1820s swifts stables which was converted into a bar and restaurant called 'The Stables' in the early 1980s. It became the focus for a canal revival when the Forth & Clyde Canal Society based a Clyde river ferry converted into a trip boat called *Ferry Queen* there. Other boats have since taken up the challenge and a jetty built to accommodate them now hosts two restaurant boats and a growing number of private boats.

A slipway built on the offside for the big boats was the first improvement to the canal since it was closed. It was necessary at the time only because the Armco culverted Glasgow Road Bridge restricted access to a slipway at Kirkintilloch, but now the bridge has been rebuilt allowing clear access to the east both for boats and pedestrians. Another pastoral section with splendid views of the Campsie Hills follows before the canal enters the town. On the offside puffers used to be repaired and launched. Today, there is the new boat house for the *Yarrow Seagull*, a trip boat specially designed for disabled people.

Townhead Bridge is a good, if melancholy, place to stop. It is a culverted mess of its former self where the clear water ends in a weed-choked pipe entry, a smelly memorial to the car-mad folly of the early '60s.

# 5 EDINBURGH & GLASGOW UNION CANAL

## Linlithgow to Falkirk

*by Guthrie Hutton*

**WALK TALK**

**Distance** – Linlithgow to Falkirk (tunnel west end), 9 miles. Tunnel to Port Maxwell, 1 mile.
**Start at** – Manse Road Bridge, Linlithgow; Grid Ref: NT 001769.
**OS Landranger Map** – 65, Falkirk & West Lothian.
**Public Transport** – Train from Edinburgh Waverley or Glasgow Queen Street stations. Local buses operate between the two towns.
**Society** – Linlithgow Union Canal Society, Manse Road Basin, Manse Road, Linlithgow EH49 6AJ.
**Remember** – A torch for the tunnel.

Just up the hill from Linlithgow station is Manse Road Basin where the Linlithgow Union Canal Society have their shop, museum and tea room. They also operate their trip boats *Victoria* and *Saint Magdalene* from here. For years boats could only go east, but the drowned culvert at Preston Road has been replaced by a new bridge. It has opened up the canal to the west where some of the Union's most magnificent and unique features can be seen on a richly varied walk. Beyond the bridge an embankment gives wonderful views back to Linlithgow and the country to the north. It too impeded navigation for years until a breach at Kettlestoun Farm was repaired.

Beyond the restored embankment, at Woodcockdale, is an old stables building now used by Sea Scouts. Ahead is the magnificent Avon Aqueduct, a cast-iron trough supported by twelve slender masonry arches. To savour it fully, scramble down the slope to the valley floor and let it tower over you – you will be impressed. At 85ft high and 900ft long, it is the longest and highest aqueduct in Scotland.

It is part of the essential character of the Union. A contour canal, winding 31½ miles from Edinburgh to Falkirk, where a flight of locks took it down to the Forth & Clyde. It is a delight to walk changing moods from wooded cuttings to open embankments, a haven for wildlife and plants of all kinds. It has few relics of an industrial past – testimony to a short unprofitable life – but just west of the aqueduct is the Causewayend Basin where an early rail/canal service between Glasgow and Edinburgh linked with the canal. It is now home to one of the many pairs of nesting swans on the canal.

At Muiravonside the bridge has been replaced by an Armco pipe restricting passage, but picnic tables have been set out beside it making it the ideal place for a rest. Just to the west is the austere but attractive Muiravonside Church.

Another drowned culvert blocks the canal at the A801, a road alive with tankers from Grangemouth Refinery. You get a good view of the refinery from the embankment east of Polmont. You get a better view of the borstal west of the town on the offside. Pity about that.

Industry once ruled at Redding. Coal was mined here – one of Scotland's worst disasters occurred at the pit in 1923 – and it was also the location of an explosives factory and chemical works. Now there is a forlorn looking industrial estate and a permanent site for travelling people. The canal returns to rural tranquillity between Redding and the Glen Village where it enters a deep cutting spanned by two high bridges. The more westerly is known as the laughin', greetin' (crying) bridge because of faces carved on the keystones. These are believed to represent contractors, the one looking east is laughing because he had an easy job while the one to the west had to construct the locks and tunnel.

The tunnel, the only one in Scotland, is not for the nervous or faint-hearted, but if you feel bold enough the experience is exhilarating. It is 700 yards long and cut from solid rock with a towpath and handrail running through it. The sound of splashing water is all around and if you don't see it first you may get a big damp. A torch is advisable. The light at the end of the tunnel never seems to get any bigger, while the light behind you gets smaller until you are out, blinking in the half light of a dank tree-lined cutting.

A path at the end of the cutting leads under the railway line to Falkirk High station, but if you have the energy, the canal continues west for another mile. Beyond Bantaskin Bridge is the impressive boathouse from where the Seagull Trust takes elderly and disabled people for trips on their *Govan Seagull*. Further on, the angled inshot, is where the locks once took the canal down to the Forth & Clyde. There is little to see now, but one chamber is visible in the undergrowth beside a rough track that runs down the line of the flight. The canal terminates beyond the lock entrance at the insignificant Port Maxwell.

The sound of the adjacent Glasgow to Edinburgh railway is a reminder of the reason for the canal's early demise and also that you have a train to catch, so retrace your steps to the station and (if you're anything like me at the end of this delightful walk) doze off happily until you return to reality at the other end.

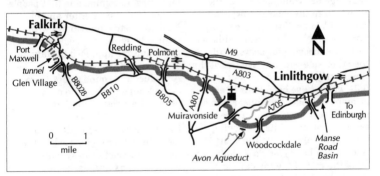

# 6 LANCASTER CANAL

## Lancaster to Glasson Dock

*by Colin Tucker*

**WALK TALK**
**Distance** – Lancaster to Galgate 5¼ miles; Lancaster to Glasson 8 miles.
**Start at** – Lancaster; Grid Ref: SD 477613.
**OS Landranger Maps** – 97, Kendal & Morcambe and 102, Preston & Blackpool.
**Public Transport** – Ribble services: Lancaster–Glasson service 139; Lancaster–Galgate services 140, 142.
**Car Parking** – Near bridge 99, Lancaster, or at Glasson or Galgate (if walk made in reverse).

The walk starts in Lancaster, where the A6 crosses the canal at Bridge 99. Walk down from the bridge on to the cobbled towpath past the Water Witch pub, converted from old stables. In summer this is a favourite mooring for boats, while on the other side you may see two of the canal's trip boats tied up near the flats which have been built in an attempt to create the appearance of warehouses. At the next bridge cross the canal on one of its few roving bridges, for apart from the short stretch you have just walked almost all of the rest of the towpath is on the seaward side. On the opposite (south) bank is the BW yard, with its facilities built in local stone. Just beyond is the remains of the building where boats used to be lifted out of the water for maintenance.

The route continues out of Lancaster, through not unpleasant terraced suburbs; if you look north from here you cannot fail to be impressed by the sight of Lancaster Castle perched atop its hill in the centre of the city.

The canal turns south at this point, and the next two miles are through a deep wooded cutting. Those who know the cuttings of the Shropshire Union will be reminded of them here, with the high stone bridges and steep tree-lined bankings. In summer it will be an avenue of green, while in autumn the turning leaves are beautiful; a winter walk would be through a myriad of stark, bare trunks and branches. There are a couple of wooden benches and tables in the cutting, useful if you reach here at lunchtime (or merely wish to rest weary feet).

At last the cutting disappears, giving way to rolling, open countryside of green fields, grazed by black and white cattle, and the occasional white-washed farm buildings, to remind one that people do live in the area. After another wooded stretch, bungalows with their tidy gardens appear on the left, heralding the approach to Galgate. The canal winds across the Conder Aqueduct and round under more stone bridges, one of the many pleasant aspects of the Lancaster Canal. At one of these, Bridge 86, there is easy access to the village of Galgate, rather dominated by the main west coast railway with its electric trains thundering across the viaduct which straddles the houses. Here it is possible to end your walk, returning by bus to Lancaster; or to obtain refreshment at the Plough Inn before continuing.

Immediately beyond Bridge 86, the canal widens out into the basin of Galgate Marina and the walker can compare the wide variety of canal cruisers tied up here, or dream about sea-going trips on the larger boats which also moor at this point. Back in the country again you need only round a couple of bends before

Lodge Hill Junction is reached. Here a number of the distinctive attractions of the Lancaster Canal – sturdy stone lock keeper's house, unusual finger-post, a delicate yet solid stone bridge, and clear, clear water – combine to make this a most pleasant and relaxing spot. At the junction your walk turns west down the Glasson Branch, while the main line continues south – it is possibly worthwhile making a short detour along it to see the unusual Double Bridge (85), one lane going to Ellel Grange and the other along the public highway.

From the top of the Glasson Branch, situated right at the junction, the canal can be seen winding its way down through the rolling green countryside, with Thurnham Hall hidden amongst trees. The locks are wide and solid, with interesting horizontal paddle gear, and the water so clear even the bottom of the lock can be seen! There is little sign of habitation on this stretch, but the views are magnificent, while in October the towpath hedge boasts enough blackberries to feed many a walker. Continue down to Glasson past the six locks, the last being located beside an old mill, powered by water from the canal. From here there is a straight walk of about ¾ mile through marshy saltings until Glasson is reached.

A long time could be spent looking round Glasson. Its features include boats; varying from small cruisers to ocean-going yachts (whose rigging provides perches for literally hundreds of birds in the evening), or perhaps a coaster unloading cargo; the locks and swing bridge leading to the dock and entrance to the Lune estuary, itself of interest either at high tide or low, when mud flats seem to stretch everywhere; and the little village streets. If you have to wait for the bus returning you to Lancaster, you could visit the post office, which sells interesting pictures of the dock and basin, or even slake your thirst with a mini-pub crawl, for Glasson boasts three pubs!

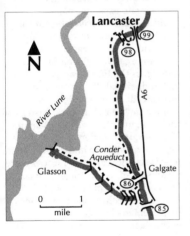

27

# 7 POCKLINGTON CANAL

## Canal Head to Melbourne

*by David Slater, revised by John Lower*

**WALK TALK**
**Distance** – Canal head to Melbourne, 5 miles.
**Start at** – Canal Head, Pocklington; Grid Ref: SE 800474.
**OS Landranger Maps** – Due to an overlap, the complete walk appears on both 105, York and 106, Market Weighton.
**Public Transport** – East Yorkshire Motor Services (01482 327146) service 195 – a very limited service.
**Car Parking** – At Canal Head and Melbourne village.
**Society** – Pocklington Canal Amenity Society, Mrs S M Nix, 74 Westminster Road, York YO3 6LY.

The Pocklington Canal runs from the river Derwent at East Cottingwith to Canal Head on the old York to Hull Turnpike Road. When proposed, prospective income from tolls ensured strong support from the then Derwent owner (Lord Fitzwilliam) and George Leather undertook the survey. Parliamentary approval was granted in 1815 and the 9½ mile canal was opened on 30th July 1818. Although cost prevented extension of the canal to Pocklington, transport of agricultural produce to the West Riding in return for lime, coal and industrial goods provided a degree of early financial success. However, trade rapidly diminished with the advent of the York to Beverley railway line through Pocklington and the York & North Midland Railway received authorisation to purchase the canal in 1847. The last commercial barge, *Ebenezer,* entered the canal in 1932 with a cargo of

roadstone and in the 1968 Transport Act the derelict canal was listed as a Remainder Waterway. Proposals to fill the canal with chalk sludge met with strong opposition and the Pocklington Canal Amenity Society (PCAS) was formed in 1969. The first of the canal's nine locks (Cottingwith) was reopened in 1971 and the restored section is now navigable to Melbourne.

This walk covers the remaining five miles between Melbourne and Canal Head. Access to Canal Head is gained from the A1079 opposite the Wellington Oak public house and is signposted 'picnic area'. Landscaping by the society has provided car parking and excellent picnic facilities and sensitive planting of trees and flowers has created an outstandingly picturesque area.

An impressive information board highlights the PCAS campaign and 21 handpainted illustrations of birds, wildflowers and insects emphasise the rich natural history of the canal and its environs. Remains of the original settlement include the lock keeper's house and a warehouse now tastefully converted into private accommodation. The piggery has been converted into a small PCAS information centre open on Sundays and members bubble with enthusiasm. At the end of the brick lined basin, Top Lock is restored and head-gates have been fitted.

Following the towpath, Silburn Lock is quickly reached, and one of the many wooden seats along the canal; a thoughtful provision for a British Waterways-designated linear walk. Traffic on the main road now becomes inaudible and colourful lichens on the lock brickwork suggest an essentially pollution free environment. The continuing route via Giles and Sandhill locks with their derelict paddle gear becomes more secluded and the canal is lined on the opposite bank by deciduous woodland containing oak, willow and chestnut. Coates Lock is the current PCAS worksite under active restoration and a notice points out that the volunteers will welcome a helping hand. Coates Bridge features restoration undertaken by British Waterways under 'Operation Bridgeguard'.

The scenery now changes in character with open skies and wide horizons, although a glance behind will reveal the distant Yorkshire Wolds. The towpath side hawthorne hedge gives way to a cleared route though wild grasses; a feature indicative of the neighbouring 'Ings'. The prominent sounds become those of birdsong and movement, only broken by distant farm tractors and occasional aircraft. In spring, mute swans may be seen nesting, and the leasing of the tree-lined Bielby Arm to York University Biology Department for research purposes seems highly appropriate. The towpath now comprises either a rough track on elevated daisy-rich embankments between canal and drainage ditches or the cleared edge of fields. A farm accommodation swing bridge has been restored with a new deck but requires the installation of a turntable to make it operative.

At last, the slow but steady march of restoration from the Derwent can be seen. Walbut Lock is fully restored complete with gates, paddle gear shrouded to modern health and safety standards and large iron hand-wheels to operate the gate paddles (locked with Leeds & Liverpool style handcuff key). These locks were built 57ft by 14ft 3in to take Yorkshire Keels but the extensive high reed beds below the skewed Walbut Bridge suggest that present day passage would be problematical. Bielby Beck suddenly appears on the towpath side, having passed under the canal. Thornton Lock is also fully restored, complete with balance beams made from railway rail and hydraulic paddlegear. Below is a new water feed to the navigated section, and the full splendour of Church Lane Bridge then comes into view with its restored mellow brickwork, curved wing walls and round buttresses.

The restored Melbourne Arm comprises the grand finale of the walk and access is obtained over a new swing bridge. The arm was officially reopened on 19th July 1987 and now boasts jetty moorings with a few resident craft and a massive new sanitary station building. The path continues into the centre of Melbourne and conveniently ends alongside the Cross Keys Inn.

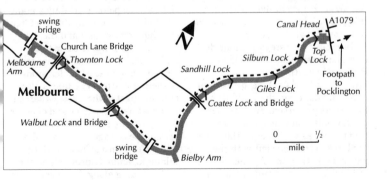

29

# 8 LEEDS & LIVERPOOL CANAL

## Shipley to Bingley

*by Tony Pierce, revised by Tim Young*

**WALK TALK**

**Distance** – Shipley to Bingley, 5 miles.

**Start at** – Shipley railway station; Grid Ref: SE 150374.

**OS Landranger Map** – 104, Leeds & Bradford; or Bradford A–Z street atlas.

**Public Transport** – Buses run from the end of the walk back to Shipley and Leeds and Bradford. Local trains from Skipton to Leeds or Bradford stop at Crossflatts and Shipley. Waterbus information is available from Apollo Canal Cruisers (01274 595915).

**Car parking** – In town centre of Shipley or at station.

Begin the walk almost opposite the exit from Shipley railway station where a signed footpath near the Black Bull public house leads you over the canal by the hauntingly named Gallows footbridge.

On reaching the towpath turn east for a short distance away from the town centre and towards the stone built Bridge 208. This is known as Junction Bridge and marks the former junction of the Leeds & Liverpool with the 3 mile Bradford Canal, long since infilled. The start of this can still be seen, as can decaying warehousing at the junction.

Retracing your steps a canalside cottage is seen near the Gallows Bridge which still carries an interesting Leeds & Liverpool Canal Company notice on the wall; it's nice to see this preserved. Further along the towpath you reach a modern bridge and, as you emerge, the centre of Shipley is on your left with the parish church on the skyline. Nearer at hand is a magnificent Salvation Army Citadel which can be seen on the opposite bank to the towpath. On

the same side as the Citadel at the water's edge stand the former BW Shipley Depot buildings. In the heyday of the canal Shipley was an important transhipment point for wool, which had to be kept dry, hence the covered loading bays still in existence. The warehouse buildings have been completely refurbished and put to new uses, including a health club, restaurant and units for offices and leisure oriented businesses.

In a section of the rebuilt warehouse Apollo Canal Cruisers have made their new home. Previously they were located just through the next bridge. They offer a variety of passenger trips including a popular licensed restaurant boat. In the summer months a waterbus service operates from here to Bingley and as you will see the 'bus' stops have been clearly marked on the towpath together with seating and linking arrangements to more conventional transport.

As you leave Shipley you may notice the remains of fencing between the towpath and the canal itself. Local legend has it that the fence was provided to prevent horses falling into the water as they passed each other on this busy stretch of canal. Local legend also has much to say about the group of cottages to your right at this point. Certainly a glance will tell you that many different ages of building exist here and the date over number 6 would seem to be authentic, but whether former stables for canal horses exist under number 9 is another matter. The tale is also told that part of the cottages served as a boatman's hostelry and of other cottages being haunted. Fact or fiction, the cottages remain and are wonderfully incongruous with the Inland Revenue Offices behind them.

Continuing along the towpath the famous mill buildings of Saltaire come into view. Built in 1850 by the philanthropic Sir Titus Salt the huge buildings having long stood empty and forlorn have now been totally rebuilt and new uses found. The mill to the right houses the Bradford Health Offices and many luxury apartments while that on the left has been converted into office space and a health club. The model village also remains intact and thriving and is well worth a diversionary visit from the canal, which passes between the Italianate church and Roberts Park with its statue of the great man.

Looking to your right you will see the river Aire with which canal and railway share the valley. Hirst Lock is soon reached with its attendant swing bridge and waterbus stop. For the next half mile or so the canal takes on a delightfully rural appearance wending its way through Hirst Wood. Oh, by the way, don't dally here after dusk: this stretch is supposedly haunted and no boatman would moor here overnight on a working run.

The end of the wood is marked by the Dowley Gap Aqueduct, a grand name for the low, seven arched structure, elegant enough but pretentious in that only two spans actually carry the canal over the river Aire. Dowley Gap Changeline Bridge brings a change of towpath sides and, soon after, the first of the 'staircase' locks is reached. On the lock keeper's house note the plaques for winning the Waterway Length Competition in 1992, '94, '95 and '96.

The Fishermans public house is very conveniently placed by the canal before you continue into Bingley. The canal actually runs through the centre of the town and access to the shops and railway station is through a hole in the wall into a carpark. On the opposite side from the towpath, factory boilers can be seen which were once fired with coal brought by the canal. The terminus of the waterbus can be reached by crossing the the road bridge. Continuing the walk, it is not long before the Bingley Three Rise is reached which, together with the Five Rise, lift the canal nearly 90ft in two giant leaps. Having reached the top of the Five Rise cross the canal and learn something of its history from the plaque on the lock keeper's cottage wall. Nearby see also the plaque for the Length Competition in 1993, the year breaking the run of plaques at Dowley Gap. Opposite the cottage are former canal stables now finding a new life. Back over the bridge note the plaque unveiled to commemorate 200 years of the canal in 1974.

No doubt you will want to spend some time at the Five Rise. The fascination never fails, but eventually tear yourself away and continue past rows of moored boats until Canal Road is seen to your left. A couple of hundred yards will lead you back to the main road with buses back to Shipley. Alternatively Crossflatts station is just along the road towards Bingley.

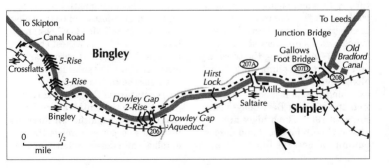

# 9 LEEDS & LIVERPOOL CANAL

## Appley Bridge to Wigan

*by Dennis Needham*

**WALK TALK**

**Distance** – Appley Bridge to Wigan, 5¹/₂ miles.

**Start at** – Appley Bridge; Grid Ref: SD 523093.

**OS Landranger Map** – 108, Liverpool.

**Public Transport** – The Manchester to Southport train service calls at Wigan and Appley Bridge. There is also a local bus service (01942 825677).

**Car Parking** – Canalside, by the bridge.

This is a well used section of towing path frequented by walkers and joggers with the addition of the latest problem: cyclists. It has been adopted by the local council and christened The Douglas Valley Way, closely following the course of that river, once the navigation from the coalfields of Wigan to the sea. The path itself is in excellent condition.

One particularly noticeable feature of this walk is the number of pubs en route; there are three within a few yards of the start. The Railway is nearest, but what about one called The Inn Between? If you try only a half in each, the end of the walk will have turned into a stagger.

From the car park by Bridge 42 turn right when facing the canal and walk only a few hundred yards before coming to the first of three swing bridges in a very short distance. Approaching the third, try and examine the piling work alongside. Although well concealed by undergrowth, it must be good. It won an award for Best Length of Piling in 1958. The bridges are allocated both numbers and names, but until almost the finish of the walk, none are identified. Is this an indication of an inactive canal society or active local vandals?

After 1¹/₂ miles of very pleasant rural scenery, your ears detect the presence of a motorway. And there it is, on top of an enormous viaduct by Dean Locks, a terrible intrusion into what was once a most delightful backwater of two locks and stone house with setts outside. Such is progress. The railway that comes into its own as return transport also crosses the canal here.

Gathurst Bridge, the next road crossing, has a pub alongside. Good food is obtainable here and the thoughtful provision of moorings and litter bins helps both boater and walker. A seat also comes in useful.

Around the next (left) corner, opposite the towing path, was the location of a colliery which once used the canal for transport. On the right just here, between canal and river, is an enormous bed of reed mace.

Another bridge, another pub: I did warn you at the start. This area is well supplied with a choice of good northern ales. By now it is possible to see the skyline of Wigan. The floodlighting towers actually belong to the soccer ground; their more famous neighbours the rugby league club are based at the far end of the town. The tall church-like tower belongs to Trencherfield Mill and is located right at the end of this walk. An arm opposite the towing path is home to quite a large selection of boats whilst the (paired) Hell Meadow Locks now hove into view. The farthest chamber is disused and derelict with clear evidence of mining subsidence.

Under the railway again, the barren nature of the land indicates quite clearly that this was once a coal mining area, although there are plans to incorporate some of the dereliction in development schemes.

There are several large lagoons on the left hand side as the walk approaches Pagefield Lock. Then a sharp left handed sweep under the (now marked) Seven Stars Bridge (the eponymous pub a few yards away) and the vista changes quite dramatically.

We have reached the area of Wigan Pier. But be careful. If you blink, you'll miss the actual thing. Built in 1822 as a waggon tippler, it's no more than a rise in the delightfully cobbled towing path. Loaded waggons were pushed along here and emptied into waiting boats. It was immortalised by George Orwell in his book *The Road to Wigan Pier* (1937) in which he set out his own particular brand of socialism. On a lighter note, it received the attention of that most Lancashire of comedians, George Formby.

There are more seats – a noticeable feature of this walk – and the redeveloped buildings around the canal. A fine pub and a museum which develops a very local theme and is called 'The Way We Were'. One exhibit is the old market stall of William Santus, a name revered by many Waterway Recovery Group gatherings. His company still exists today, manufacturing 'Uncle Joe's Mint Balls'.

The aforementioned Trencherfield Mill is just around the corner, past Pottery Changeline Bridge. This is the L&L name for a turnover bridge. There is lots to see and do in this area, well worth allowing some time for.

Leave the canal by Pottery Bridge and on joining the road turn left. Walk straight ahead into the town, past North Western railway station on the right to Wallgate station, a hundred yards further along on the left. If you plan to return by bus, turn left at Wallgate and second right. The bus station is at the top on the left.

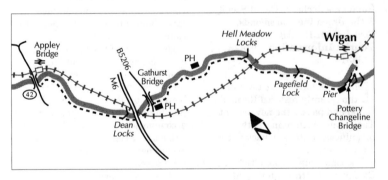

33

# 10 ROCHDALE CANAL

## Sowerby Bridge to Hebden Bridge

*by John Lower*

**WALK TALK**

**Distance** – Sowerby Bridge to Hebden Bridge, 5½ miles.

**Start at** – Sowerby Bridge Basin; Grid Ref: SE 065238.

**OS Landranger Maps** – 103, Blackburn & Burnley and 104, Leeds & Bradford.

**Public Transport** – Rail: Sowerby Bridge–Mytholmroyd–Hebden Bridge. Bus: Frequent service on A646, alight at the top of Tuel Lane and walk ½ mile down to the start. Metro Travel Centre (0113 245 7676). A vintage Halifax Corporation open-platform bus also operates on this route, service 46A (01422 343557).

**Car Parking** – At Sowerby Bridge Basin.

**Society** – Rochdale Canal Society, 3 The Broad Ing, Passmonds, Rochdale OL12 7AR.

**Tourist Information** – 01422 843831.

This walk follows the towpath of the recently restored Rochdale Canal and passes the new lock at Tuel Lane which connects this magnificent waterway back to the national system.

The canal runs deep in the narrow Calder Valley, through rugged millstone scenery, with the steep Pennine Hills on either hand. Though major development took place here during the industrial revolution, the building material chosen was local moorland stone and so woollen mills and terraced houses blend into the exciting landscape, always dominated by the high moors.

The walk commences at Sowerby (pronounced Sawby) Bridge where there is a car park in front of The Moorings public house at the canal basin. The basin forms the terminus of the Calder & Hebble Navigation, home to Shire Cruisers, and the interesting warehouses are worthy of exploration.

At the bottom of the cobbled lane, Lock No 1 of the Rochdale Canal can be seen. Access to the towing path is by a small footbridge over the lock.

Turning right, a further lock is encountered before Wharf Street Bridge, dominated by the Parish Church. Above this point were formerly two locks. After the legal closure of the canal in 1952, Church Lock was infilled in the late '60s for the Tuel Lane road improvement whilst Tim Bates Lock disappeared beneath the town centre car park. In 1996, the canal was reopened, passing through a tunnel formed from the old Wharf Street Bridge and a concrete capped Church Lock, before curving into the new, deep lock, claimed to be the deepest in the country.

Cross Wharf Street by the pelican crossing and follow round The Commercial public house to Tuel Lane Lock. Note the twin sets of bottom gates designed to use the minimum amount of water when accommodating Rochdale boats (72ft) or Calder & Hebble (57ft). A lock keeper here collects the licence fee from passing boats.

Beyond the new concrete channel lock approach, Tower Hill Bridge carries the former Tuel Lane. Beyond is a chasm between tall mills and then a short stone-lined tunnel through a rocky bluff.

Leaving Sowerby Bridge behind, the scenery becomes more rural with magnificent views across the valley. The towpath is wide and trees arch over the canal like a leafy avenue in summer. Approaching Luddenden

Foot (for this is an area of singular place names), houses which appear to be normal two-storey constructions from the road back onto the canal at four or five storeys, indicating the steepness of the hillside. In the village is an interesting aqueduct over a mountain torrent and plenty of opportunities for refreshment, including the Coach & Horses on the main road.

At two and a half miles, this pound is exceptionally long by Rochdale Canal standards and it is protected by an interesting towpath-side overflow weir. Next are the two Brearley locks and, above the top lock, a short diversion down the lane is rewarded by the sight of an attractive packhorse bridge over the river Calder.

Continuing along the towpath, the modern Armco steel culvert carrying the access road to the Moderna Industrial Estate replaces a fixed swing bridge. Unfortunately, there is no towpath through several of these new bridges. The canal now passes through Mytholmroyd (don't read this description aloud!). The A646 crosses on a stone arch bridge showing signs of being widened several times, and carrying buildings on one parapet. The next (new) bridge at Midgley

Road does have a towpath and is the nearest point to Mytholmroyd Station if it is desired to finish the walk here.

Above Broadbottom Lock, and across the main road, is Walkley's Clog Mill, where wooden footwear is still made. A small charge gains entry both to see clogs being made and also to a range of speciality and craft shops. Whether visiting Walkley's or not, the walker then has to brave crossing the A646, for a long, curved Armco tunnel ducts the canal under the road. A horse-drawn trip boat operates to Walkley's and it is interesting to watch the crew leg through the tunnel.

The road bridge above Mayroyd Mill Lock is the nearest to Hebden Bridge Railway Station, but it is worthwhile exploring this 'Pennine Centre' before returning to Sowerby Bridge. The canal passes through the middle of the town's park and on the far bank a wharf has been recreated on the site of a former petrol station, complete with slipway for visiting trailboats.

Turn right at Blackpit Lock over the lock bridge. Immediately above the lock, the canal crosses the river Calder on an aqueduct. Head into town and by the traffic lights is the tourist information office with much of local and waterway interest.

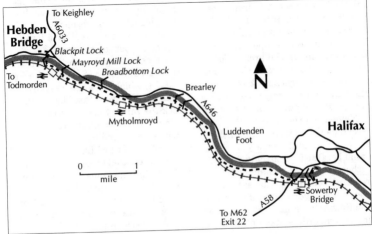

# 11 ROCHDALE CANAL

## Mills Hill to Rochdale

*by Frank Shackleton*

**WALK TALK**

**Distance** – Mills Hill to Rochdale is about 5 miles.

**Start at** – The Rose of Lancaster pub; Grid Ref: SD 889062.

**OS Landranger Map** – 109, Manchester, Geographers A–Z Manchester.

**Public Transport** – Trains on the Manchester Victoria–Rochdale–Halifax–Bradford–Leeds route and other local services stop at Rochdale and some stop at Mills Hill. Local buses connect Mills Hill directly with Manchester and Oldham. A bus journey from Rochdale to Mills Hill requires a change at Middleton. Rochdale bus station buses to Manchester and surrounding towns. (Timetable enquiries for both buses and trains 0161 228 7811.)

**Car Parking** – At both Mills Hill and Rochdale stations.

**Society** – Rochdale Canal Society, 3 The Broad Ing, Passmonds, Rochdale OL12 7AR.

The first part of this walk from Mills Hill to Castleton is through relatively open country; from there into Rochdale the scene is increasingly urban and industrial. The walk gives the opportunity to look at the industrial archaeology not only of the Rochdale Canal but also of the Manchester & Leeds Railway which closely accompanies the canal along much of this length.

Navigation rights along the Rochdale Canal were extinguished in 1952 and until recent years the canal became increasingly derelict although the water channel remained open since the sale of water is a major source of income to the Rochdale Canal Company. Much improvement has taken place more recently through the efforts of the Rochdale Canal Society and Rochdale and Oldham councils and parts of the canal which had been drained are now restored.

With car parking at both Mills Hill and Rochdale stations the walk can be made from either end. Leave Mills Hill station and turn right towards Oldham and cross the main A669 at the traffic lights. Cross the recently widened bridge over the canal and bear left along the B6195 (Haigh Lane). Take the passageway by the side of the Rose of Lancaster which leads down to the towpath on the eastern side of the canal. For the first half mile the canal follows a wide semi-circle to cross the valley of the river Irk on a small but substantial aqueduct.

After passing the restored Walk Mill and Coneygreen Locks (63 & 62) a bridge carries a track over the canal to the hamlet of Coneygreen. Remaining locks on the walk are as yet derelict. Shortly the railway crosses the canal for the first time just before the Scowcroft Lock (61). The original Stephenson railway bridge of about 1840, known locally as the Iron Donger, is still in place.

On the west side of the canal, just before Boarshaw Lock (60) are the remains of a basin formerly connected by tramroad with local collieries. Continuing towards Slattocks we come to the lowest of the six Laneside or Slattocks Locks (59–54) which raise the canal 57ft in about half a mile. Just beyond the lock the railway again crosses the canal, carried on an impressive skew bridge with winding brick courses.

Above the third Laneside Lock the canal is crossed by the A664 road. The Ship Inn stands on the corner near the now vanished site of a boat building yard and by Slattocks Top Lock (54) stands a brick lock cottage. Shortly the line of the canal is crossed on the level by the M62 motorway. The M62 westwards was built over the first section of the one and a half mile long Heywood Branch opened in 1834. The M62 crossing is a major barrier to the restoration of the canal. Various options including lowering the canal or the building of a new alignment have been considered. To regain the towpath turn right by Maiden Fold Farm then left under the M62 before turning left again.

The next locks are the three Bluepits Locks (53–51) with a changeline bridge at the middle lock. At this point we meet the busy A664 road and care is needed in crossing here. Near the Arrow Mill (1907), March Barn Bridge carries a track across the canal. The bridge is a single arched stone structure skew to the line of the canal and is believed to be the first bridge built with this type of construction.

About ¹/₂ mile from Castleton at Sudden the canal is again culverted, this time under the A627(M) and its link road Edinburgh Way. To regain the towpath turn right through the industrial estate along Gorrel's Way and pass under the motorway. On reaching the main road turn left along Queensway and cross the end of Edinburgh Way, turning left to regain the canal. This section has been landscaped with culverted bridges and in one place the canal has been narrowed. Close by stands the new headquarters of the Co-operative Retail Society.

At the Well i'th Lane Bridge the towpath again changes sides. Our walk ends just beyond the bridge which carries the A671 Oldham Road over the canal. Immediately before the bridge is the junction with the former Rochdale Branch. The western face of the bridge carries a cantilevered changeline bridge to accommodate the traffic that formerly used the branch. Cross the changeline bridge and pass under the road and leave the towpath at Moss Lower Lock (50).

If you are returning by bus to Manchester or Oldham then this is a convenient place to end the walk. For Rochdale station turn along the main road towards the town centre. On the left is a group of industrial buildings standing by the remains of the branch canal. The branch is cut short at Durham Street Bridge. Continue along Oldham Road until just before the railway bridge. Turn left and cross the iron Halfpenny Bridge of 1831 which crosses the line of the Rochdale Branch. Turn right under the railway and then left to the station. If you are returning to Mills Hill by bus then walk down Maclure Road past the Fire Station to Drake Street where you can take a bus for Middleton. Rochdale bus station can be found by continuing down Drake Street towards the town centre.

Rochdale
Moss Locks 49-50
A671
Castleton
A664
A627 (M)
N
Bluepits Locks 51-53
M62
Slattocks or Laneside Locks 54-59
Slattocks
Coneygreen Lock 62
Boarshaw Lock 60
Walk Mill Lock 63
Scowcroft Lock 61
A664
B6195
A669
A669
0     1
mile
Mills Hill

# 12 ROCHDALE CANAL

## In Manchester

*by Joseph Boughey*

**WALK TALK**

**Distance** – Manchester Victoria to Failsworth station, 5 miles (Redhill St to Ashton Road West, 3¹/₂ miles.)
**Start at** – Ancoats Lane Lock; Grid Ref: SJ 849984.
**OS Landranger Map** – 109, Manchester, Geographers A–Z Manchester.
**Public Transport** – Rail: Failsworth to Manchester Victoria.
**Society** – Rochdale Canal Society, 3 The Broad Ing, Passmonds, Rochdale OL12 7AR.

This walk includes the full length of the award-winning Rochdale Canal Park, created in 1970 by shallowing the canal to 6in depth and weiring the locks; a similar fate was planned for the Ashton Canal.

From Manchester Victoria station, find Miller Street and follow this into Swan Street and Great Ancoats Street. At Redhill Street you are beside Ancoats Lane Lock, with a handsome footbridge immediately above it. Shortly beyond this, the shallowed section beings. It is a melancholy sight, with the shallow canal filled with rubbish and looking much as it did in 1970, before the conversion began.

There was no towpath here, and horses had to be drawn along Redhill Street to the turnover bridge. A recently created path can be followed on the offside. From here ran the Potter Street arm, to which timber was delivered until the late 1930s. Just before the bridge, Radium Street runs off to the north; a hump in this road shows the line of the Bengal Arm. In the 1930s paper bales from Birkenhead were received here, with waste paper being shipped out, one of very few later

downstream traffics. These arms were to be closed just before the main canal itself, under a separate closure Act of 1950.

Beyond the bridge, some remains of the junction with the Bengal Arm can be discerned on the offside, before a concrete 'bridge' at low level, one of several pedestrian bridges provided under the shallowing scheme. Just before the next one is the site of Butler Street Mills. These were also receiving coal in 1940, and this was probably the last traffic above Dale Street, in 1944. From this point eastwards, there was very little traffic by the end of the 1930s.

After the next bridge, hump-backed and probably original, the Miles Platting locks begin. This section featured, very briefly, in the film *A Taste of Honey*, which indicated an interest by children which persists today. The Navigation Inn, nearby, is an unusual reminder of the past in an area which has been successively redeveloped. By the pound above, a playground now occupies the site of the Albert Mills, served with coal in the 1930s. A newly renovated mill stands by the third lock.

The final lock of the flight is converted to a rough weir, the next pound, supplying a dye works, being left full of water but with massed reeds and rubbish, showing the canal's pre-shallowing appearance. It is necessary to divert and walk up Varley Street to Hulme Hall Lane. Bridges carrying both roads have been replaced in the 1990s, with full navigational headroom.

Anthony Lock was also converted to a weir, and the long pound above has been narrowed to half width with four stepped weirs providing a gradient to improve flow. After a large railway bridge, the Ten Acres flight of locks begins. Beginning in older industrial surroundings, this ascends into a more modern landscape, with the canal narrowed in places and the banks planted with trees. Modern housing alongside the canal, which replaced mills and slum properties, has been carefully oriented towards it, with a walkway on the offside. Unfortunately, this scene is marred by the large quantities of rubbish dumped in the canal. Beyond a concreted swing bridge and former basin, the canal passes Newton Heath Lock and enters the last pound of the shallowed length.

About 100 yards along, the shallow section suddenly ends, at the City boundary, and the Failsworth section begins, just below Tannersfield Low Lock. The canal itself is reeded and full of rubbish, but the section into Failsworth is deep and used for fishing in places. The three locks, however, have been filled in and converted to weirs. Two lowered road bridges on this section were among the earliest blockages in the 1950s, but an attractive original brick and stone bridge survives.

This final pound was the last to be regularly maintained after through traffic collapsed in the 1920s. A later revival in trade involved maintenance sufficient only to pass narrowboats. The Marlborough Mills, which still stands by Tannersfield Top Lock, received waterborne coal until the mid 1930s. The Top Lock and 400 yards to the north suffered from subsidence which reduced the depth of the canal from 4ft to 3ft in the 1930s until repaired in 1941–43, by which time all traffic had left this length.

A large low level pipe crosses, and then Ashton Road West, another major obstacle to restoration, lies ahead, beyond a short strip of watered canal. The canal has been filled in to accommodate the Failsworth superstore, and considerable works will be required to re-site the canal. Beyond here the canal has been tidied up but not yet reopened. Since the M66 Inquiry was won in 1988 it is likely that the whole canal will be restored, and the 3-mile length in Manchester and Failsworth will form a major barrier. The M66 crossing is about a mile north. From Ashton Road West, head west, across Oldham Road into Old Road, along Hardman Lane to Failsworth station and the rail journey back to Manchester.

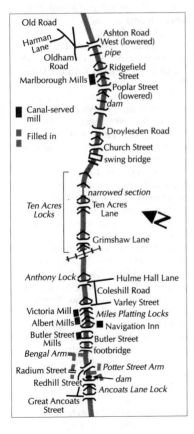

Old Road
Harman Lane
Oldham Road
Marlborough Mills

Ashton Road West (lowered)
pipe
Ridgefield Street
Poplar Street (lowered)
dam

■ Canal-served mill
■ Filled in
■

Droylesden Road
Church Street
swing bridge

Ten Acres Locks

narrowed section
Ten Acres Lane

Grimshaw Lane

Anthony Lock
Hulme Hall Lane
Coleshill Road
Varley Street

Victoria Mill
Albert Mills
Butler Street Mills
Bengal Arm

Miles Platting Locks
■ Navigation Inn
Butler Street footbridge

Radium Street
Redhill Street
Great Ancoats Street

Potter Street Arm
dam
Ancoats Lane Lock

# 13 HUDDERSFIELD NARROW CANAL

## Huddersfield to Marsden

*by Tony Pierce, revised by Dennis Needham*

**WALK TALK**

**Distance** – Huddersfield to Marsden, 7 miles.

**Start at** – Manchester Road, Huddersfield; Grid Ref: SE 135161.

**OS Landranger Map** – 110, Sheffield & Huddersfield.

**Public Transport** – Metro bus services 351 and 352 operate from close to Marsden railway station and stop outside Charlie Brown's at Longroyd Bridge. Frequent service including Sundays. Details on 01484 426313.

**Car Parking** – Side streets in Huddersfield.

**Society** – Huddersfield Canal Society, 239 Mossley Road, Ashton-under-Lyne, Lancashire OL6 6LN (0161 339 1332).

Locks by the dozen, smoke-blackened mills gaunt on the skyline and hills: an exquisite blend of beauty and starkness. In February 1985, this was the first walk published in *Waterways World* and it's as dramatic today as it was then.

The Huddersfield Narrow was a prime example of a bad investment. There were huge engineering problems to overcome: 74 locks on a 20-mile navigation and what would turn out to be the longest canal tunnel in the British Isles. It also climbed to 646ft above sea level, making it the highest as well. The Act was obtained in 1794 and through navigation between the Ashton and Huddersfield Broad canals was possible by 1811.

It was legally abandoned in 1944 but a passage was forced by Robert Aickman in 1948 as described in *Waterways World* in April and June 1974. Soon after, the locks were cascaded and bridges felled. Then came the restoration movement, people with far more vision than this writer who explored the derelict line in the late 1960s and declared it irrevocably dead.

With complete restoration and re-opening expected early in the next century the moral is: never back a horse I select.

The easiest place to start this walk is on Manchester Road – the A62 heading west – at Longroyd Bridge. Road crosses canal at this point and on the right is an access road to Charlie Brown's Auto Centre. The towpath entrance is to the left of the canalside building.

Turn left, by Lock 4E. The lock numbers on this, the east side of the summit are suffixed with the letter 'E'; those to the west with a 'W'.

The line turns sharp left at the next Lock, 5E; and what an oddity it is. Constructed integrally with Paddock Foot Aqueduct over the river, the bywash exit is in the centre of the aqueduct.

There is an air of dereliction around the canal so far. Many of the old industries that used it for transport have themselves gone. The towing path is fine here and remains so for the duration of the walk.

At the next lock, Britannia Mill looms large. This is the first Parry-style 'dark satanic mill', but certainly not the last. Beautiful? No, but, along with the many others that line this walk, full of interest. It took Parry only one verse to reach 'England's green and pleasant land'; this walk manages it almost as quickly.

The Milnsbridge flight of locks follows. A road bridge beyond Lock 11E is a fine example of sympathetic restoration. Widened of necessity, the stone is a close match to what was there before, blending seamlessly.

The valley then narrows. On the skyline to the left is an unbroken row of terraced houses with grey roofs. The main A62 is up there, but at no stage does it impinge on the peacefulness of this line. A sharp right and left takes the canal over Golcar Aqueduct which crosses the river Colne. There is a pretty horseshoe waterfall below.

Yet another mill on the left is followed by a millpond. This had a series of canal-facing openings, now filled with newer sandstone. Nearby, a carved stone milepost indicates '3 Miles'. The valley is now at its narrowest and most exquisite, but suddenly, at Lock 16E, the valley opens out with a large water meadow to the left.

The first derelict lock (21E) is reached. This is the start of a short infilled section through Slaithwaite. Surprisingly, as recently as 1938, this mill town used to be a noted spa.

The line is easy to follow through the town. There are pubs, shops and food here.

The canal route crosses a road into a landscaped area. At the far end, the parapet of a bridge indicates the route to follow. Beyond, an infilled lock complete with picnic table, and then water again. Funding from the lottery will allow restoration of this section and other major obstructions to navigation.

Civilisation retreats and the Pennine peaks dominate the far

view, although the valley sides are easing, forming pasture. At Lock 26E there are footings of what once was quite a large building; another mill. Through Waring Bottom the locks become more frequent. Yet another mill on the left has a footbridge connecting it to a row of cottages on the right bank. Built in 1860, these were mill-owned until its closure a decade ago.

Through a series of low stone bridges and by lock tails, the walk eventually arrives at Lock 42 and Marsden railway station. Leave the canal here and bear left to the bus stop.

One magnificent building some yards from the water has strong canal connections. The Marsden Mechanics holds the town's library, but is also home base for the Mikron Theatre Company. They are deservedly popular in the town, and Artistic Director Mike Lucas played a pivotal role in getting the building re-stored to use.

Although the walk is over, a short distance further is the eastern portal of Standedge Tunnel. The old keeper's cottage has been turned into a Visitor Centre with information and displays about the canal, its fascinating past and exciting future. If you really cannot walk another step, it is accessible by road.

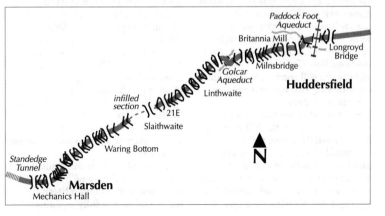

# 14 HUDDERSFIELD NARROW CANAL

## Greenfield to Diggle

*by David Slater, revised by John Lower*

**WALK TALK**

**Distance** – Greenfield station to Diggle Hotel, 3 miles.
**Start at** – Greenfield railway station; Grid Ref: SD 992047.
**OS Landranger Maps** – 109, Manchester and 110, Sheffield & Huddersfield.
**Public Transport** – Greater Manchester bus service 427 (0161 228 7811).
**Car Parking at** – Limited at Greenfield station, public car park at Diggle (SE 007080).
**Society** – Huddersfield Canal Society, 239 Mossley Road, Ashton-under-Lyne, Lancashire OL6 6LN (0161 339 1332).
**Trip Boat** – *Pennine Moonraker*, details from HCS (above).

The success of the Huddersfield Canal Society in obtaining Millennium Commission funding means that boats should soon be crossing the Pennines on this long-derelict waterway. This walk provides spectacular evidence that a great deal has already been achieved.

The Huddersfield Narrow Canal opened in 1811 and was the shortest route between Manchester and Leeds. It was never as great a commercial success as the nearby Rochdale Canal which opened seven years earlier. Hopefully, these two waterways will soon form a popular cruising ring through spectacular mountain scenery.

Starting at Greenfield railway station, walk down the hill past The Railway public house, turning sharp left round the hairpin bend. The canal is encountered at a newly constructed stone-faced bridge, built to replace an embanked culvert. To the right are old wharf cottages, but our route is to the left. Steps lead down to the towpath where we enter a world of banked deciduous trees and intermittent views of the steep Pennine Hills which hem in the valley all around.

Overlooked by tastefully renovated cottages, Halls Lock (20W) is restored and its stone tail bridge typifies many on the Huddersfield by its narrow arch and absence of towpath. Towrope grooves can be seen in the bridge parapet.

The towpath now forms a divide between canal and river Tame. A milestone engraved '13 miles' is set in the towpath wall just before the A670 High Street, crossing in Uppermill.

Above Wade Lock (21W), the towpath changes to the left-hand side, but a diversion along the main road is recommended to explore Uppermill. This attractive little town with its quaint stone architecture has become a popular tourist venue with cafés, antique and book shops. Saddleworth Museum and Tourist Information Centre is the start point for trips on the *Pennine Moonraker* narrow boat. Indeed, this was the first section of the Huddersfield Narrow to be restored, and rejuvenation of the canal and the town have gone hand in hand.

The towpath is rejoined by turning left up Moorgate Street. Once again, the Tame comes alongside, and stepping stones cross to St Chad's Playing Fields. The offside bank is lined with oak, sycamore and horse-chestnut as far as Dungebooth Lock (22W). The scene is then dominated by the slender, tall, curved Saddleworth railway viaduct, with a special skewed span to accommodate the canal.

Immediately after the viaduct, the canal crosses the Tame by a single-arch aqueduct and its colloquial name 'Old Sag' is fully explained

HUDDERSFIELD NARROW CANAL

when viewed from the picnic area opposite. The aqueduct also forms the head chamber of Lime Kiln Lock (23W). There are well preserved masons' marks in the lock stonework and more rope grooves in the bridge parapet.

Pause at the canalside Brownhill Visitor Centre which not only provides extensive information, but also has public toilets. The canal beyond Brownhill Bridge was formerly infilled and has been restored as a narrow concrete-lined channel. It then widens into a basin

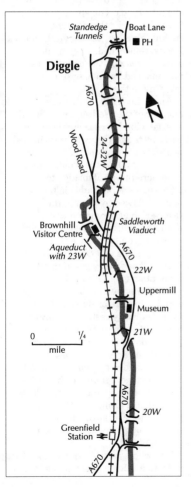

where a transhipment warehouse on the far bank has been restored by the Society.

The canal is again culverted at Wool Road and reopening is planned for 1999. At this point, the scenery changes abruptly, as the canal begins its steeper climb up the heather-rich Pennines by means of the nine lock Diggle Flight. These locks have been restored and show unique features for they were built later than the others on the canal, to coincide with the eventual opening of Standedge Tunnel. As constructed, there was a clear route for the hauling rope, for the locks are provided with single gates top and bottom and paired ground paddles top and bottom, all mounted on the side opposite to the towpath.

The 12 mile stone is in the towpath at lock 26W. The Gothic-style buildings and clocktower of the old Dobcross loom works form a prominent landmark by locks 29W and 30W. Just before the railway footbridge, look out for the leaky, mysterious pedestrian subway which crosses beneath the canal and is hidden by bushes in summer.

At Ward Lane Bridge, it is better to cross to the left-hand bank. In company with the railway, the canal now crosses high above Diggle Brook before plunging into the pitch black end of Standedge Tunnel. The date 1893 on the portal indicates that the canal tunnel was extended with the opening of the double track rail tunnel. By crossing over the railway bridge and heading down to the bus turning circle, it is possible to see a short length of original canal and the original Diggle Brook Aqueduct on the opposite side of the railway.

At over three miles, Standedge is the longest canal tunnel in Britain. It is an arduous high altitude walk over the old horse path, clearly signposted Boat Lane, next to the Diggle Hotel. Perhaps it would be wiser to walk to the latter.

# 15 HUDDERSFIELD NARROW CANAL

## Ashton to Stalybridge

*by Joseph Boughey*

**WALK TALK**
**Distance** – Ashton to Stalybridge, 2¹/₂ miles.
**Start at** – Whitelands; Grid Ref: SJ 942988.
**OS Landranger Map** – 109 Manchester, Geographers A–Z Manchester.
**Public Transport** – Greater Manchester Transport, bus routes 236 and 237, Mottram Road to Beaufort Road (0161 288 7811).
**Society** – Huddersfield Canal Society, 239 Mossley Road, Ashton-under-Lyne, Lancashire OL6 6LN (0161 339 1332).

This walk follows recently restored sections of the Huddersfield Narrow Canal through the major barrier to further restoration. This length was one of the most heavily-trafficked in the canal's later history, and the walk indicates some surviving buildings, mainly former cotton mills, which the canal once served.

From Beaufort Road, walk down Mossley Road into Scotland Street and Whitelands. Look over the bridge to the end-on junction with the Ashton Canal. Before restoration, a sewer crossing had to be removed here. As first built, there was no towpath at the road bridge, but now a small horse tunnel is followed to emerge by Ashton Lock (1W), now re-excavated. The original bridge has been widened here, and the unusual mechanism to open the restored bottom gates (also featured at Lock 2W) can be seen.

Ahead is a long straight narrow section. As built, this was Whitelands Tunnel; although later opened out, the canal was never widened. This is probably the place

where Robert Aickman's boat was holed in August 1948 on the final cruise for many years. It ends with a portal to the vanished tunnel, beyond which water intakes to Wellington Mill, on the offside, are a reminder of the disruption to water supplies which ended navigation in 1948.

The next bridge, again with no towpath, was widened after closure and had to be altered to restore navigation. The locks ahead were among the last to be 'cascaded', in the late 1970s. The short pound between marks the site where Aickman's crew, having sunk in Lock 2W, were beached. They made a causeway across the canal to a site now marked by an asbestos-clad building to the offside.

Above Lock 3W, on the offside, is another of the Wellington Mills, with a large wharf in reasonable order, perhaps that which was refurbished in 1932. It was proposed in the mid-1960s to transfer the whole length from here to Stalybridge to adjacent owners. Had this taken place, followed by piping, the restoration of through navigation would have been almost impossible.

Just beyond Clarence Street Bridge, on the offside, is Clarence Mill, still served by canal in 1899. A straight stretch follows, halfway along is the unusual Tame Aqueduct, with a separate bridge for the towpath. Early restoration proposals planned to bypass Stalybridge by locking down into the Tame here. Beyond the aqueduct, the site of a swing bridge is passed, and then Peel Street Bridge, rebuilt in the 1980s. The towpath beyond here was long blocked, but it may now be followed past rather precarious retaining walls through the new bridge at Bayley Street.

The whole canal from the aqueduct to Mottram Road was transferred to

Stalybridge Corporation in 1965, with the section to Bayley Street piped by the late 1960s. The line to Caroline Street has been re-excavated, exposing the site of a coal yard owned by the Dukinfield Coal & Cannel Co, whose colliery on the Peak Forest Canal served points on the Huddersfield Canal up to Mossley Gas Works. This area is now known as Staley Wharf.

Beyond here, you leave aside restoration and enter detective work. A ramp alongside the Wharf Tavern led up from the canal; parts of the bridge remain. The canal line, including Lock 4W, was through waste ground by the filling station and under Castle Hall Exhibition Centre. Divert via Caroline Street

and Castle Street. In the Exhibition Centre car park is another reminder of the canal. A steep ramp leads to the line of the canal, with some remains of masonry, notably the tail, visible to Castle Hall Lock (5W).

Below Lock 5W was the boiler house and part of the Castle Mills complex, served by canal into the 1890s. Look across to Castle Street; on the far side can be seen the main Castle Mills buildings. Follow Castle Street and turn up Leech Street. A paved way can soon be seen leading through bridge parapets, all that is visible of Melbourne Street Bridge.

The derelict warehouse on the left was one of the buildings forming the Stalybridge Depot of the Manchester Ship Canal Co, closed in the 1920s. From here, and from Mottram Road, the Ship Canal Company ran narrowboats which served Stockport, Marple, Runcorn, Liverpool and Todmorden in the 1890s. Across the Square, the line of the canal, including Lock 6W, disappears, and you must divert along Corporation Street and turn right into Mottram Road.

Here the bridge and lock have been filled in, but the canal starts again. Look back along the canal line; this is obliterated and built upon, but a group of older buildings includes the former Stalybridge Mills of Buckley & Newton. Until 1913 these were supplied with grain via Huddersfield, and it appears that they were supplied from Manchester into the 1920s. From the wharf itself the London & North Western Railway Company claimed to run daily services to Manchester, Huddersfield and Wakefield over a hundred years go. It will not be too long before the canal links these places once again. The site of the Mills and adjacent works which obstruct the canal line are to be redeveloped, and this may make it possible to reinstate the canal line through Stalybridge.

45

# 16 BARNSLEY CANAL

## Walton to Notton

*by David Slater, revised by John Lower*

**WALK TALK**
**Distance** – Walton To Old Royston, 3 miles. Walton to Ryhill, 4$\frac{1}{2}$ miles.
**Start at** – Shay Lane, Walton; Grid Ref: SE 356173.
**OS Landranger Map** – The complete walk appears on both 110, Sheffield & Huddersfield and 111, Sheffield & Doncaster.
**Public Transport** – Enquiries, Metroline (0113 245 7676). Note for walkers arriving by public transport, there are regular services from Wakefield to Walton and Notton Cross Roads (see map), but no route between.
**Society** – Barnsley Canal Group, 93, Swinston Hill Road, Dinnington, Sheffield S31 7RX (01909 565225).

The Barnsley Canal was another success of the eminent engineer William Jessop. Opened in 1802, it linked Barnby Basin above Barnsley with the river Calder at Heath, just below Wakefield. Trade, based on the 'coal down – corn up' practice, remained adequate despite later improvements to neighbouring road and rail facilities. However, subsidence from coal mines necessitated the canal's abandonment in 1953. Barnsley Canal Group was set up in 1984 and campaigns both for the Barnsley and Dearne & Dove canals.

The walk commences in Walton, a village 2$\frac{1}{2}$ miles south of Wakefield, on Shay Lane (B6378) at the site of the former Soap House Bridge, just to the East of the New Inn. A public footpath sign directs the way but initially the canal is infilled. The towpath is fenced from the line of the canal which forms a private driveway to several houses. A high retaining wall and embankment then supports the towpath above a modern housing estate, but stonework remains of Lock 14 coincide with a rural transformation.

The canal in fact climbed through twelve locks as it passed through Walton, Lock 11 was immediately above Soap House Bridge, but Lock 14 is the first with visible remains. Walton Top Lock (15) is intact and reveals the sizeable dimensions which permitted craft 79ft long and 14ft 10in wide. From here, the canal largely remains in water for some distance.

Walton Hall Bridge displays stop plank slots between the arch and towpath and deep towrope grooves on the metal uprights. The canal now enters Haw Park Cutting with access to Haw Park over the bridge. The cutting is dramatic with near vertical sides of iron stained rock and an overhanging blanket of trees.

Clay Royd Bridge with its stone abutments, collapsed towpath and wooden deck marks the start of a passage through rambling and unspoilt Haw Park Wood. On the sharp bend just beyond is a horizontal towrope pulley mounted on a large block of stone on the towpath edge – this was to prevent the long towrope from pulling the barge sideways into the bank as the horse disappeared round the corner.

Haw Park Mine Bridge bears the date 1828, and there is a further towrope pulley on the following sharp bend. Cold Hiendley Reservoir suddenly comes into view and its embankment, of which the infilled canal forms part, is reached by a modern footbridge over a concrete spillway. At the head of this reservoir can be seen the dam and spillway for the larger and later built (1854) Wintersett Reservoir, where sailing takes place. A feeder from this leads into the canal near the footbridge. The whole area is a haven for wildlife.

At the far side of the reservoir, the canal is back in water, but suffers from being used as a linear rubbish tip. The Chevet–Cold Hiendley road bridge has been culverted. Cold Hiendley Cutting is as spectacular as Haw Park Cutting, but the topography has resulted in wider, more gently sloping sides.

Strong, layered rock sits on an underlying weaker shale which weathers and crumbles. Large boulders become unsupported and have fallen onto the towpath and into the canal. In places the towpath must be negotiated with care. However, the walker is presented with a naturalist's dream of traditional English woodland including oak, ash, elder, beech, willow and honeysuckle. Pass beneath the appropriately named High Bridge at Old Royston and the canal-side walk ends where a railway embankment replaces an original viaduct with no towpath access over the line.

Take the steps which lead up the bank and turn back left along the track which runs along the bank top. Follow the footpath straight across the minor road. After a short distance, the unmistakable remains of a railway embankment are on the left; take the ramp up on to the embankment and follow this disused railway footpath until it leads up onto Station Road, Ryhill. Follow uphill into the village; at the give-way turn right into School Road. Just round the corner is a bus stop (same side) where the regular bus service will take you back to The New Inn, Walton. From the top deck there are splendid views across the reservoirs.

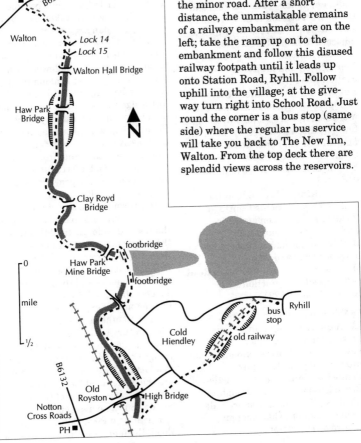

# 17 MANCHESTER, BOLTON & BURY CANAL

## Pendleton to Clifton

*by Joseph Boughey, revised by Frank Shackleton*

**WALK TALK**

**Distance** – Pendleton Church to The Beehive, Clifton, 3½ miles.

**Start at** – Pendleton Church; Grid Ref: SJ 813995.

**OS Landranger Map** – 109, Manchester, Geographers A–Z Manchester.

**Public Transport** – Although trains serve Clifton station they are so infrequent that they do not form a practical means of transport for this walk. Pendleton station is closed and the nearest station is now ¾ miles south at Salford Crescent, which is adjacent to Broad Street (A6). Swinton station is about ¾ miles from Clifton and is situated on Station Road (B5231).

Buses connect the Salford City Shopping Centre at Pendleton with Manchester, Bolton and surrounding towns. Clifton is served by bus from Manchester via Pendleton and Swinton station. Timetable Enquiries for both buses and trains: 0161 228 7811.

**Car Parking** – Available at the Salford City Shopping Centre at Pendleton. In Clifton kerbside parking is to be found near The Beehive public house at the junction of Queensway and Rake Lane. Queensway is a turn off Bolton Road (A6) opposite its junction with Station Road (B5231).

This walk involves a ruined canal, running through unprepossessing landscape, which nevertheless displays evidence of an interesting past. It begins at Pendleton Church at the junction of Broad Street (A6) and Broughton Road (A576). This is a short walk from the Salford City Shopping Centre at Pendleton.

Pass the site of Pendleton station and continue east to a second railway bridge. The canal bridge was immediately adjacent to this but has been lost in the reconstruction of the railway bridge. However, the line of the filled-in canal can still be seen. The railway was built by the canal company under an Act of 1832, an earlier plan to convert the canal to a railway having been abandoned. The line of the canal was much altered in places when the railway was built. The company amalgamated with the Manchester & Leeds Railway in 1844 and became part of the Lancashire & Yorkshire in 1845. It thus became one of the first to be taken over by a railway company.

The first section of the canal line is inaccessible and the parallel Langley Road South must be followed with diversions. The first is along Holland Street, where an extraordinary tall footbridge can be climbed. Spanning both canal site and railway, Cock Robin Bridge's height is derived from the massive mining subsidence which dogged the canal from the 1880s onwards. Unfortunately the anti-vandal fencing prevents any view of the canal.

To the south, the site of the Walker Carver wallpaper works is on the towpath side. In 1942 this was the only remaining user of the canal, receiving coal from the Worsley Collieries, on the Bridgewater Canal, via Hulme locks and the river Irwell. Just north of the bridge was Pendleton Colliery, which served this works and other users from the early 19th century until closure in the 1930s. Before this, at the end of Indigo Street, is a ramp giving access to a factory. The walls of the ramp are the stone-lined banks of the canal, making this one of the few canals you can drive along!

Turning up Park House Bridge Road, the middle section of the walk begins, with a canal filled partly with water, at least in winter! Park House Bridge has been filled in, but a firm towpath with fine stone banking leads north.

Almost immediately, the remains of a wharf and layby are seen on the offside. This served Agecroft Colliery, which closed in 1932. A former boatman, Harry Vaughan of Burscough, recalled loading here in the 1920s after delivering pottery materials to Clifton. Across the canal is the site of the now vanished Agecroft pit, modernised and reopened after the war to serve a new power station. This section sometimes contains water, and always contains rubbish, the latter

much in evidence at Agecroft Road Bridge (A6044), which remains intact after over 30 years of closure and over 50 years of disuse.

By the towpath is the site of the Agecroft Power Station, now no more. Never served by canal traffic, this installation destroyed the rural tranquillity of a valley much patronised by Edwardian rowing clubs, which used both the canal and the nearby Irwell. There was a 1960s plan to use ash from this station to fill in the canal. As the canal moves onto an embankment, the desolation surrounding the power station is apparent.

Just before the site of Lumbs Aqueduct the canal is dammed; the

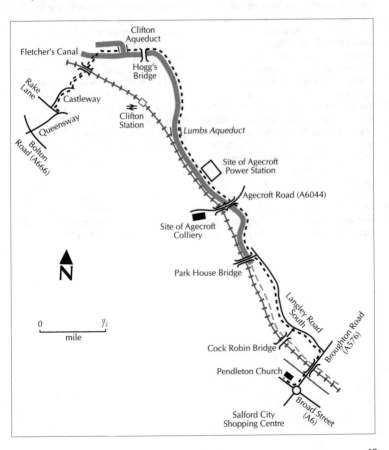

aqueduct has been removed, and it is necessary to scramble down and up to rejoin the towpath.

The next section was dammed, drained and piped after September 1939, when this work was ordered to avoid flooding to the adjacent Magnesium-Elektron works. This immediately cut traffic to Clifton Junction, but piping of the 1,107 yard length was allowed to continue after 1945. The broad and deep bed of the canal, with the pipe clearly in place, continues northward, a strangely mummified reminder of the past closure. The pipe was used to convey water to British Rail at Agecroft and Pendleton for their steam locomotives until 1966. Water was supplied at its far end via Fletchers Canal until 1955, and then via a pumping station from the Irwell at Clifton, which was abandoned when the canal downstream was de-watered.

From here the path can be muddy after rain. A short length has been filled in and used for storage. Then the canal suddenly reappears, full of water. Under Hogg's Bridge, which was strangely replaced in the late 1970s by a modern concrete bridge with full headroom, there is a short length which almost looks navigable.

Flanked by an impressive (but closed) railway viaduct, this short section is used as a cooling pond by the local works. It is here that, up to 1939, pottery materials from ships at Runcorn were unloaded from narrowboats, unloading sometimes taking up to a week.

Just north, but now filled in, was Fletcher's Canal, which was used up to 1935. The junction bridge was demolished in 1966, amid plans to demolish the adjacent Clifton Aqueduct over the Irwell. This three-arched aqueduct, along with a dam across the canal bed, erected in the 1930s, is still intact. Much of the canal beyond is infilled but can be followed if you are determined to do so.

The path by the side of Fletcher's Canal should be followed north past Pilkington's Tile Factory which has made a concrete roadway out of the canal. At the end of the fence the canal bed reappears and continues towards Wet Earth Colliery with its association with James Brindley. Take the footpath which turns off left and climb the valley side passing under the railway bridge. This brings you to Castleway where a right turn should be made. At the T-junction turn left into Rake Lane and a short distance along this will bring you to The Beehive public house and its adjacent bus stop.

Although alongside a ruined canal which may never see boats again, this walk offers an interesting journey through the past. The future of the remains is doubtful.

*A boat descending the tree-fringed Marple Lock flight which is explored on page 52*

# 18 PEAK FOREST CANAL

## Marple Flight

*by Stephen Barrett, revised by Rodney Corrie*

**WALK TALK**
**Distance** – Bridge 2 to Aqueduct & return, 2½ miles. Bridge 2 to Romiley, 4 miles.
**Start at** – Macclesfield Canal Bridge; Grid Ref: SJ 961883.
**OS Landranger Map** – 109, Manchester, Geographers A–Z Manchester.
**Public Transport** – Regular daily train service between Manchester Piccadilly and Sheffield via Romiley and Marple. Also Manchester to Romiley and Rose Hill, Marple (not Sundays).
**Car Parking** – On streets and car parks in Marple.

The Peak Forest Canal climbs 214ft through Marple Flight, giving the canal an overall height of 500ft above sea level. Each of the sixteen locks gives a rise of about 13ft and they are in good working order. The lock flight was not built until about 1804; before this the upper level was connected to that below by a 1¼ mile tramway. From the top of the flight there are majestic views eastwards towards the Peak District National Park.

From Marple town centre walk eastwards to a triple fork in the main road. Take the right hand fork, Church Lane, until you cross Bridge 2 of the Macclesfield Canal. Go on to the towpath on the far side of the canal.

The first thing of interest is the attractive warehouse on the opposite side from the towpath. Just past the warehouse there is a fine example of a roving bridge typical of the many on the Macclesfield Canal. Here we are at the waters meeting and need to cross the bridge to take the towpath of the Peak Forest Canal northwards. The Macclesfield is behind us, the upper Peak Forest Canal goes off to our right.

It is at this point that one Samuel Oldknow comes on the scene. Oldknow was a local tycoon, owning a mill, coalmines, quarries etc. He was even instrumental in the construction of the canal. The first of his enterprises was at waters meeting. His lime kilns lie behind the boat basin. They were built into the solid rock face and were made to resemble medieval ruins; Oldknow's home was quite close by and he objected to having the views from his windows upset with ugly kilns. The kilns were fed limestone from quarries around Doveholes in Derbyshire, a tramway being used to take the limestone to the Peak Forest Canal where it was brought down to the kilns by boat. They were fired by coal from Poynton on the Macclesfield Canal. These kilns were in use right up to the twentieth century. What remains can be reached by crossing the bridge below the top lock and taking the lane between the houses to the hillside beyond.

As we walk on down the lock flight it is apparent that the local people take great pride in their canal: well-kept gardens lead down to the water.

Possets Bridge is between locks 12 and 13. It is said that Oldknow, who had the bridge built, offered his workmen a posset of ale a day if they could construct the bridge in the time allowed. It is not known if the bridge was finished in time. Possets Bridge is unusual in that it has three tunnels: one for the horse, one for the boatman, as there is a lock directly alongside, and of course, there was a tunnel for the boat. Originally, however, there was a fourth tunnel now blocked off; this carried a private canal arm off to Oldknow's lime kilns. There is a wonderful warehouse about halfway down the flight on the opposite side from the towpath. In 1976 it was completely renovated and restored to its former glory. Originally one of Oldknow's properties used to store cotton that came from his mill in nearby Mellor, it is now converted to office use. The fabric of the renovated building still shows the whereabouts of the covered loading bay and chain hoist.

Next a busy main road (A626) crosses the canal and here the towpath swaps sides. Immediately on the other side of the towpath wall a lane enters Brabyns Park. At Lock 7 there is access by a ramped path and steps to the park and so to the Goyt

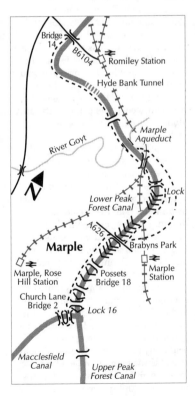

Valley. Between Locks 5 and 4, where the railway burrows under the pound, there are picnic tables beside the towpath.

By Lock 1 the signposted Goyt Way, having shared the towpath from south of Marple, diverges to drop to the floor of the valley. At this lock there used to be a pub called the Queen's Hotel. There was a passenger flyboat service from Ashton to Marple. It is recorded that many passengers would leave the boat at the bottom lock and walk the rest of the way into Marple instead of the often slower passage through the locks by boat.

One of the finest sights on the whole of the canal network is just round the bend: Marple Aqueduct. When constructed people came from all over the country to view this great achievement. The canal spans the valley 90ft above the little river Goyt.

This is the end of the Marple Flight walk. Beyond the west end of the Aqueduct the Etherow/Goyt Valley Way, first descending towards the floor of the Goyt Valley and offering better views of the aqueduct and viaduct, permits a circular route up-stream. A return can be made through Brabyns Park to Lock 7 or the lane at the A626 road bridge noted on the way down.

The Etherow/Goyt Valley Way, forming part of the Midshires Way, shares the towpath beyond the aqueduct as far as Hyde Bank. There are signposted ways leading to the valley floor in the neighbourhood of Chadkirk Country Estate. For those seeking the train from Romiley, continue on the towpath from Marple Aqueduct for about 1¼ miles to Bridge 14 which carries Stockport Road (B6104). It is less than half a mile to the right up the road to the station.

# 19 SHEFFIELD CANAL

## Sheffield to Rotherham

*by Dave Dawson*

**WALK TALK**

**Distance** – Sheffield Basin to Rotherham, 6 miles.

**Start at** – Sheffield Basin; Grid Ref: SK 368879.

**OS Landranger Map** – 111, Sheffield & Doncaster, or, better, Sheffield & Rotherham Geographia Street Atlas.

**Guide** – *The Complete Guide to the Sheffield & South Yorkshire Navigation* published by the Hallamshire Press.

**Public Transport** – Bus service 69 (01709 515151).

**Car Parking** – Ample parking on Sheffield Wharf.

It's a wonder the Sheffield to Rotherham canal was ever cut. The interested and not so interested parties bickered on for years, but eventually, in 1819, the canal was opened along 'The high line'. The engineers took this high level to make it easier should any future folk wish to link up with the Peak Forest and Chesterfield canals. Anybody got a shovel?

The terminal buildings can be found at the back of the Sheaf Market, just by the enormous ramp which once served the Victoria station. The whole basin has recently been dredged and all the original buildings, including the terminal warehouse, the grain warehouse and the straddle warehouse of 1895, have been restored. The developers discovered the original dry dock, which had long been buried, and this too has now been brought back to life.

The towpath leads directly from the right hand side of the basin, and, as so often with a canal cut, that step onto the towing path takes you to a world of peace and tranquillity centuries away from the roaring traffic.

The path was not always so peaceful. When the Victorian 'mesters' built their steelworks along the Don valley, it was said that this whole area was 'Divided from Hell wi' a sheet of tissue paper,' and every old bridge has deep towrope grooves which remind us of the bustling activity of that time.

After the first of these old bridges, a railway viaduct built in 1859, we come to the new boatyard, where *Ethel*, the last remaining wooden Sheffield Keel, sits on the side awaiting restoration.

Next comes Bacon Lane Bridge. The bridge hole here was only just high and wide enough to allow a Sheffield keel to pass through, hence the boatman's nickname for it: 'the eye of the needle'. The bridge guard here is scored deeper than the rest.

Shortly after this we come to the three mile post, the canal continuing along its quiet corridor between the factories.

After the next bridge though, the factories are gone and we walk between high green banks. These again are eventually replaced by a wharf and winding hole which must be an industrial archaeologist's dream. A short yet heavily built stone aqueduct next carries us over Darnall Road and the prospect opens out as we walk on towards Tinsley Locks.

We come on the top lock quite suddenly, the flight sweeping down endlessly but, before exploring, cross to the other side. The locks are broad gauge but only 62ft long and originally there were twelve of them, two of these being later combined to make room for a railway bridge. It's here you'll find the one mile post and the inscription noting that one of the locks was blitzed during the Second World War. Look out as well for the roof bearing the legend 'Cafe'. We have to cross over a lock gate to where an excellent compleat angler has cut an impressive hole in the wire fence, just opposite the café door.

The place is the best transport café in the world and to hell with nouvelle cuisine!

The footsore can finish the walk here, the 69 bus stop being just one hundred yards away. Those who wish to continue, however, must now cross back to the towpath and walk under the M1 viaduct. The locks take us down to where the canal joins with the river Don which is here deep, wide and placid, but in a moment there is a dull roaring sound as the river plunges over the enormous arc of a weir, the navigable channel and the towpath going quietly their own way through what is still, at least by the side of the cut, a rural valley.

At the next lock, take the bridge over Holmes Goyt.

Soon you are on the edge of Rotherham town where the path changes sides for the last time. Here there is a new railway bridge with the ruins of the original stone construction, rope scars and all, beneath it.

Now we leave the canal, following the path behind the New British Waterways' cottage at Ickles Lock. Take the road to the right which will lead you into the central bus station and the fast and frequent 69 bus back to Sheffield.

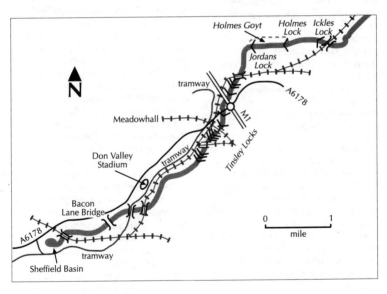

# 20 CHESTERFIELD CANAL

## Staveley to Chesterfield

*by John Lower*

**WALK TALK**

**Distance** – Mill Green, Staveley to Chesterfield, 5 miles.

**Start at** – Mill Green, Staveley; Grid Ref: SK 430747.

**OS Landranger Maps** – 119, Buxton, Matlock & Dovedale and 120, Mansfield & Worksop.

**Guide** – *A Walkers & Boaters Guide to the Chesterfield Canal and Cuckoo Way* published by the Hallamshire Press.

**Public Transport** – A regular bus service, seven days a week, operated by Stagecoach (01332 292200). The end of this walk is two hundred yards from Chesterfield railway station.

**Society** – Chesterfield Canal Society, 01246 559054.

**Trip Boat** – *John Varley*, 01246 274077.

**Countryside Ranger Service** – 01246 433186.

**Tourist Information** – The Peacock Centre (01246 207777).

With the final collapse of the Norwood Tunnel in 1907, the Chesterfield Canal from here to Chesterfield was abandoned and fell into disuse. Eighty years later, restoration commenced on the 5-mile section between Staveley and Chesterfield which had remained to supply water to a factory. An interesting one-way walk is possible, returning by the frequent bus service.

The walk commences at Mill Green, Staveley, at the foot of the side road which veers off from the entrance to the large Morrison's store. The towing path is reached over a small hump-backed bridge, much affected by mining subsidence, and held up by arches bent from old railway rails. To the right towards Worksop, the canal is infilled, but to the left there is a good new towpath surface all the way to Chesterfield.

The first mile of canal as far as Hollingwood has been restored by local opencast mining contractors Fitzwise. For a publicity stunt at a Chesterfield Canal Society Open Day, they set out to see how much canal could be dredged in a day. Over four hundred yards were cleared by two large excavators and a bulldozer. They have also opencast and restored much of the land alongside, including the site of the former Staveley Works and a quarter-mile length of canal.

There are five locks on the climb up to Chesterfield, all of which have been restored by the Chesterfield Canal Society. The first at Hollingwood was built in the 1890s when the Great Central Railway diverted the canal in order to build their Chesterfield Loop Line. The remains of a railway bridge and Staveley Works station can be seen immediately above the lock.

Beyond the deep cutting which abounds with wild flowers in spring, the canal crosses the former Dixon Opencast Site. Dixon's Lock is a completely new structure (see January 1996 *WW*); the design, supervision and fund-raising were all undertaken by the Canal Society. Above, viewing the variety of wildlife, it is difficult to believe that this is a new section of canal crossing a new landscape.

The next lock reached is Bluebank and there follows the most attractive section through Bluebank Woods. The canal from here to Chesterfield has been dredged by Derbyshire County Council as a derelict land grant scheme and indeed the surrounding woods and pastures are also being opened up as a country park and wildlife area. Here also is another narrow section built in the 1890s when the canal was diverted to permit construction of the railway and several loops of the nearby river Rother were cut off, now forming artificial ox-bow lakes and miniature nature reserves.

At Wheeldon Mill Lock, the culverted bridlepath bridge is still to be rebuilt, as is the main road crossing at Station Lane. Together with Cow Lane Bridge (above) these will form a third contract of the County Council restoration scheme, hopefully in the near future, allowing navigation of the full section.

Passing beneath the twin railway bridges, pause and examine the rope marks in the stonework, caused by the horse-drawn boats and proving that trade on the canals did not die

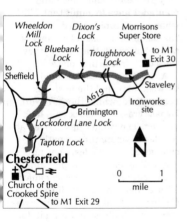

the moment the railways opened.

Tapton Lock was the first to be restored by the Canal Society and is the base for the *John Varley* trip boat. Here also is a slipway, and the lock cottage (rebuilt in the 1960s!) is earmarked as a visitor centre by the canal's owner, Derbyshire County Council's Countryside Ranger Service.

A little further on is Tapton Mill Bridge, a floodgate and the waterway enters onto the river Rother and obtains a water supply by St Helena's Weir. Following the towing path along the riverbank through Arnold Lavers Timberyard, the original terminal basin was located on the far side, just before the steel lattice footbridge. The new footbridge over the Chesterfield Inner Relief Road (A61) is on the line of the basin but all that remains on the far side is one massive stone gate-post and the name Wharf Lane.

Continuing on the towpath, the river is now very shallow but in the 1890s was straightened and made navigable to a new terminal basin which now lies buried in the yard of the Trebor-Bassett Sweet Factory and beneath the canal information panel. On the main road, a frequent bus service will carry you back to Staveley (the stop is a few yards to the left), or if you have a little energy left, why not explore the interesting town of the famous crooked spire.

# 21 CHESTERFIELD CANAL

## Shireoaks to Worksop

*by Louise Mathurin, revised by John Lower*

**WALK TALK**
**Distance** – Shireoaks station to Worksop Town Lock, 2¹/₂ miles.
**Start at** – Shireoaks station; Grid Ref: SK 556813.
**OS Landranger Map** – 120, Mansfield & Worksop.
**Guide** – *A Walkers & Boaters Guide to the Chesterfield Canal & Cuckoo Way* published by the Hallamshire Press.
**Public Transport** – No trains on Sunday.
**Car Parking** – at Worksop station.
**Society** – Chesterfield Canal Society, 01246 559054.
**Tourist Information** – 01909 501148.

This walk is along the newly restored part of the Chesterfield Canal, and it is extremely pleasant, with an abundance of wildlife. I have done the walk in both directions, and recommend taking public transport to Shireoaks and walking to Worksop rather than from it.

Shireoaks is a hamlet on the outskirts of Worksop, as delightful as its name. It is very old, pottery from 250BC having been found where a wood once stood.

The walk starts at Shireoaks Row, just by the station. The new bridge here, built in 1996/7, replaces an 'earthed up' embankment and small pipe which had blocked the canal for over thirty years.

A short walk brings us to the site of Shireoaks Colliery, which dated back to the 1850s. The pit had its own foundries and brickworks, and later produced its own electricity and gas. A lot of the coal mined here was transported by canal, which of course is the most sensible way to do it. The

site has been landscaped, the entrance bridge to the colliery basin restored and the basin itself enlarged for pleasure boat moorings and to form the focal point of new housing development.

Just past here can be found the three Shireoaks Locks. Alongside the top chamber stands the (much modified) lock keeper's cottage, now in private hands and one of the few remaining on the entire Chesterfield Canal. Shireoaks Low Bridge is below the bottom lock.

After a fairly straight length, Doefield Dun Lock is reached. It is possible to see the spoil tips from Shireoaks Colliery here, though now they are being landscaped and planted. I have to admit that I like what some people regard as an 'intrusion' of industrial scenery on a canal – after all, that is why they were built in the first place.

A railway crosses the canal between here and the next lock, Haggonfield, whilst the A57 Worksop Bypass crosses the lock on a high viaduct. The walker has arrived at Rhodesia, where the towpath changes sides. Rhodesia has no connection, as some people think, with South Africa, but was named after a chairman of the Shireoaks Colliery Co, and in the 1920s it was a 'new town' built as an overspill for Shireoaks.

There was another major obstacle to restoration at this point, two road crossings which were so low that it would have been impossible to get even a punt through. These were the first major obstructions above Worksop and their replacement is a major triumph for the Chesterfield Canal Society.

The stretch following is bounded, behind the towpath hedge, by a large dredging tip, constructed by British Waterways to accommodate all the dredgings removed from the restoration scheme. The aptly named Deep Lock is followed by High Ground Bridge, deeply scored by the passage of towing lines, and Stret Lock. Below is a link road to the Worksop Bypass – that this crosses a bridge and not an embankment is an early success of the canal society.

From this point, Worksop itself can be seen, and looks very attractive across the meadows. The bypass is plainly visible, but we did not find it obtrusive, although there was plenty of traffic on it at the time. A new winding hole has been constructed at the entrance to the former Lady Lee Arm. This branch which ran three-quarters of a mile to a quarry has been infilled but the towpath is a public right of way.

Continuing on the main canal, to the left can be seen the Rockware glass works, which produces several million glass containers each month. There is also a wire works, which moved here from Sheffield during the last war. This makes a wide range of steel wires, from about 1in diameter to about 2ft 6in.

Morse Lock is now reached, the first to be restored by British Waterways, and reopened with a rally on 7th June, 1996. The scenery is still rural, with Sandhill Lake on the left and sports fields on the right. Below the lock is the winding hole which for thirty years formed the head of navigation of the cruiseway from the river Trent.

It is just a short walk now to Town Lock, near the centre of Worksop. There is a stone and plaque on the lockside which commemorates the bi-centenary of the canal which took place in 1977. The towpath is usually closed by a gate beneath the bridge, so it is necessary to return to the car park to get up onto the road. Beyond is the fascinating straddle warehouse, formerly used as the British Waterways yard and now converted as a pub.

Cross over the canal bridge and at the traffic lights in front of the Co-op car park, take the middle of three roads. The station is about ten minutes walk from the canal but is signposted.

The navigable part of the Chesterfield Canal is a jewel, and I hope it is not too long before the campaigning of the flourishing Canal Society will result in the re-opening of the remainder as far as the place whose name it bears.

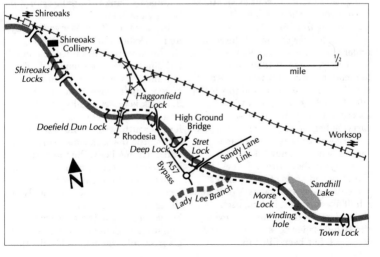

# 22 ST HELENS CANAL

## Earlestown to Bank Quay, Warrington

*by Joseph Boughey*

**WALK TALK**
**Distance** – 6 miles canalside; 8 miles total.
**Start at** – Newton Common Lock; Grid Ref: SJ 565948.
**OS Landranger Map** – 108, Liverpool.
**Public Transport** – Regular Inter-City trains between Warrington Bank Quay and Earlestown.
**Car Parking** – close to Newton Common Lock.

This walk follows the Sankey Brook Navigation, or St Helens Canal, the oldest in England, along a route which demonstrates the different ways in which a derelict canal, now the subject of restoration plans, has been treated.

It is best to begin at Earlestown station or park next to the site of Newton Common Lock, which marks the boundary between sections closed in 1931 and 1963. To the north is a low bridge which replaced a swing bridge after 1935. Recent excavations have revealed the location of the walls of the filled-in lock.

A path follows the line of the canal under the arches of Earlestown Viaduct, where from 1830 the first locomotive-worked railway crossed the 1757 canal. Just beyond this is the site of the Sankey Sugar works, served until 1959 by motorised barges carrying bagged sugar from Liverpool.

Barges used to turn in a basin (part of whose stonework is still visible) just above Bradley Lock. Its chamber and parts of its top gates are still intact, and the next mile and a half are in water, having been cleaned out in the 1970s. However, the swing bridge does not work and Hey Lock has been filled in.

The canal here forms part of the Sankey Valley Linear Park, with the surrounding area landscaped by tree and bush planting. The recent planting means that only the section below Hey Lock suggests the view when the canal first opened. At Newton Brook, marking the boundary of the Park, the scene changes abruptly: the next two miles have been obliterated, although a path remains.

The infilled canal here is spanned by an overbridge which was provided in the 1950s to cross it and the adjacent railway. The St Helens Canal was unusual in that all the early bridges were swing bridges and sailing was used in this flat country. The next section is covered by a landscaped rubbish tip, dating from the 1970s; a path may be followed over the top of this, following a wire fence which marks the canal line.

The next, uninteresting, length follows a lane towards a scrap yard next to the M62 embankment. The canal line has been filled in and planted with bushes, but, curiously, Winwick Lock retains much of its chamber and four battered gates, re-painted by Sankey Canal Restoration Society members.

Beyond the M62 is Winwick Quay and workshops, where craft using the canal were maintained. Some buildings here date from the 1750s, and these have been revived (if altered) by the present occupier. The dry dock is intact and has been cleared recently; beyond, a straight length south, with former dredging tips on the towpath side, leads to the site of Hulme Lock, the top parts of which have recently been excavated.

Below here the Sankey Brook formerly crossed the canal, partly on the level; although generally bulldozed, part of the sluice gates remain. The Sankey Brook has been diverted into the next half mile, the channel being deepened so that it no longer looks like a canal. This should be followed past successive modern crossings, until the path crosses a footbridge over the stream. This should then be followed until the canal line draws away into a short dry length acting as a flood relief channel, leading to Bewsey Lock.

Although gateless, the lock and a swing bridge over its chamber are well preserved, and the lowest level of the canal is in excellent, if unnavigable, order. This part of the Sankey Valley Park is more formal than that further north, with well-tended bushes and paths. Below Bewsey either side of the canal can be followed. The offside leads past an unusual children's playground with a giant archery target; long-standing plans for a trip boat on this length have not materialised. This can be followed to a footbridge over Sankey Way, or the latter can be accessed from the towpath.

The alternative line follows the towpath under the Cheshire Lines Railway viaduct, with a rebuilt centre section; beyond is a 1980s footbridge with over 8ft headroom! The next crossing is Sankey Way, whose construction in 1965 provided the immediate reason for the closure of the canal.

Bank Quay station is about a mile from here. If time permits, the towpath can be followed round to Sankey Bridges (or Sankey Way followed to a footbridge over this major road). This section has been transformed from earlier semi-rurality to form the centrepiece of an urban park forming a green wedge between recent housing areas.

The 1980s footbridge crosses both Sankey Way and the canal as the latter curves round to Sankey Bridges. There were three bridges here, including a large main road bascule bridge, removed in 1972, and a swing bridge, which has recently been restored. The third bridge is a former railway swing bridge; a path across this can be followed with caution. Beyond this, the original line of the canal, discharged into Sankey Brook here an insignificant stream; there are few remains. The canal turns onto the extension line which rapidly replaced the first terminal.

Returning to Sankey Bridges, the old main road can be followed to Bank Quay station. The short journey by rail back to Earlestown enables views of the centre section of the walk and provides an opportunity to visit one of the canal's competitors and eventual owners, the London & North Western Railway.

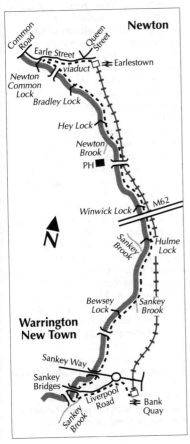

61

# 23 SHROPSHIRE UNION CANAL

## Ellesmere Port to Chester

*by Dennis Needham*

**WALK TALK**
**Distance** – Ellesmere Port to Chester, 8½ miles.
**Start at** – The Boat Museum, Ellesmere Port; Grid Ref: SJ 407771.
**OS Landranger Map** – 117, Chester & Wrexham.
**Guide** – *Waterways World Guide to the Shropshire Union Canal.*
**Public Transport** – Frequent service from Delamere bus station (passing Bridge 133 *en route*). (Details from Cheshire Bus Information Line 01244 602666.) Rare trains from Ellesmere Port to Helsby give access to an hourly service to Chester. The service obviously does not aim to compete with that by bus!
**Car Parking** – On site at the museum.

Much of this walk has industry and motorways in close proximity. But subscribers to the theory that beauty is in the eye of the beholder will find a wealth of interest starting right at the beginning with The Boat Museum. Use their car park. It's large, free and you will patronise them afterwards.

The Manchester Ship Canal is close and you may be fortunate enough to see some large vessels passing. But the towpath beckons. This was the Wirral Canal, built as a broad line by the Ellesmere Canal Company as part of their plan to link Shrewsbury with the river Mersey. Chronologically, it was the second part of what was to become the Shropshire Union Canal. The quality of its construction must have been assured with William Jessop in overall charge and Thomas Telford

supervising day-to-day. Two hundred years ago, Ellesmere Port did not exist; only Netherpool, just a hamlet. From Roman times, Chester (then Deva) was the port for this area, but silting of the river Dee reduced its effectiveness and made the establishment of an alternative imperative.

Turning left – away from the museum – the towing path immediately passes under a rustic old accommodation bridge. Today, this looks utterly incongruous, surrounded as it is by concrete as the M53 sweeps by overhead. The construction of this road reduced the width of water available and eliminated any possibility of barge traffic. Almost immediately you are in the industrial heart of Ellesmere Port. After passing under a railway bridge, the signal box alongside with its windows enclosed in wire mesh is a comment on the quality of local youth.

Across the water was once the home to a very important local industry and heavy user of the SUC. The Wolverhampton Corrugated Iron Company started producing their wares here in 1906.

Industrially, the worst is now behind. The motorway crosses again and a factory complete with mysterious pipework which leaks wisps of steam in a most threatening manner is discovered on the left. The water here is clear with luxuriant weed growth and the inevitable floating rubbish always associated with urban canals. It is also heavily fished making Hurdling the Roach Pole part of the walk.

By the time the next bridge is reached, the whole of the Mersey vale is visible. The higher buildings of Runcorn and Widnes can be seen on the skyline with the petro-chemical complex at Stanlow closer. Ugly as it appears now, by night it takes on an altogether different appearance and can be quite attractive.

The accompanying motorway now leaves to pass west of Stoak village whilst the canal hugs the contour in a big sweep to the east. The most remarkable thing about this village is the way it appears to have escaped the dead hand of developers eager to build housing close to Chester and Merseyside. The Bunbury Arms offers a pleasant break in the walk. Leave at Bridge 138 and it is on the corner of a crossroads. To regain the towing path, either retrace your steps

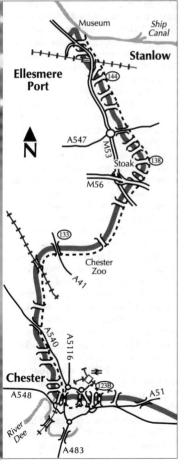

or turn left from the pub which will pick up the towing path some 200 yards later.

Then follows the final concrete cavern as the M53 and M56 intersect. Green starts to rule. An extensive linear mooring is then reached with boats of distinctly variable quality.

Beyond, the far side of the canal is heavily overgrown with reed mace. It also houses one of the most concentrated assemblies of waterhens I have seen anywhere on the canal system. Two pipe bridges and humps in the ground indicate the presence of oil storage tanks here but they do not interfere with the pretty woodland views. Bridge 133 is reached and with it the opportunity to cut short the walk, an Ellesmere Port bus service running along this road.

But the beauty of this walk is not yet over. Under a delightful stone railway bridge the canal turns sharp left running on an embankment past a copse, an enchantingly peaceful section of rural water.

Chester soon makes its presence felt though. Tranquillity may be lost but there is in increasing canal interest. The expanse of Tower Wharf is reached via a delicate little turnover bridge. On the right, a dry dock and beyond the first of three locks that drop canal into the river Dee and the open sea. These are 'new' locks, built when the Wirral length was opened. It joined the existing Chester Canal which already made its connection, the locks being at the far end of this basin area.

Follow the path up past the Northgate staircase flight, though a solid rock cutting at the base of Chester City Wall and round into a lively redeveloped area with an excellent Cantonese restaurant and canalside pub. Leave the canal here to reach the bus station. For the train, carry on along the towing path until you reach Bridge 123B. Pass under it, turn back, up the steps to the top and turn right.

# 24 SHROPSHIRE UNION CANAL

## Acton to Hurleston

*by Joseph Boughey*

**WALK TALK**

**Distance** – Acton to Hurleston, 2 miles.

**Start at** – Acton Village; Grid Ref: SJ 633532.

**OS Landranger Map** – 118, Stoke-on-Trent & Macclesfield.

**Guide** – *Waterways World Guide to the Shropshire Union Canal.*

**Public Transport** – Hourly bus service (CAD 4). Contact Cheshirebus (01270 505350).

**Car Parking** – In Acton village.

This short walk covers some of the most heavily trafficked cruising waterway – but also part of the least successful of the early canals – the Chester Canal.

From the bus stop in Acton, walk north and down Wilbraham Road; in the far corner is a footpath leading across a field to Acton Bridge. Tom Rolt moored *Cressy* here in 1941 and walked up the path to visit the Star public house. Acton itself is little changed, apart from the post-war housing estate which covers part of the path, but it would now be impossible for a narrowboat to moor by the bridge.

This length was the last section of the Chester Canal to be completed, being opened in 1779. Conceived only as a branch, it was built as cheaply as possible, with seven swivel bridges between Nantwich and Barbridge. Brick overbridges replaced these after 1805; all have been altered in turn. Acton Bridge, originally Church Turnbridge, had its arch removed and replaced by former railway girders in 1924, for no clear reason, while Bluestone Bridge, the next north, was removed entirely after the war.

The Chester Canal Company was so impecunious that it cut this length of the canal on land for which it had not paid; on two occasions, enraged landowners blocked the canal with a chain and demanded payment. In 1785 Samuel Hulse placed a chain across the stretch to Bluestone blocking all traffic for the whole year. It was only removed after the company agreed to pay rent for the land.

This length is a simple contour canal, running through fairly flat but pleasant countryside. A shallow cutting approaches with what is now the A51 Henhull Bridge, a massive concrete bridge constructed in 1931 to replace an original overbridge. Beyond, the canal widens out considerably.

On the towpath side, and still recognisable as such, was Henhull Wharf, one of many roadstone wharves maintained by Cheshire County Council. Traffics, latterly in cinders from Anderton, were recorded here up to 1936. As the canal goes over a small embankment it is crossed by a pipe, one of three supplying Dee water to mid-Cheshire; another will be encountered above Hurleston Locks.

Around the corner is Cornes Bridge, named after a local farming family; it was altered in the 1970s to take farm vehicles. It replaced Oulton's Turnbridge. Land on the offside beyond formed a dredging tip into the 1940s; its successor is to be seen beyond Hurleston Junction Bridge. The four Hurleston Locks can be seen in profile as this bridge, altered in the 1950s, is approached, with the high embankment of Hurleston reservoir beyond. Before the junction was made, Dyer's Turnbridge crossed the canal here.

The locks mark the start of the Ellesmere Canal, whose opening in

1805 fostered the revival of the then almost moribund Chester Canal.

There are no stop gates at the junction, due to an arrangement to return Dee water extracted at Llantysilio for the canal to the Dee below Chester. This agreement played a part in the closure and revival of the canal.

The lowest lock at Hurleston is one of the narrowest on any British canal; smaller craft were built for regular use of this canal. After only 20 years, works needed to be carried out on these locks in 1825, including the installation of cast iron gates at this lowest lock.

Instead of following the towpath to the top lock, cross the gates and walk up to view the reservoir from the top of the embankment. From here a path can be followed round past the spillway to the top lock. This reservoir is used to store domestic water for mid-Cheshire, abstracted from the Dee at Vron or Llantysilio and brought by canal to the top lock. The scheme took from 1949 to 1959 to come to fruition; it included purifying works and the special spillway, which aerates the canal water.

Looking south from the embankment, the spire of Acton Church, where the walk started, can be seen. The reservoir was built in the late 1830s to store water to supplement supplies to the Middlewich branch. At least one labourer was killed in its construction, by a fall of earth in 1838. He was buried in the churchyard at Acton, although no stone can be traced now.

The purification works can be seen on the offside above the locks; boats used to moor here until the mid-1960s. Ahead is a road bridge from this period, followed by its predecessor from 1805, now disused. The bus stop is by the front of the North West Water works.

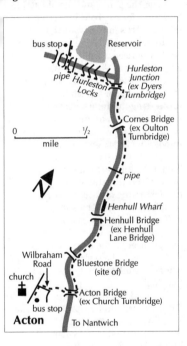

# 25 TRENT & MERSEY CANAL

## Kidsgrove to Sandbach

*by Tom Foxon*

**WALK TALK**

**Distance** – Kidsgrove station to Sandbach station, 8 miles.

**Start at** – Kidsgrove station; Grid Ref: SJ 837543.

**OS Landranger Map** – 118, Stoke-on-Trent & Macclesfield.

**Public Transport** – Hourly trains from Crewe to Kidsgrove or Sandbach.

**Guide** – *Waterways World Guide to the Trent & Mersey & Caldon Canals.*

Over thirty years had gone by since I had boated my last load of Trentham gravel down to Manchester and the time was overdue, I thought, to revisit a waterway, which, in its trading day, had always had a special attraction for me. So it was, that, one beautiful June morning, I caught the train from Crewe to Kidsgrove.

Walk out of the station, turn right and take the path that passes behind the signal box and you come out on the towpath of the Trent & Mersey Canal, hard by the entrance to Harecastle Tunnel. As soon as I set foot on the towpath I felt the old atmosphere come flooding back. The rings to which I had often tied to await the tunnel tug were still there and the area around the top lock was little changed.

'Cheshire Locks' is not usually thought of as a particularly scenic waterway, but, once clear of Kidsgrove, the countryside is very pleasant, especially around Church Lawton, although it grows a little duller below Hassall Green. There is a great deal of interest to see. Despite the fine weather, I encountered only about half a dozen pleasure boats on the move and the few walkers seemed to be locals exercising the dog or taking a short cut. The towpath is in excellent condition being wide and well maintained; the grass had been cut and walking conditions were very good.

By the time I reached Rode Heath, which appeared to be much more up-market than in days of yore, I was ready for a pint. The pub here is right on the canal and the old stable buildings for the boat horses still stand. It was just as well that I had fortified myself as, on resuming my walk, I noticed a small promontory projecting into the canal. With a shock I realised that this was once the site of one of the canal's most interesting landmarks, a tall warehouse with an arch under which boats could unload. Obviously it is impossible to preserve every old building but it seemed very sad to have lost this particularly striking piece of canal architecture. The T&M has lost many of its canalside buildings and its atmosphere has suffered in consequence. A unique feature of this canal which has also disappeared is the enamel signs which used to be fixed to many of the bridges extolling the virtues of Petter Oil Engines.

As I walked down towards Hassall Green it was difficult to believe that I would never again hear the distinctive croak of a 'Knobstick' klaxon heralding the appearance round one of the bends of a 'Barlaston' style fore-end as a low-loaded boat forged uphill, its load of white china clay contrasting with the long black hull; nor would I be overtaken by a fast travelling crate boat hell bent for Runcorn to the accompaniment of rattling paddles, banging gates and urgent cries of "Draw!"

I was, of course, casting a professional eye at the locks and was glad to see no sign of hydraulic paddle gear. The original ground paddle posts were wooden but they all seem to have been replaced by steel. The top gate paddles with their long spindles projecting beyond the balance beam had gone, as had the side paddles connecting each pair of locks. When these were opened, the incoming water would cause the bottom gates of the empty lock you were ascending to close.

The arrangement for strapping the top gates on the T&M was also unique to that canal. Instead of an upwardly projecting post a piece of iron projects horizontally, the strap being placed under this and held, which closes the gate and stops the boat at the same time. Many of these old strapping irons survive, although some locks had been fitted with the Shropshire Union style of strapping post.

I was also on the lookout for old trading boats and encountered *Fox*,

now a full length conversion and resplendent in full FMC livery, Barlow's old *Beatty* and, finally, deep loaded with bricks just removed from a lock being re-built, the ex FMC *Gailey*, which I had last seen thirty years ago looming out of the morning mist with a load of firebricks from Brierly Hill to Burslem.

Another pint at the Romping Donkey at Hassall Green and then on down to Wheelock, its canalside little changed over the years. I left the towpath at Sandbach, eight miles from Kidsgrove, and from here the train whisked me back to Crewe in a few minutes. Despite the changes I had observed, plenty of the old atmosphere remains in Cheshire Locks; and with an excellent towpath, plenty of pubs and good accessibility by public transport it is a towpath walk to be recommended.

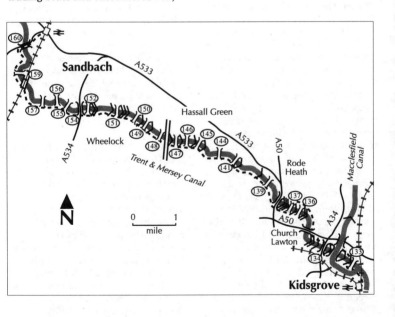

# 26 TRENT & MERSEY AND MACCLESFIELD CANALS

## Kidsgrove to Congleton

*by Dennis Needham*

**WALK TALK**

**Distance** – Kidsgrove station to Congleton station, 7 miles.

**Start at** – Kidsgrove station; Grid Ref: SJ 837543.

**OS Landranger Map** – 118, Stoke-on-Trent & Macclesfield.

**Public Transport** – Trains between Manchester and Stoke.

**Car Parking** – Station (pay) or side streets close by.

Although almost entirely in Cheshire, this pleasant walk is never out of sight of the rugged Staffordshire moorlands, giving the illusion of a rather hilly route.

Kidsgrove railway station is our gathering point. On the right hand corner behind the signal box take the flight of steps that will bring you to the towing path. You have an immediate choice then; turn left to start the walk or a short stroll to the right. This will bring you to the northern portal of Harecastle Tunnel. Actually, it's portals, because on the right of the current bore is the old, original, Brindley tunnel, long since disused, being badly affected by subsidence.

Back to the walk proper. After passing under the railway you will arrive at Hardingswood Junction. A stone set into the parapet here informs you that this is the start of the Macclesfield Canal.

Wrong! It's actually the Hall Green Branch of the Trent & Mersey Canal. Over the bridge leads to the first lock where the towpath changes sides. You can walk under the road bridge, down a steep flight of steps, or over and down the ramp beyond.

Ahead is a large aqueduct. Cross the canal below the second lock and walk up the steps to the left hand side of that aqueduct. Turn right. On the left, in the corner, is the David Piper empire. Builder of high quality steel narrowboats, there are always several examples of his workmanship around.

Over Pool Lock Aqueduct and the walk leaves Staffordshire for Cheshire. Just beyond, one stormy night several years ago, the embankment failed and a torrent of water flooded the roads below. The canal was closed for several months whilst repairs were effected.

Now the scenery will improve. High on the hill to the right is a ruin; or pretends to be. It's actually a folly, Mow Cop, now owned and managed by the National Trust. The shape you see is almost exactly the way it was built a couple of centuries ago by a local landowner who wanted to improve his skyline. It also created a pretty spot for him to picnic. The views from up there are magnificent – well worth a visit after your walk.

An attractive cutting brings you to Hall Green Stop Lock. This is the start of the Macclesfield Canal, and the 1ft rise here is controlled by the most unusual set of gates: single bottom, double top.

The change of ownership is now very clearly evidenced by the bridges. Graceful curves constructed from soft local stone mingle with rusted and decayed swing bridges. And they come thick and fast in this section. New housing now backs to the canal with an old building somewhat incongruous. This was once the famed Bird in Hand pub and a faded legend on the wall confirms that fact. Until the death of the owner, Mrs Whitaker, in the late 1980s, beer came from the cellar in a jug – nothing modern like hand pumps here.

Heritage Narrowboats can be discovered beyond the next bridge. They operate a fine fleet of hire boats together with a day boat if you fancy a more extensive exploration of this canal. Next on the right is the impressive, brick Ramsdell Hall, its

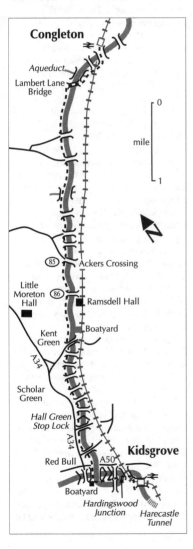

carefully manicured lawns reaching right down to the water's edge.

Over to the left, almost a mile away and with no easy access at the moment, is Little Moreton Hall. This is one of the finest Tudor buildings still in existence today and another 'must' for a road visit after the walk. It's also in the care of NT.

Bridge 85 gives access to a cluster of houses known as Ackers Crossing. Now follows a straight section of canal with more stone bridges in quick succession. After crossing a small aqueduct, Astbury church spire can be seen on the left. This is unusual in that it's constructed separately from the main body of the church. The original spire fell down many centuries ago and the current one was built to replace it.

Billy Tight's Swing Bridge is no more, replaced by a rather boring footbridge, but the golfers who use it to get from one side of the Astbury course to the other probably prefer it instead of relying on boaters to close the original.

Now, as we reach the end of the walk, the opposite bank has housing – good quality with most of the owners appearing to regard the canal as an integral part of their gardens rather than something to be shut off behind 6ft high lap fencing. The next bridge is, for me, the highlight of the walk. The elegant curving lines of Lambert Lane turnover bridge must surely be the apogee of 19th century bridge-builders' art.

A wide expanse of water takes you past Congleton Wharf, over another aqueduct followed by more housing, this time on both banks. Another roving bridge returns the towing path to the left bank. Then ahead is a large, quite modern, millers with the railway crossing the water. Just before here are steps that take you off the canal to a choice of local hostelries and the station for your journey back.

69

# 27 TRENT & MERSEY CANAL

## Stoke to Barlaston

*by Dennis Needham*

**WALK TALK**

**Distance** – Stoke to Barlaston, 6 miles.

**Start at** – Stoke-on-Trent station; Grid Ref: SJ 879457.

**OS Landranger Maps** – 118, Stoke-on-Trent & Macclesfield and 127, Stafford & Telford. The A–Z street atlas for Stoke-on-Trent covers much of the walk.

**Guide** – *Waterways World Guide to the Trent & Mersey and Caldon Canals.*

**Public Transport** – Local trains from Barlaston and Wedgwood halt to Stoke. PMT bus service 45B from Barlaston to Stoke (01782 747000). Neither service operates on Sundays.

**Car Parking** – Stoke railway station or adjacent streets.

It would be stretching the truth somewhat to describe this walk south from Stoke-on-Trent as the most beautiful in this book. Nevertheless, it is full of interest, pretty in parts and manages to achieve that most marvellous of canal feats: solitude in a city centre.

Starting point is Stoke railway station. There is a (pay) car park opposite the splendid frontage. And, if frontages appeal, what about the North Staffordshire Hotel across the road? Turn left as you leave the station and left at the end into Stoke Road. Under the railway bridge turn right and there is a small road to the right which gives access to the canal towing path by Stoke Bottom Lock. This is now a concrete cavern since the arrival of a ring road (A500) in the 1970s meant that the canal hereabouts was re-routed slightly. This involved construction of the new chamber.

Head south, away from the lock. A glance here to the right over the valley and you can see the delightfully named 'Our Lady of the Angels and St Peter in Chains' brick-built church on the hillside with St Dominic's Convent also in the complex. Industry crowds the far bank as traffic on the new road to the right roars along. Down on the towing path, we're almost alone.

Each factory has some kind of interest. Jones & Shuffs might look ordinary, but it's only because the signwriter ran out of space and paint. The full name: Shufflebottom. There is a delightful amalgam of faded and smoke-blacked old Trent & Mersey brick with newer, scruffy looking, concrete. The stream passing under the canal now is the infant river Trent and alongside is what remains of the only traditional pottery on our walk. Known locally as pot banks, there's only an old bottle kiln with a few crumbling brick walls left. And, it's not even used as a pottery now.

The towing path is well maintained along this section which passes a new, small industrial unit followed by a boatyard. There is a wide variety of craft tied up here, some looking as though they may never move again.

Under the next bridge and the factory on the left makes sanitary ware. It's stored a little further along on the right: is it really possible to sell so many toilets?

That is the last canalside factory and we head out of town past the refuse incineration plant (I did say it wasn't all pretty) into open fields with occasional derelict tracts of land. The railway closes in from the right and beyond is Hem Heath colliery. Or it is at the moment. One moment it is scheduled to close, the next, a reprieve is granted. Whether or not it's there when you walk, my crystal ball does not reveal. On this stretch – if you're lucky – a young man engaging in falconry can be seen. He regularly walks the area, hawk on his arm, looking for a stray rabbit.

Bridge 106 is your first opportunity for refreshment. The Trentham attends to your liquid needs whilst there is a restaurant attached which provides good food at a reasonable price.

The housing has moved distinctly up-market now although this will quickly give way to trees and fields. Around the next bend is Trentham Lock. It's quite deep – almost 12ft – and the area is smart and tidy, the result of a Manpower Services scheme a decade ago. Rustic seating is provided and the remains of the lock cottage, demolished in the 1960s, have been repointed and made safe providing a little snippet of history.

Beyond the lock you can see the last bit of industry on your walk, the Wedgwood china factory. A few hundred yards below the lock (and beyond the only length of towing path that is not in good condition) is Bridge 104. Leave the canal here, cross the bridge and you can be in the Wedgwood Visitor Centre in five minutes.

It's open weekdays and for a small admission charge you can wander around a large hall watching demonstrations of some of the manufacturing processes. A small cinema gives a comprehensive account of the company, its history and work. The museum holds a superb collection of their products old and new and the inevitable gift shop will tempt you unmercifully.

As you return to the canal, Wedgwood halt will provide a train back to Stoke if you are now too heavily laden to continue the walk. For the rest, return to the canal and continue. There is another half mile or so of typically pretty Trent Valley scenery. Atop a hill to the right is a statue to local nobleman the Duke of Sutherland whilst the Plume of Feathers waits to greet us canalside at the next bridge. Here again, food that can be washed down with Bass or Worthington beers. Then turn left for the station, right for the bus.

If you do visit this pub, don't overdo it because, on your return to Stoke, the Railway in Harthill Road just south of the station demands a visit. Ansells at its very best. There's also a chip shop across the road which includes Wright's Pies in its repertoire. This is a local brand and of supremely high quality.

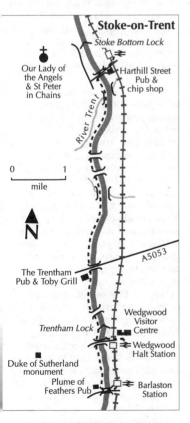

Stoke-on-Trent

Stoke Bottom Lock

Our Lady of the Angels & St Peter in Chains

Harthill Street Pub & chip shop

River Trent

0    1
mile

N

A5053

The Trentham Pub & Toby Grill

Wedgwood Visitor Centre

Trentham Lock

Wedgwood Halt Station

Duke of Sutherland monument

Plume of Feathers Pub

Barlaston Station

71

# 28 TRENT & MERSEY AND STAFFS & WORCS CANALS

## Colwich to Stafford

*by Dennis Needham*

**WALK TALK**

**Distance** – 7 miles.

**Start at** – Colwich Church; Grid Ref: SK 011212.

**OS Landranger Maps** – 128, Derby & Burton-upon-Trent and 127, Stafford & Telford.

**Guide** – *Waterways World Guides to the Trent & Mersey and Caldon Canals* and to the *Staffs & Worcs*.

**Public Transport** – The 825 Stafford to Lichfield/Tamworth bus stops outside The Trumpet. This is operated by Midland Red (0785 223344). Alight at Colwich by the church.

**Car Parking** – Free in the side streets of Colwich close to the church.

**Shugborough Hall** – A National Trust property of truly magnificent proportions. Ancestral home of the Earl of Lichfield and a 'must' for anyone with even the vaguest appreciation of beauty.

This pleasant, almost entirely rural, walk in the vale of the river Trent has most of the constituents of a good canal walk: a wide selection of canal infrastructure, good views and plenty of boating activity in season.

Start by the church in Colwich, just off the A51 Rugeley to Stone road. Across from the church, to the right of the buildings, are two paths. Take the right hand one which will bring you to Colwich Lock on the Trent & Mersey Canal.

Turn right and pass under the vast railway bridge where the lines to Scotland and Stoke-on-Trent diverge. It was here in 1986 that an horrific train crash occurred when a northbound express turned right into the path of a London train. Seeing the speed that they pass the spot, it was a miracle that it did not turn out to be a disaster of Harrow & Wealdstone proportions.

Beyond and to the left, the hills of Cannock Chase can be seen. There are over 20 square miles of heathland, designated an Area of Outstanding Natural Beauty, with herds of fallow deer roaming wild. Ahead, a pretty (un-numbered) iron bridge spans the canal. This used to be the drive to Shugborough Hall which can be seen through the trees on the left. The river Trent is at the other side of the towing path here and rhododendron bushes line the far bank offering a spectacular floral display in the right season.

A little further along, look to your left. There is a delightful stone bridge crossing the river. But it is not all it seems from this angle. Closer examination reveals it to be a packhorse bridge, the longest in the country, and only about 4ft wide. The 17th century Essex Bridge was originally a 40 arch structure; now only 14 are left. It gives access to Shugborough Hall, a National Trust property, and very well worth a visit.

Opposite Haywood Lock is a house that used to threaten all kinds of mayhem to any boatcrew daring to step on their ground. Now it is The Lockhouse Restaurant, licensed, offering hot meals all day, and bed & breakfast; altogether more welcoming. The elegant and much photographed bridge spanning the northern end of the Staffs & Worcs Canal can be seen now. This busy junction always has a collection of boats moored whilst the hire company across the way is a scene of frenetic activity at weekends as holidaymakers change over.

Here the walk turns left, into the Staffordshire & Worcestershire Canal. Opened in 1772, its aim was to make a cross country link between the rivers Severn and Trent, and later the Mersey. James Brindley was again the engineer, and its tortuous wanderings, his hallmark, can be seen almost at once. First, the line crosses over the infant river Trent on an aqueduct, and then under a bridge. Notice the large cast plates that carry not only the bridge number but its name as well.

The far bank then starts to move away as we enter the reed lined expanse known as Tixall Wide. A popular location for fishermen, it still retains a remarkable collection of bird life. Moorhens, mallards, herons and kingfishers all use the Wide as home. Beyond, the stables and gatehouse of Tixall Hall.

The original Tudor hall was sited here in 1580, built by Sir Walter Aston. A replacement was built alongside in the 18th century by Thomas Clifford, a descendant of the Astons. Mary, Queen of Scots was imprisoned here for a fortnight in 1586, only a few weeks before she met her end at Fotheringhay.

Although both halls are now long gone, the newer building was there when the canal arrived. In agreeing permission for the cut to pass through their land, the owners demanded a scenic passage; thus the broad expanse of water.

At the far end is Tixall Lock. A cast iron boundary post can be seen across the lock bearing the legend 'SWC'.

A very des. res. is situated across the canal by Bridge 105, Milford Bridge, with swimming pool, greenhouse, and (seemingly) acres of carefully tended lawn. A pretty picture.

Swinging sharp left, the line crosses the river Sow on another heavily built aqueduct before turning right, avoiding the railway. Trains here can creep up on you. There is a tunnel close by, masking the noise until the last minute.

Alongside the railway for over a mile now. Predominantly rural still, at the far end are some attractive chalet type dwellings cut into the embankment with glorious sun lounges: north facing! Several owners here have their boats moored outside the back door. As the canal makes a left turn under the railway, notice the concrete slabs in the towing path. Just here, the Stafford branch used to leave the canal. Baswich Lock once took the canal down into the river, which was then canalised into the town. It's been abandoned and unused for many a decade now.

The houses of Baswich now line the far bank, with the towing path side still offering unimpeded views to Stafford. Less than a mile then to Radford Bridge (98). Leave the canal here by the Trumpet pub. Outside their front door is the return bus stop.

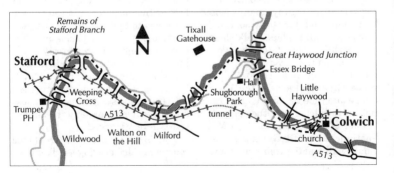

# 29 Trent & Mersey Canal

## Shardlow Circular

*by John Roddis*

**WALK TALK**

**Distance** – Shardlow to Trent Lock and back, 7 miles.

**Start at** – Shardlow; Grid Ref: SK 447305.

**OS Landranger Map** – 129, Nottingham & Loughborough.

**Guide** – *Waterways World Guide to the Trent & Mersey and Caldon Canals.*

**Public Transport** – Barton/Midland Fox/Kinch jointly operate services 121–124 from Derby and Leicester every hour, which call at Shardlow (2-hourly service on Sundays). Ring Busline on 0116 251 1411 for further details.

**Car Parking** – In Wilne Lane, Shardlow, just beyond Lady in Grey Restaurant. There is also a large car park at Trent Lock. Both are free.

**Moorings** – On towpath opposite Dobson's boatyard.

Shardlow is the starting point for this interesting and attractive walk along the Trent & Mersey Canal and the river Trent.

From the car park walk up Wilne Lane to the canal bridge, and turn left onto the towpath. Houses have been built here on the site of the former Trent Brewery and Cowlishaw's Wharf. Opposite is the Malt Shovel public house dating from 1799. There are always many moored boats here, and this stretch of canal is popular with anglers. Walk along the towpath to the A6 road bridge, observing on the way a well-preserved crane near a disused wharf. Cross the canal by the A6 bridge and take the first lane on the right, which leads past the entrance to Dobson's Boatyard, and No 1 Mill. Continue along Mill Green past the village hall and the Iron Warehouse

to eventually reach a pathway between some houses. This brings you to a back road where you turn right, past the impressive Wharf House to the Malt Shovel pub, and so back onto Wilne Lane.

Here, turn left up the lane, away from the canal. In about half a mile you pass a few isolated houses and a converted old chapel. Continue to where the lane ends at a field. Here there is a path waymarked 'Midshires Way' on the right.

The path runs to the right, along the edge of the field towards a footbridge which you can see in the distance. When you reach the bridge, do not cross it, but follow the river bank to the right. This is the river Derwent, draining a large chunk of Derbyshire, on the final stage of its journey to the Trent. There are a few stiles to negotiate, but the path is well marked. Eventually, at a left hand bend in the river, it leaves the bank and heads across a field, and then between two boggy pools, to reach the Trent & Mersey Canal at Derwentmouth Lock.

The nearby sewage works manages to be quite inoffensive, and the general surroundings of the lock, with its overhanging chestnut tree and blackberry bushes, are very pleasant.

For some reason, the bottom gates of the lock always seem to swing open if the lock is empty, so cross the lock by the top gates, and walk down the towpath to the point where the canal joins the river. This is one of our more impressive waterway junctions – a real cross-roads where the wide waters of the Trent are met by the Derwent running in from the left. The contrast between the almost secret canal entrance and the large rivers is very marked.

The towpath crosses the Trent on a concrete bridge bearing the Trent

Navigation Co's initials. Continue down the river bank, under the pipeline bridge and the M1 bridge to reach the lock cut leading to Sawley Flood Lock (usually open at both ends).

Across the main road is Sawley Bridge Marina where there is a coffee shop for snacks, light lunches, teas etc. Our walk, however, follows the towpath on the opposite side of Sawley Cut, down to the twinned Sawley Locks. These are always well kept, with a good display of flowers, and are usually very busy, especially at weekends. Both the locks are mechanised. The balance beams have been removed giving the lock gates an unusual appearance.

Now cross the Trent by the footbridge which runs alongside the railway viaduct, and then continue down the north bank of the river, on a well-maintained towpath, for about a mile to reach the cluster of houses, pubs, boatyards and houseboats that form the settlement known as Trent Lock. At this point the Erewash Canal (an outpost of the former Grand Union empire) runs into the Trent. The lock surroundings were much improved a few years ago. A British Waterways office and information point is situated near the lock. No matter what time of year, or what time of day, you visit this spot, it is always full of interest, and there is much to see. Both the pubs here do good bar snacks and lunches, and can be recommended. There is also a tea room in one of the lock-side houses.

The return journey to Shardlow could be made by retracing your steps up the towpath all the way. An alternative is to walk up the lane from Trent Lock, away from the river, for about a mile, over the level crossing, to reach the main road at Sawley village. Turn left past the filling station, then take Wilne Road on the right opposite the church. This soon bears left and reaches more open country. Cross the M1 and then take the lane on the left which, in about a mile, brings you back to the footbridge over the Derwent that was encountered on the outward journey. Rejoin the path to Wilne Lane, and walk back down here to Shardlow.

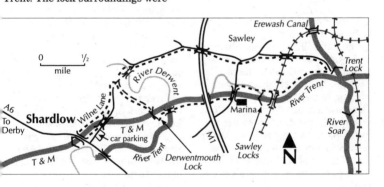

75

# 30 CALDON CANAL

## Etruria to Stockton Brook

*by Dennis Needham*

**WALK TALK**

**Distance** – Etruria to Bridge 18, Milton – 4 miles; Etruria to Stockton Brook – 6 miles.

**Start at** – The China Garden pub, by Etruria Marina in the Festival Retail Park, off the A53; Grid Ref: SJ 869475.

**OS Landranger Map** – 118, Stoke-on-Trent & Macclesfield. The A–Z Street Atlas to Stoke-on-Trent covers all the walk at a scale of 4in to a mile.

**Guide** – *The Waterways World Guide to the Trent & Mersey and Caldon Canals.*

**Public Transport** – PMT service 101 Leek to Stafford covers both return points. Alight at Cobridge traffic lights and walk down the hill to Festival Park, about 600 yards.

**Car Parking** – Plenty around the pub and all around the area.

Stark industry, staircase locks, an elegant city park and pretty countryside all in this short distance makes a quite irresistible walk.

At the China Garden pub turn left. This was built in 1986, along with the marina, as part of the National Garden Festival held that year. The whole area was derelict prior to the event, part of a huge steelworks. The marina is a particularly attractive mix of private boats, hire fleet and restaurant boat in an entirely urban setting.

Just beyond the marina, a busy dual carriageway forms a roving bridge. As you arrive on the right hand side, note the newspaper publishers, the site of Josiah Wedgwood's original works. Also look down on the round brick building.

Once canalside, it provides a graphic illustration of the effects of subsidence. This domed-roof building was constructed in 1769 in the same style as the old bottle kilns that once belched smoke and fumes into the atmosphere here. Round, brick, and with a thick metal strap around its waist, it had a variety of uses over the years. The newspaper company restored it in 1985 to house a display of printing techniques used in both the newspaper and pottery trades.

Gone are the days when this area was a seething melee of boats delivering coal and clay to the pottery, and taking the finished product away to Liverpool docks for export. With the local steelworks, who were also extensive users of the canal, it really must have been something to behold.

Passing under the main road, Etruria Junction is soon reached with the Caldon Canal leaving to the left. Opened in 1779 to feed raw materials from the hills to the pottery and steel industry, the line was classified a Remainder Waterway under the 1968 Transport Act. Thanks to an early example of co-operation between British Waterways, a vibrant canal society, and local authorities, it was re-opened in 1974 and up-graded to Cruising standard in 1983.

Cross the footbridge just beyond the top lock to gain the towpath. Two hundred yards ahead, the canal makes a sharp right turn towards Bedford Street Staircase Lock. Above the two-chamber lock, the housing is old and depressing, as are the factories; a really run-down area. Planet Lock is next. With a 3ft 10in rise, this is a real oddity: it was not built until 1916. Subsidence was again the culprit.

There then follows a real oasis of green. Hanley Park is a well-used recreation area, very popular with locals. An overbridge signifies the return of industry. Commercial narrowboats worked on this length until 1995. Two unusually shaped narrowboats that could be driven from either end were used with another of more conventional style to take pottery a few hundred yards between two works, Eagle and Imperial. A longer run to the Milton warehouse finished with rationalisation in the 1980s.

Ivy House Lift Bridge signifies the end of the factories. This once had a fearsome reputation among boat crews, but sweat and effort have now been replaced by electric operation. Sometimes. When new, the local yobbery discovered a new game called 'Block-up-the-Keyhole-with-Matchsticks/Chewing Gum'. However, the joy of this sport was attenuated somewhat by having to wait so long to see any results, and they seem (thankfully) to have turned their destructive proclivities to other targets.

By Bridge 16, the flattened factory on the left was the destination of the pottery boats mentioned earlier. The pottery industry has undergone many upheavals in recent years. So too has the coal industry. Virtually every colliery in this area is now closed; including Norton. The existence of this mine was the main reason for a 1,000 yard arm that ran off to the left alongside the Foxley pub. There was

also an ironworks, but that also disappeared, and the infilled arm is now virtually impossible to trace. The pub is inaccessible from the towpath, but if refreshment is needed, there are several pubs within a few yards of Bridge 18 just around the corner.

At the next bridge (19) it is possible to conclude the walk, but if you have another 1½ miles left in you, there is increasingly attractive scenery to come. Four locks, two lift bridges and the canal's feeder from Knypersley reservoir to the north.

As the canal reaches the main road by the Holly Bush pub, leave the towpath and catch the return bus, the same one that will pick up at Bridge 19.

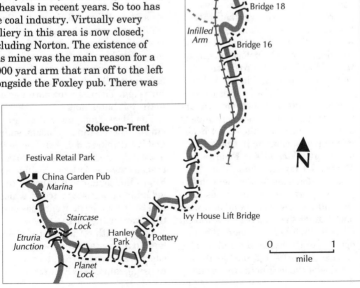

# 31 CALDON CANAL

## Cheddleton to Froghall

*by Ann Lee*

**WALK TALK**
**Distance** – Cheddleton Flint Mill to Froghall Wharf, 5½ miles.
**Start at** – Leek town centre; Grid Ref: SJ 987564
**OS Landranger Map** – 118, Stoke-on-Trent & Macclesfield.
**Public Transport** – Buses from Leek to Cheddleton are operated by Proctors. From Froghall to Leek, PMT services 234 or 236. Details from Staffordshire Bus on 01785 223344.
**Car Parking** – Plenty in Leek.

Generally acknowledged as one of the prettiest canals in the country, it has only recently been possible to add this walk to the *WW* list owing to a lack of public transport. This is now remedied courtesy of the council subsidised Staffordshire Bus.

The first step is a somewhat unusual one: we do not start at the beginning of the walk. Leek town centre is where we forgather, there to catch the bus to Cheddleton. Alight at the Flint Mill and examine this delightful relic before leaving on the walk. It's a few yards to the right on the main road and in a very pretty location. Open summer afternoons and weekends, waterwheels turn and a whole range of splendid machinery operates. The canal played a crucial role in transportation in this area and a butty *Vienna* – in Fellows Morton & Clayton colours – is moored alongside to represent this.

Having walked the few yards to the mill we now turn round and walk back, under the road bridge towards Cheddleton Top Lock where the re-opening of the restored canal was carried out in 1974. A plaque at the far side of the lock notes this great

day. Beyond, another lock and a right hand bend brings bridge 44 into view with either liquid sustenance to the right or a visit to the North Staffordshire Steam Railway on the left. Steam train rides are available at weekends during the season.

The river Churnet is close now as it vies with railway and canal for space in the narrow valley. Wood's Lock is passed and the lush greenery that typifies this line is much in evidence. No public roads reach this part of the route so our only company will be kindred spirits and a few boats. Indeed, considering the beauty of this canal, it is relatively unused. Apart from Tuesdays, when hire boats reach the end of their outward leg, and weekends, you can find real peace, even at the height of summer.

Oakmeadow Ford Lock then drops the canal into the river. Notices warn boats against proceeding when the river levels are too high, but walkers are seldom affected. The smell of wild garlic pervades now and trees crown the banks. Before long, the human race is in evidence again as we approach Consall Forge. On the right, set against the valley walls, are the remains of industry that used to operate here. Now canal and river split as the towpath crosses a pretty bridge over the river and the canal turns left. Then, the towpath moves to the left hand bank.

The Black Lion pub is also here, offering a good range of beers, snacks and hot drinks; a delightful place for a break in the walk. The canal soon reaches the last lock on this line at Flint Mill, so named because of the old building across the water which had the canal for its front door and the river for the back.

The towpath returns to the right hand bank as the canal passes Cherry Eye Bridge (53), a very unusual, almost Gothic arched construction. The word 'sylvan' was surely invented to describe the scenery on this length of canal so beautiful is it. The river and railway now lie far below in the valley bottom as the first signs of industry are discovered.

An enormous copper works lines the right hand bank before Froghall Tunnel is reached. There is no towpath through so you need to cross the road and follow the path opposite. This regains the water at the other end of the 76 yard bore where a winding hole effectively marks the end of the line. This is a popular gathering place for an afternoon out from the Potteries. However, by crossing the next road, you can reach the limit of water where a tearoom can also be found. As built, this canal used to continue to Uttoxeter, but when a railway was needed, much of the canal's line was taken for that and it closed in 1847. There are also lime kilns to be discovered here.

Leave the area and head towards the main road, there to catch a return bus to Leek.

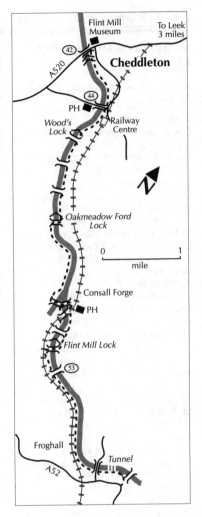

# 32 CROMFORD CANAL

## Bullbridge to Langley Mill

*by David Slater, revised by Mike Harrison*

### WALK TALK

**Distance** – Bullbridge to the Great Northern Basin, 9 miles.

**Start at** – The Canal Inn, Bullbridge; Grid Ref: SK 357523.

**OS Landranger Maps** – 119, Buxton, Matlock & Dovedale, 120, Mansfield & Worksop and 129, Nottingham & Loughborough.

**Public Transport** – Return by Trent Bus Company (01332 292200) routes 120, 124 (change at Wilmot Street, Heanor) or train (change at Nottingham & Derby).

**Car Parking** – Easy car parking (and sustenance) at both Bullbridge/ Ambergate and Langley Mill.

**Midland Railway Centre** – Butterley, Derbyshire (01773 570140) open daily in summer, otherwise weekends and Wednesdays.

This walk explores the largely forgotten nine miles of the Cromford Canal from Bullbridge to where it joins the Erewash & Nottingham canals at Langley Mill. It commences on Bullbridge Road near the Canal Inn. Here the canal is in water but is soon obliterated by a bungalow. The path descends a steep grassy slope, crosses the railway and the A610 and continues up an embankment behind St Mary's Mission. This gap, high above the river Amber, was the location of Bullbridge Aqueduct until 1968.

The canal bed continues above the houses of Sawmills and passes through a four arched stone bridge before being lost briefly under a small car park. Remains of an earlier line of the canal can be seen under a half infilled bridge along the lane to the right. At Ladygrove, garages,

greenhouses and even a hen run are built on the line. The infilled canal then becomes more secluded until the short Buckland Hollow Tunnel is reached. Pass through the tunnel and across the Excavator public house car park, turn right under a railway bridge and then across farmland. At Stevens (or Starvehimvalley) Bridge a short section is in water and used as a fishery. A footpath is then followed across two fields to Lower Hartshay. A raised pipe here adjacent to a neat terrace indicates the position of the canal. Shortly beyond are the remains of a wharf where a rivetted iron narrowboat hull lies decaying.

The channel now contains some water and having passed the Gate Inn and negotiated the 125 concrete steps over the new A610 embankment, one continues along a wooded cutting leading to the western end of the 3063 yard Butterley Tunnel.

Follow the route over the tunnel by walking under the A38 and turning first left onto a track between a private drive and Hammersmith station of the Midland Railway Centre. Pass over the railway (watch out for steam trains at weekends!) and alongside Butterley Reservoir, then turn left to the main road. Pass by the entrance to Butterley Engineering Works then turn right towards Derbyshire Police Headquaters. This road then bears left and continues for a straight mile virtually over Butterley Tunnel, confirmed by adjacent ventilation shafts.

The canal is rejoined by turning left to the Newlands Inn. A sign to the Midland Railway Centre Country Park directs us along a recently dredged section to the eastern portal of Butterley Tunnel in a cutting with a cascading feeder.

On returning, the canal continues past the hamlet of Golden Valley towards Ironville. The towpath is on a narrow strip of land between the canal

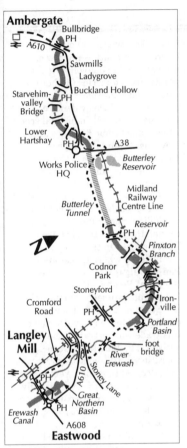

The overgrown remains of the once extensive Codnor Park Ironworks give an idea of the area's industrial past.

After a Bailey bridge, a stone side bridge indicates the entrance to what was Portland Basin. The cast iron aqueduct which carried the branch over the river Erewash has been demolished and the basin infilled. The only remaining evidence is the wharf wall, adjacent to which ran a tramway.

In water, but very overgrown, the canal heads straight to the remains of an LNER bridge. From here only a track continues through the fields. Traces of Stoneyford Top Lock (9) may be seen before the small settlement of Stoneyford and the Boat Inn.

The canal has now been completely obliterated by opencast mining, but a footpath signed 'Cromford Canal Walk' follows the line. Crossing the river Erewash by a footbridge, which indicates the position of another aqueduct, the path continues through wetlands which are the result of mining subsidence.

One now passes a small copse on the right. The determined explorer will here discover the remains of Vickers Lock (12) and adjacent cottage. The path then arrives at Stoney Lane. At the time of writing, the Cromford Canal Walk between here and the site of Strutt's Lock (13), which is not a right of way, has been obstructed with barbed wire. Unless prepared for some mountaineering via the A610 embankment, it is best to turn right along Stoney Lane, recross the river and pass under the A610 to join Cromford Road. Continue down into Langley Mill and turn left at the main road by The Mill public house to shortly arrive at the Great Northern Basin.

Langley Bridge Lock (14) was restored in 1973 giving access from the Erewash Canal to moorings on both the Cromford and Nottingham canals. A plaque and Amber Valley tourist map give more details. The swing bridge and Great Northern public house complete the scene.

and Codnor Park Reservoir. A major flood relief scheme in the 1980s entailed lowering the water level and removing the top lock. The towpath is diverted via two modern footbridges over this flood relief channel. However, the stone arch bridge at the entrance to the two mile Pinxton Branch survives as does the remainder of the Codnor Park flight.

Canalside buildings on the right include the former pottery (adjacent to Pottery Lock No.3) and the Mechanics Institute. On the left below Gas House Lock (5) are the remains of the lock keeper's cottage, stables and maintenance yard. Marshalls Lock (6) has an interesting dry dock alongside.

# 33 LLANGOLLEN CANAL

## Chirk to Llangollen

*by Dennis Needham*

**WALK TALK**

**Distance** – Chirk centre to Llangollen Wharf, 9 miles.

**Start at** – The centre of Chirk off the B5070 (ex-A5); Grid Ref: SJ 291376.

**OS Landranger Maps** – 117, Chester & Wrexham and 126, Shrewsbury.

**Guide** – *Waterways World Guide to the Llangollen and Montgomery Canals.*

**Public Transport** – Operated by Bryn Melin (01978 860828), not Sunday.

**Car Parking** – Plenty of side roads.

**Caution** – There are two tunnels and one high aqueduct; sufferers from vertigo and claustrophobia should take note. A torch for use in the tunnels is a useful accessory.

A walk of sheer beauty, incorporating the only section of the Llangollen Canal that can really make that claim. With virtually no industry, and long lengths out of range of strollers, this is waterside walking at its finest. No locks, but enough infrastructure to uplift the weariest spirit.

There is a choice of starting point. For those with claustrophobic tendencies, take Station Road from Chirk town (or village) centre and, just beyond the railway, a path on the right reaches the canal at the north end of Chirk Tunnel. For the full walk, follow the westerly road (B4500) towards Chirk Castle, and take a flight of steps on the left which leads to the southern portal of the tunnel. Turn right, into the ¼ mile gloom.

The cutting beyond is exquisitely beautiful, falling gently back to water level as it rounds a right hand bend. Beyond here, a winding hole marks what was once Black Park

Basin. This was a rail/canal interchange point. A narrow gauge railway used to deliver slate and granite from quarries further up the valley, and coal from local collieries. There is now little evidence of what was once a vibrant industrial scene which ended some 60 years ago.

A huge leisure development now dominates the scenery, the centrepiece of which is a marina with hire boat base. Soon, Whitehouses Tunnel appears. This is only a short one – 190 yards – and is not too forbidding. Soon after leaving this tunnel, the canal turns sharp left at Irish Bridge. On this corner was once a rail siding where limestone from Pen-y-Craig quarry was loaded by the Great Western Railway.

The quarry itself is further along the canal, on the left. They used the canal in earlier days, but much of this trade was lost when the railway arrived. The lime kilns were operating until the last war. It was then decided that they were a beacon from the air, and the strategically vital steelworks in Wrexham were only a few minutes away in a Luftwaffe bomber.

The canal is now contained in a concrete trough, the result of chronic ground instability over the years. A lift bridge at Fron heralds a right turn leading to the Pontcysyllte Aqueduct. This structure has had superlatives hurled at it from anyone who can lift a pen, and every one fully justified. If vertigo rather than claustrophobia is your curse, there is a road alternative. Leave the towing path at Fron, heading left towards the main road. Here, a right turn signposted Trevor drops down into the Dee valley (allowing views of the aqueduct from river level) and up the other side to Trevor Basin.

At the far end of the aqueduct is the basin and a low bridge to the left which takes the canal towards

Llangollen. This was originally intended as a water feed for the main canal which was to continue ahead to Chester, servicing pits and steelworks on its way. It would then give a direct link between the town of Ellesmere and the sea.

A wooden footbridge over the canal gives access to the hire company's shop and, through the gate, to the continuation of the walk. Alternatively, carry on to the next road bridge, turn left to the road and left again. This takes the walk past The Telford Inn before meeting up with the short cut.

Pick up the canal again by the road bridge, with the towing path on the right. This crosses after a few yards, and stays to the left for the rest of the walk. The term 'contour canal' is now re-defined. It sticks rigidly to the north side of the Dee valley and contorts itself dramatically in so doing. This length of canal is contained in an older trough, but before long the new style concrete takes over. This approaches the once notorious length that was very prone to failure: the most recent, in 1985,

having produced the present reconstruction.

Ahead is Castell Dinas Bran, 1,100 thrombosis-inducing feet up in the Welsh hills. Here, Eliseg, Prince of Powys, defended his land against the English invaders. Today, they are called visitors and Eliseg's descendants welcome them with open cash registers.

Sun Trevor Inn marks the start of a very narrow section with a blind bend. It's a good spot for those with a sadistic streak to watch often inexperienced boaters meeting and trying to cope with a perceptible current. A couple of bank failures occurred here in the 1940s. One released sufficient debris and water to take out the railway track below. A goods train was wrecked, unfortunately resulting in fatal injuries to the driver.

High above the rooftops, the Llangollen Canal reaches the town. The walk finishes at Bridge 45. Here, a horse-drawn trip boat will convey you to the source of the water at Horseshoe Falls. Leave the canal, turn left down the hill, over the river and into the town for the return bus.

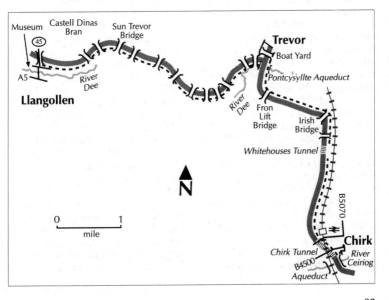

# 34 LLANGOLLEN CANAL

## Ellesmere to Hampton Bank

*by Joseph Boughey*

**WALK TALK**

**Distance** – Ellesmere Wharf to Hampton Bank, 4 miles.

**Start at** – Ellesmere Wharf; Grid Ref: SJ 398345.

**OS Landranger Map** – 126, Shrewsbury.

**Guide** – *Waterways World Guide to the Llangollen & Montgomery Canals.*

**Public Transport** – Cambrian Midland Red 226 Whittington–Ellesmere Whitchurch service (Fridays only); Fishers 423 Whitchurch–Ellesmere–Oswestry (Wednesdays only). Contact Shropshire Traveline (0345 056785). At Hampton Bank buses stop on request (no actual bus stop).

Bus timings make it best to begin by the canal at Hampton Bank and take the bus to Cross Street in Ellesmere. From here, walk through the town to Ellesmere Wharf, where a warehouse wall still proclaims the carrying services offered by the Shropshire Union company until 1921. This branch featured coal and timber wharves, and a gas works and iron foundry. To the west was the former United Dairies creamery. This reflected Ellesmere's earlier importance to the cheese trade, with canal traffic still passing in 1920. For many years United Dairies was a major user of canal water, and the water returned to the canal was often at a high temperature!

This part of the canal featured a number of early pleasure boating activities. On the offside just before White Bridge is the site of a boathouse, demolished in 1951, which was used by a local rowing club from the Victorian era onwards; while in the 1930s trip boats were operated by Albert Hobson Greenwood, a Shrewsbury coach operator, between Ellesmere and Colemere, a route which this walk will follow.

Along the main canal to the right can be seen the BW Ellesmere Depot, while opposite is Beech House, formerly the Ellesmere Canal Company's offices. The towpath to Red Bridge runs opposite the side of this house. An open section beyond leads into a wooded approach to Ellesmere Tunnel. Some 87 yards long, this is a fairly shallow tunnel but with a major road junction and a car park on top. Beyond, a wooded section leads to Blake Mere, one of several in the Shropshire lake district; it is separated from the canal only by the towpath. One or two paths run close to the Mere, while there is some access to the woods beyond.

Beyond Burns Wood Bridge, on the offside, is a large dredging tip in active use, well screened by trees. A winding hole is followed by an open stretch, with an unusual thatched cottage and glimpses of Cole Mere in the distance. To take a closer look at the Mere, with a boathouse on its far side, leave the towpath at Little Mill Bridge, follow the path close to the shores of the lake, and then up to rejoin the towpath at Miss Each Bridge. The path partly follows the base of the canal embankment here, which is marked by some Shropshire Union boundary posts. A large overflow runs off excess water into Cole Mere.

A high wall punctured by a series of arches marks the remains of lime kilns. The latter were filled directly from the top from loaded boats; a bungalow now stands on the site above, and there are few signs of the wharf from the towpath. This wharf was disused by 1890. The towpath coping under Miss Each Bridge is one of a number made from bricks manufactured by Wood & Avery, of Albion brickworks, West Bromwich, alongside the Birmingham Canal Navigations. The management of both the Shropshire Union and the BCN were closely connected from the last century, and presumably the bricks were brought here by canal.

The towpath to Lyneal Road Bridge has only been restored relatively recently; this is shown by the unusual vegetation. The canal curves sharply round under the bridge, an original one which has been heavily reinforced. Lyneal Wharf was in regular use in the early part of the century, until 1921; from here the Lyneal Trust operate *Shropshire Lad* and *Shropshire Lass* for handicapped people. Ahead, the canal runs past a wooded area before passing under Greaves Bridge, beyond which there is a slight cutting, crossed by Lyneal Lane on a level if much-patched bridge. The landscape then changes; this area is known as Balmer Heath, and the vegetation on both sides of the canal reflects this. There is the site of a small estate wharf on the offside just beyond Lyneal Lane Bridge, before the canal runs on to a low embankment. Whilst all of the bridges so far have been original bridges, albeit altered, Hampton Bank Bridge dates from the 1990s; however, it has been reconstructed with a hump-backed form and faced

in brick. Beyond the bridge, a number of wharves can be seen in the distance, but this is the point to return to the bus stop.

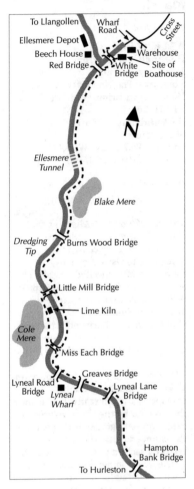

# 35 MONTGOMERY CANAL

## Frankton to Maesbury Marsh

*by Ann Lee*

**WALK TALK**

**Distance** – Maestermyn to Maesbury, 7½ miles.

**Start at** – The Narrowboat Inn at Maestermyn Bridge; Grid Ref: SJ 351326.

**OS Landranger Map** – 126, Shrewsbury.

**Guide** – *Waterways World Guide to the Llangollen and Montgomery Canals.*

**Public Transport** – The very limited service from Oswestry to Ellesmere is operated by Bus Clwyd, services 278 or 423. Alight at the Narrowboat pub one mile beyond Whittington. Service 576 from Maesbury to Oswestry is by Cambrian Midland Red. Details of all services from 01691 652402, 01691 662488 or 0345 056785. None operate on Sunday.

**Car Parking** – Large off street car park in Oswestry, or on a side road close to the bus stop in Maesbury.

A very difficult walk to achieve due to the paucity of public transport, any effort involved is more than repaid by the sheer volume of canal interest, gorgeous scenery, and the chance to visit the newest restored section of the Montgomery.

The bus is joined in Oswestry, a town not noted for its canal association. Alight at the Narrowboat Inn, Maestermyn Bridge. To gain the towpath, cross the bridge, and on the left is an opening. Once on the towpath, you are across the water from the Narrowboat Inn. Turn left. The towing path initially leaves something to be desired but it doesn't last too long before the first bridge is reached and matters become altogether better.

A roving bridge takes the path to the right hand bank and then, as you approach Frankton Junction, another one returns to the left. Ignore the second and bear right to reach the Montgomery Canal; or Llanymynech Branch of the Ellesmere Canal if you want to be pedantic. The locks, a staircase of two followed by two singles, were re-opened in 1987 by Dr Alan Robertson CBE, then Vice Chairman of British Waterways. The house on the offside of the canal between the third and bottom locks was once part of the boatyard from which the young L.T.C. Rolt was a passenger on the newly converted narrowboat *Cressy* that he would eventually buy.

Some 500 yards from the locks is a 'T' junction where the walk turns right. The section to the left was originally proposed as the main line, connecting Chester with Shrewsbury via Wrexham, Trevor, and Frankton. In the event, Shrewsbury was never reached, the canal ending at Weston Lullingfields, six miles away, still several miles short of Shrewsbury. The defined course of this ends after only a few yards, and, although some traces can be found further beyond, they are on private land. Moorings have been constructed here; it's a delight to see the boats again after so many years.

Now the Monty adopts the style that will become its hallmark for the next three miles: total peace. The countryside is open, beautiful, but somewhat featureless, due to the fact that farmers here seem to be arch-proponents of hedgerow destruction. Past the site of the 1936 breach that hastened its closure, the new (Graham Palmer) lock and a new aqueduct over the river Perry. The towpath forms a raised island between river and canal. It's so delightfully remote now, with very few boats around. This seclusion also brings a bonus: no dogs being taken 'walkies' and no mountain bikes bearing down on hapless walkers at breakneck speeds.

The entrance to Rednal Basin is then reached. This housed, amongst other things, a fertiliser works operational until 1921, and an interchange with the Great Western Railway, closed over 100 years ago.

A sharp right turn takes the canal under the railway into a mile long arrow-straight length. The old building on the left has an unusual history. A small door at water level is believed to have been used by passengers on the Newtown to Rednal flyboat that operated nearly a century and a half ago. The bridge beyond takes the towpath to the left bank and the whole peaceful vista is complemented by the presence of swans, mallard and moorhen. These are well established, having been in residence when the canal was still derelict.

At Queens Head the A5 London to Holyhead road roars noisily overhead on a new bridge with navigable headroom. The old bridge here was culverted when it carried the A5 but the new route has allowed reconstruction to take place. The pub itself is a pleasant watering hole whilst on the towpath side is an old warehouse. There was a flour mill and sand quarry here once, both providing work for the canal. The milepost, erected in 1989, is in memory of Graham Palmer.

300 yards along, the first of three Aston locks is reached and navigation is at an end for the time being. The wildlife conservation people have been active here after finding some rare plants growing in the canal. Declared a SSSI, reserves

have been created alongside, into which they have been moved to allow restoration of navigation.

Below Aston locks is another remote and pretty length with very few accommodation bridges. Beyond one of them, the towpath enters an avenue of mature trees. Roots break the surface, creating quite a hazard for the unwary.

With the channel clear of weed, Maesbury Marsh hoves into view. At the Navigation Inn, leave the towpath, turn right, and the bus stop is 200 yards along on the left.

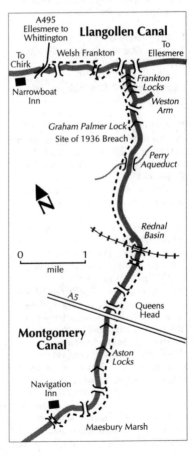

# 36 MONTGOMERY CANAL

## Four Crosses to Welshpool

*by Ann Lee*

**WALK TALK**
**Distance** – Clafton Bridge to Severn Street Bridge, 7 miles.
**Start at** – Clafton Bridge, Four Crosses; Grid Ref: SJ 264185.
**OS Landranger Map** – 126, Shrewsbury.
**Guide** – *Waterways World Guide to the Llangollen and Montgomery Canals.*
**Public Transport** – Cambrian Midland Red Welshpool to Oswestry service D71 – Not Sundays. Service details on 0345 056785.
**Car Parking** – Roadside on the B4393.

The towpath can be gained from the B4393 by following the path to the left just before the road starts to rise for the bridge. Turn left for Welshpool.

The first of many flattened bridges appears before too long but, fortunately, local authority commitment will see this and the others rebuilt before too many more years are past. The first canal infrastructure of real interest is at Burgedin. Just above the top lock, the course of the 2¼ mile Guilsfield Branch diverges to the right. Some of it still exists, and a nature reserve has been established on the line, making it possible to explore parts. Trade was almost exclusively coal and limestone, a feature of so much of the main line as well. The two locks, dropping the canal to its lowest level, are currently under restoration: the next lock will be 'uphill'. From here, the canal is navigable all the way into Welshpool.

By the next bridge, surplus water runs off to the river Severn under the towpath and through an intriguing weir. This curious structure diverted water to the nearby corn mill, thus ensuring it was of some use before finally being discarded. The scenery is starting to open out at this point, and the Severn valley in all its majesty is plain to see. As are the Briedden hills; over 1,300ft high in places.

Soon, the next lock is reached. It is Bank Lock, the first of four chambers that will lift the canal 35ft to the Welshpool level: thus the last locks on this walk. If you are fortunate, there will be a boat using the flight, allowing the opportunity to see the distinctive 'Monty' paddle gear in operation. The word 'flight' is something of an exaggeration as the distance between bottom and top is over a mile.

The name of the top lock, Pool Quay, may mislead. It does not refer to a canal quay, but to one by the river Severn, which closes to the canal just beyond the lock. There is no trace of the quay now, or of the industry that once operated. There were mills for corn, lead and wool, all operating until well into the last century and providing trade for the canal.

Steeply sloping hills to the right add to the attractiveness of this length, and are soon covered by trees. The only intrusion into this pleasure is the incessant noise from the trunk road which is never too far away. The line weaves somewhat as it clings tenaciously to the contour. There are a number of lift bridges along here, mostly operational, of the old fashioned hang-on-to-a-chain-and-heave type; not the 'easy' type so beloved of current BW management that need 90 or more turns of a windlass to operate.

The Moors Bird Sanctuary is just beyond Bridge 114 on the towpath side. Those with an interest ornithological will doubtless want to make the few yards detour to examine this fine collection of exotic creatures. Then comes Buttington Wharf. This was a canal wharf, as evidenced by the carefully restored lime kilns. Picnic tables, mooring rings and an interpretation board all make this a very pleasant spot. Just beyond the wharf is a huge area of land, now the nascent Buttington Ross Enterprise Park.

Gallows Tree Bridge, once another of the levelled crossings, is now restored, but without a towpath. Walk up the slope, cross the road that is not now so busy with the opening of a Welshpool bypass and regain the path on the other side. The old course of the canal has been abandoned to allow construction of the new bridge. The two lines converge after just 100 yards. Now, for the first time on this walk, it really gives the impression of a canal walk. Good firm towpath, the water is weeded only in the margins, and plenty of silt stirred into the water. Even a bit of rubbish. The several wharves and factories that lined both sides of the canal in this length are now no more, but under Mill Lane bridge across the water is a slipway and some end-on moorings for boats.

The iron girder bridge crossing the canal next was originally used by the Welshpool & Llanfair Light Railway, and linked with the Cambrian Railway station a little to the left. Opened in 1903, the W&L ran for nine miles up the valley and was built to the (unusual) gauge of 2ft 6in. It closed in 1956, only to be rescued by a Preservation Society formed soon afterwards. But even they could not beat the might of Welshpool council who wanted some of the route for road widening. Now, the section between the main line

and the western edge of town is gone, and no more will delightful little steam engines shuffle their way across the canal.

The next bridge sees the end of the walk. Turn right into Severn Street, and to High Street for the return bus.

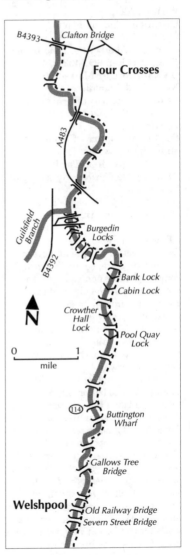

# 37 MONTGOMERY CANAL

## Aberbechan to Garthmyl

*by Ann Lee*

**WALK TALK**

**Distance** – Aberbechan to Garthmyl, 7$^1$/$_2$ miles.

**Start at** – Aberbechan Road Bridge (152); Grid Ref: SO 142934.

**OS Landranger Map** – 136, Newtown & Llanidloes.

**Guide** – *Waterways World Guide to the Llangollen and Montgomery Canals.*

**Public Transport** – Cambrian Midland Red bus service D75 stops across the road from The Nags Head. (Details 0345 056785). No service on Sundays.

**Car Parking** – Roadside in layby close to river Severn.

The southernmost 1$^1$/$_2$ miles of the Montgomery Canal at Newtown are now no more, being dry, with the course virtually non-existent. To the north, exquisite beauty and stark ruggedness interchange with startling rapidity. And, as this section is still some years away from seeing boats again, the towpath is the only way to enjoy this rather special waterway.

It was the final length of the Montgomery to be completed, Garthmyl being the southern terminus for over twenty years before funds were found to reach Newtown, the link finally opening in 1821.

The walk starts at the hamlet of Aberbechan, a couple of miles north of Newtown on the A483 road to Welshpool, effectively the first left hand turn after Newtown. 250 yards along the B4389 from the turn is a widish layby for parking, right by the river Severn. One hundred yards further along is the canal bridge. Turn left. The towpath here, and for

virtually all this walk, is in good condition, and only causes a few problems after sustained heavy rain. After 600 yards you will reach the limit of the canal at Freestone Lock. An incredibly decrepit bridge spans the tail of this lock, looking as unsafe as the lock chamber itself. Here is a water feed from the river Severn, just a few yards away. There were a couple more locks between here and Newtown, but much of the canal's course is now on private land.

Return to the road bridge and examine a superb cast iron span. A plaque records that it was manufactured at Brymbo in 1852. Brymbo was a steel works near Wrexham that is no more. Beyond, a pretty aqueduct takes the line over Bechan Brook to a flattened Bridge 151 at Aberbechan. Here was a wharf with lime kilns. Now, fairly modern bungalows line the canal each side. Restoration of the bridge is not a very complex problem. The scenery in this length of the Severn valley is of the dramatic variety with hills towering over the water to the left, and gentler slopes to the right.

After another half mile, locks start to appear. Newhouse and Byles are first, with the river having closed very tightly to the right. Beyond here the walk reaches one of the early triumphs of the preservation (later restoration) movement. In the early 1970s, a by-pass was due take the A483 away from the village of Abermule, and a culvert was scheduled for the proposed route over the canal. Vigorous lobbying eventually resulted in a navigable tunnel being built, albeit without a towpath. Just before the entrance, take the gate to the right, and follow the path around, to the left, under the road to regain the towpath. Canal and road are close companions for the next 2$^1$/$_2$ miles, but several lengths are well sheltered, and the traffic is not too intrusive.

A double bridge takes the old road over both canal and river, another

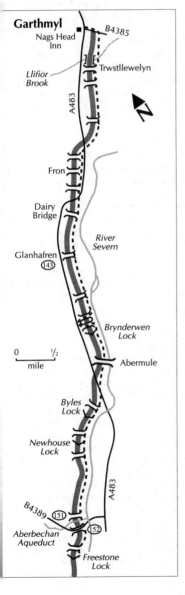

**Garthmyl**
Nags Head Inn
B4385
Trwstllewelyn
Llifior Brook
A483
Fron
Dairy Bridge
River Severn
Glanhafren (143)
Brynderwen Lock
Abermule
0    ½
mile
Byles Lock
Newhouse Lock
A483
B4389 (151)
Aberbechan Aqueduct
(152)
Freestone Lock

exquisite iron structure, and brings the walk to Brynderwen lock. At the head, on the far bank, is an old warehouse still carrying the legend, 'Shropshire Union Railway & Canal Co'. Below is a wharf and lock cottage. Here, the towpath changes sides to bypass the wharf.

Another pretty bridge, cast iron platform resting on brick abutments, takes the towpath back to the right. Glanhafren Bridge (143) is even prettier with blue and white painted iron railings. The stark beauty of the previous lengths has now given way to tree-lined elegance. The hills are never far away, but the whole feeling here is one of intimacy.

At Dairy Bridge, the first major blockage is revealed. A brick wall dated 1949 records the dirty deed. Cross the road, and a gate gives access to the towpath again, and to the settlement at Fron. Here, there were wharves and more lime kilns. In only half a mile, another flattened bridge is reached. Beyond, the canal leaves the road for its last mile and wanders through pure agricultural land with a few accommodation bridges before Trwstllewelyn (and you thought you had trouble pronouncing Pontcysyllte) Bridge takes an unclassified road towards Montgomery over the water. As for much of this walk, the canal here is very weedy, but only requires a good dredging.

A brick aqueduct carries the canal over Llifior Brook, and to the B4385 which marks the end of this walk. The canal is now dry for some 250 yards. This was occasioned by a re-alignment of the road a little further ahead. Leave the towpath and turn left, walking the few yards to the main road. On the right, just opposite the pub, is a layby where the return bus stops. Alight at Aberbechan Turn, cross the road, and walk down the lane to the start.

# 38 SHREWSBURY & NEWPORT CANAL

## Newport – Out and Back

*by Joseph Boughey*

**WALK TALK**
**Distance** – By-pass to Polly's Lock,
1½ miles (3 miles total).
**Start at** – Newport Wharf; Grid Ref:
SJ 743194.
**OS Landranger Map** – 127,
Stafford & Telford.
**Car Parking** – at Newport Wharf.

This short walk covers the only major length of the Newport Branch of the Shropshire Union Canal which remains in water. Although it closed in 1944, and with its draining and sale approved in 1960, a brief campaign to restore the Newport Branch lasted until 1966. Newport UDC was the only local authority to support restoration, and acquired the canal, improving it as a local amenity, albeit by cascading the locks, in 1971. There are no facilities at either end, and it is best to start this walk by Newport Wharf, where there is a car park, retracing steps from each end.

The Wharf is by Newport Road Lock, which has been cascaded and the canal below filled in, but with one Shropshire Union ground paddle – now a very rare sight – intact. Opposite, only one wharf building survives, the main warehouse having been demolished during the last 25 years. This was operated by the Shropshire Union company until it ceased carrying in 1921, when the Chester & Liverpool Lighterage Co took over, bringing grain from Ellesmere Port into the 1920s. There is a large basin here; many traffics terminated at Newport, beyond which coal was the main traffic. Coal, mainly from

South Staffordshire, was still arriving at the coal wharf in 1943, while gas tar passed from here to Oldbury in the 1930s.

Above the lock, the walk follows a neat towpath towards Haycock's Lock. Again cascaded, the offside features moden housing which has blended in well with the retained canal. Summer House Bridge, on a slight skew, follows. A weed screen blocks the canal here; five separate angling bodies fish this section, and keep it in good order. Along this length, small stages have been constructed, part of Newport's bid to host a national competition for disabled anglers in 1994.

The next section enters open countryside, across an embankment. The cost of piling embankments for powered craft was one British Waterways Board justification for their dismissal of the restoration proposals in 1965–66. At the end of this section, a small and unobtrusive pumping station provides the water supply for the canal, diverting it from a stream. The water ends abruptly at the tail of Meretown Lock; this has been firmly filled in, with the empty canal beyond heavily overgrown. Shortly after, the Newport by-pass cuts through the canal line; it is worth walking up the sloping path alongside this to get a view of the canal embankment.

Retracing steps to Newport Road, the canal is filled in under the former A41 road bridge, which has survived unscathed. However, it is necessary to duck one's head underneath, as the infilling process attempted to provide a slope to keep the canal water flowing. A very thin channel emerges for a short length before the canal continues at full width. The road bridge was also a turnover bridge with a very definite

ath before the 'restoration'
roclaimed on a plaque on the far
ridge parapet. Unfortunately, this
s surfaced incongruously in tarmac.
The next section was semi-rural
ntil recent housing development,

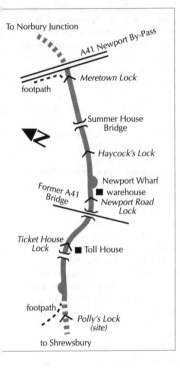

To Norbury Junction

A41 Newport By-Pass

footpath

Meretown Lock

Summer House
Bridge

N

Haycock's Lock

Former A41
Bridge

Newport Wharf

■ warehouse

Newport Road
Lock

Ticket House
Lock

■ Toll House

footpath

Polly's Lock
(site)

to Shrewsbury

which comes close to the towpath at
one point. As elsewhere, the central
channel is flanked by reeds on
either side; this section is home for
aquatic wildlife, including a family
of (sometimes rather aggressive)
swans. In the distance, just before
Ticket House Lock, is a typical lock
cottage, like that at Audlem Top
Lock on the Shropshire Union
Canal main line, although this has
been enlarged. The lock has been
rather scruffily cascaded, with an
ungainly steel deck over the
accommodation bridge below.
However, the grooves in the
ironwork have been carefully
painted. The towpath below is poor
by comparison with the rest;
probably walkers use it less, as the
canal runs out into open
countryside. A stream culvert under
the lock is worth viewing here.

This last length upon which
leakages were detected features a
wide pool towards its end, with
reeds forming an island in its
centre. Beyond, the canal ends
abruptly. A pipe takes the water
into a stream; the culvert and
Polly's Lock have been bulldozed
away, and there is absolutely no
sign into the distance that the canal
ever proceeded further, besides a
short length of footpath which takes
up its line.

# 39 GRANTHAM CANAL

## Gamston to Cropwell Bishop

*by David Slater, revised by Jack Lynam*

**WALK TALK**
**Distance** – Gamston to Cropwell Bishop, 7½ miles.
**Start at** – Tollerton Bridge (7); Grid Ref: SK 609367.
**OS Landranger Map** – 129, Nottingham & Loughborough.
**Public Transport** – Barton Transport (0115 924 0000). Services 22 and 22b. Timetable obtainable from Broad Marsh bus station or the Tourist Information Office in Nottingham. The bus stop in Cropwell Bishop is opposite the Post Office on Church Road.
**Car Parking** – Road parking at both Gamston and Cropwell Bishop. Also there is a very convenient small car park (8 places) at the start of the walk at Bridge 7 on Tollerton Road.
**Societies** – The Grantham Canal Restoration Society, 76 St Michael's Avenue, Gedling, Nottingham NG4 3PE (0115 953 1153).
Grantham Navigation Association, 36 Brockwood Crescent, Keyworth, Nottinghamshire NG12 5HQ (0115 937 5696).

The Grantham Canal was another success for William Jessop and much of its 33 miles from Nottingham to Grantham meanders in a contour fashion through the vale of Belvoir. Opened in 1797, it served to exchange coal in the Erewash Valley for agricultural produce in the Vale. However, after 1851, the new railway between Nottingham and Grantham caused a decline in canal traffic and this finally resulted in its legal abandonment in 1936.

The walk commences at Tollerton Bridge (7), Gamston, where Tollerton Lane crosses the canal. Access is gained from the Lings Bar Road (A52).

The vista is instantly rural with broad horizons and the canal, although shallow, is still in water and weed free. The towpath is wide and well maintained but stout footwear is recommended in winter. A characteristic Grantham Canal Restoration Society milepost soon indicates that we are 2½ miles from the Trent. Tollerton Airport occupies the land immediately to the south. Lowe's Bridge (8) has now been culverted and Hallam's Swing Bridge (9) has been replaced by a low, fixed, concrete crossing.

The canal then crosses Thurlbeck Dyke by an aqueduct (designated bridge number 10) and this is best seen by scrambling down the Dyke's steep bank. Polser Brook soon runs along the offside having passed under another canal aqueduct close to Skinner's Lock Cottage. This isolated stretch may, however, assume vital importance in the future as one restoration proposal is to canalise Polser Brook and navigate it to the Trent at Holme Pierrepont.

Passage by Sanders' Lock takes us to the culverted Cotgrave Bridge (12) where an information board is provided by the Restoration Society and Trust. Cropwell Bishop is stated to be 4½ miles distant and Grantham, for marathon walkers, 29 miles!

At this point the canal is overrun by weed and grass and the water level diminishes gradually. However, despite the low water level, the canal is home for several swans and in late spring nesting birds and cygnets are frequent sightings.

Several locks on the canal still possess wooden quoins bolted to the stone and this is well seen in the next two: Cotgrave Bridge and Hollygate Lane. Astute eyes are necessary to see the remains of Bridges 13 and 14 but Colliery Bridge (14A) is appropriately named as it once served to convey British Coal traffic from the now dismantled Cotgrave Colliery. We enter a pleasant wooded section which takes us over Hollygate Lane Bridge (15), past Joss's Lock and by the Hollygate feeder. The area is rich in wild flowers and butterflies and identification of the former (for non-botanists such as myself) is helped by an excellent Society booklet.

As we approach Mann's Bridge (16) with its silted winding hole, the return of civilisation is heralded by cars speeding along the distant Fosse Way (A46). The Fosse (or Cropwell) flight of three locks passes under the A46 at Bridge 18 and the top lock displays an unusual construction suggesting that here were originally two sets of head gates. An attractive picnic site now replaces the original Cropwell Wharf canal settlement. Fosse Lock Swing Bridge (19) is of interest to canal historians as the poorly documented 3½ mile Bingham Branch is thought to have originated in this vicinity, although no definitive evidence now remains.

The 20 mile long pound continues through Hole Hill cutting to Cropwell Town (Nottingham Road) Bridge (21) and the canal bed is now sufficiently pastoral to allow cattle grazing and traditional Sunday picnics on a blanket of buttercups and daisies. An unfortunate feature for elderly walkers, however, is the presence of three stiles which require a degree of agility to negotiate. The towpath changes sides at Bridge 22 and the present culvert gives no visual hint of the attractive sounding 'Cropwell Roving Bridge'.

To the west of the canal between Bridges 21 and 22 there is a large open cast mine operated by British Gypsum but the area adjacent to the canal has been worked out and landscaped so it is not obtrusive. Past canal prosperity is indicated by the old wharf and winding hole. The canal now enters the wooded Blue Hill Cutting and irony reigns with the realisation that its quarried blue clay was used for plugging the gypsum bed leaks! We finally leave the canal at Blue Hill Bridge (23) and a public footpath sign directs the way to Cropwell Bishop. The church tower is a useful landmark in following the track across the fields.

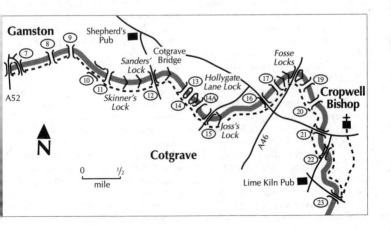

# 40 BCN

## Cannock and Anglesey Circular

*by David Sewell*

**WALK TALK**
**Distance** – 8¼ miles.
**Start at** – Chasewater; Grid Ref: SK 034071.
**OS Landranger Map** – 139, Birmingham. Larger editions of Birmingham A–Z.
**Public Transport** – Midland Red Chaserider services 154 and 156 from Birmingham bus sation. West Midlands buses 345 and 349 from Walsall.
**Car Parking** – Chasewater Park.
**Refreshments** – There is a café at Chasewater. The Turf by the A5 bridge over the Cannock Extension Canal serves Ansells Ales and meals which includes lunches on Sunday. The Jolly Collier by the bridge of the same name serves M&B, plus Walsall brewed Highgate Mild and Wolverhampton brewed Springfield Bitter. Food is also available.

This walk starts on the banks of a canal feeder reservoir made into a large recreation area with water ski-ing, speedboats, preserved steam trains, toilets, cafés and picnic sites with adequate car parking. Built to provide water for the Wyrley & Essington Canal, which it still does, it is now known as Chasewater.

Start the walk from the car park and follow the track around the lake in a clockwise direction as far as the preserved railway. Follow the railway to where the path crosses the line at the rear of a carriage shed. Follow the path to Brownhills Road, turn left onto the road. Take the first turning on the right which is Albutts Road and carry on along the lane. The houses give way to fields and after about ½ mile is a path with a sign pointing to Watling Street. This is the site of Norton Green Bridge on the dry bed of the Cannock Extension Canal.

Many disused canals are used as footpaths but it is usually the towpath which is retained; here the local authority has surfaced the bed of the canal for this purpose. The towpath was on the top of the brickwork which follows the path on the left. Carry on to the main A5 Watling Street and cross to the gate on the other side of the road. This next part of the Cannock Extension Canal is in water.

The canal was opened in 1858 to serve the coalfields of Cannock. By this time the Wyrley & Essington had been amalgamated with the Birmingham Canal Navigations for 18 years. It was the Birmingham Canal Navigations system's last canal to be built and was their most northerly.

Follow the towpath on the left side of the waterway. By Wyrley Common, the wood has extended across the path so walking may be difficult in summer. There is a way through however and the towpath is soon clear. On the opposite side are boatyards with residential boats, one with its own tame ducks. On the day I passed their thoughtful owners had broken a gap in the ice for them. Further down is a coal tip on which an attempt is being made at landscaping with trees and grass. Apart from this the scenery is quite pastoral until the junction with the Wyrley & Essington at Pelsall.

Here on the far side are derelict canal stables in which the stalls can still be seen. Friar Bridge is at the end of the branch. Cross over the other bridge to the main line towpath and turn left. The next bridge, Yorks Bridge, has a convenient pub. All the bridges are named rather than numbered, incidentally, on the BCN. The next is Yorks Foundry Bridge, followed by a new bridge which has its name on it: High Bridge. Next comes Jolly Collier Bridge.

Further on, the canal runs alongside Brownhills Market which is on the opposite side to the towpath. However a footbridge gives access to it and the nearby supermarket. This area is also being landscaped with grassy banks and trees. Further on is Catshill Junction. Go over the bridge and turn left. This is the Anglesey Branch. This once connected with the Coventry Canal at Huddlesford, via Lichfield. From Ogley Junction it has now been closed. Stand on the bridge over the truncated section and the line of the former canal can be seen; also, in the distance, is Lichfield Cathedral.

The Anglesey Branch carries on under Anglesey Bridge. This bridge displays its name and underneath is the date 1850. Before 1850 the rest of the branch to the reservoir was only

a feeder but in the year of 1850 it was made navigable because of coal mines in the area. This branch was still used commercially until the late 1960s to carry coal from these mines in the area, some via the Staffordshire & Worcestershire Canal to Stourport Power Station. The towpath is in good condition so carry on over the railway aqueduct and under the main A5 to Anglesey Basin. Here, still intact, are the chutes used to load the coal on to the boats.

Continue to the end of the waterway and the wall of the dam can be seen. At the bottom is a house; head for this and there is an exit on its left side and from here a track to the lane on the top of the reservoir. Follow this to the entrance of Chasewater Park and on to the car park. This is a nice place to park in. For those interested in wildlife there are many different species of waterfowl at the park with seabirds in the winter. The water is also populated by fresh water crayfish.

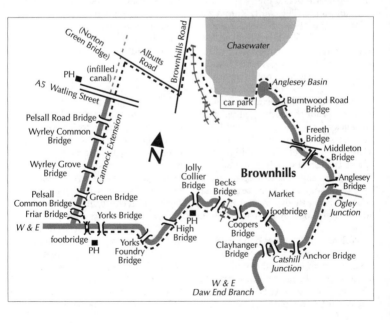

# 41 BCN

## Tame Valley Locks

*by Joseph Boughey, revised by John Lower*

**WALK TALK**
**Distance** – Hamsted station to Aston station, 4½ miles.
**Start At** – Hamstead station; Grid Ref: SP 050926.
**OS Landranger Map** – 139, Birmingham.
**Public Transport** – Rail, Aston to Hamstead, frequent service (not Sundays). (Centro Hotline 0121 200 2700).
**Car Parking** – On street near Hamstead station.

The Tame Valley Canal was one of the less developed, rural parts of the Birmingham Canal Navigations (BCN), built to avoid the Farmers Bridge Locks. It was built in an uncompromising fashion, crossing the hilly landscape straight and wide in deep cuttings and high embankments. This walk follows the lower section through the thirteen locks of the Perry Barr Flight to Aston where the junction with the Birmingham & Fazeley and Grand Union canals is dominated by the modern day Spaghetti Junction.

The walk starts at Hamstead station. From the traffic lights, walk up Rocky Lane and turn left at the roundabout up Tower Hill. Tower Hill crosses Freeth Bridge high above the canal which is in a deep cutting but there is no access here, so it is necessary to join the towpath at Walsall Road Bridge by turning right at the main road by the Clifton Bingo Club.

Walsall Road Bridge is a large 1930s structure whose wide span crosses an unnarrowed canal, a feature of all bridges on this stretch. The BCN had a small wharf here and the canal has towpaths on either side. It is probably better to choose the one on the right.

The first seven locks descend the hillside in a straight line although an original footbridge spoils the view. These locks have some BCN paddle gear, one curiosity being the gate paddles on the top lock, the only ones on the flight. Until 1958, water was backpumped up from the Salford Bridge level and the remains of pumping equipment can be seen at various points. Before the seventh lock, Perry Reservoir can be seen on the right.

A longer pound follows, punctuated by a wide bridge carrying the M6 motorway. Just before Aldridge Road Bridge was a manure wharf, the lowest of a number on the canal taking night-soil from urban Birmingham to what was then a farming area. Two locks, part of the second flight, follow, and then a short pound before Lock 10 and Sutton Road Bridge. Basins formerly ran off this short pound to east and west. The east basin served Stonehouse Works and Edward Tailby built boats here from about 1881 until about 1925. The opposite basin, now built over, was the site of Perry Barr Wharf.

It is advisable to cross here to the left-hand towpath which is in better condition. A long length of the right bank below Sutton Road Bridge is dominated by a huge container depot, whose construction in the mid 1960s drew some bitter comment from the Inland Waterways Association concerning transport priorities. The locks were extremely busy at one time, rising from a total of 10,980 passages in 1849 to 29,406 in 1898 – the latter corresponding to some 95 lockings per working day.

Beyond Witton Bridge, an original footbridge, an elevated section of the M6 crosses the canal and a basin with concrete roving bridge. This served Brookvale Road destructor which opened in April 1924. Refuse brought here by road was burnt and the ashes transported upstream to tips at Great Barr. The basin was out of use by 1961.

Witton Road Wharf lay just before Witton Road Bridge; the latter, carrying Brookvale Road, was reconstructed in 1912. A short distance beyond, the right hand towpath ends at the site of the former BCN Engine Wharf. Here also was Forgings & Presswork, a factory which dispatched 7,977 tons of forgings by canal to Tyburn on the Birmingham & Fazeley as late as 1964. Then follows the top lock of a pair, sometimes called Witton Locks, which included Witton Toll Office. The office closed by 1920, but the lockhouse and cottages which served another pumping engine remain.

A new bridge duplicates an original at Deykin Avenue, between the locks. Below on the right hand side was the source of the canal's final traffic. The General Electric Works was established at Witton about 1903 and in 1962 received 5,890 tons of coal from Holly Bank on the Wyrley & Essington Canal. The site is cleared for redevelopment.

At the roving bridge, cross to the right hand side. The rest of the canal is dominated by the M6/A38 intersection known as Spaghetti Junction, with an LNWR viaduct squeezed in for good measure. The motorway viaducts are mostly at high level, with tubular legs into the canal. The canal itself is little altered, but a long length is covered over like a tunnel. A stop place, where cargoes were checked, remains in the middle of the canal, together with Salford Road Bridge, rebuilt in 1926, it is unaltered by the motorway works.

Salford Junction with its two canal junctions and two aqueducts over the river Tame must make this area the most complex transport intersection in the country. Turn right at the first junction, over an aqueduct and along the towpath of the Birmingham & Fazeley Canal. A 'Welcome to Heartlands' sign together with a new highway crossing and aesthetic towpath improvements proclaim that this area of former dereliction is subject to massive redevelopment. Soon the bottom chamber of the eleven lock Aston Flight is reached, with its single gates top and bottom.

Leave the towpath here, cross over the canal and Aston station is just ahead across the main road.

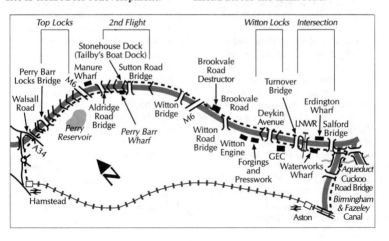

99

# 42 BCN

## Dudley No2 Canal

*by John Lower*

**WALK TALK**

**Distance** – Windmill End to Gas Street Basin, 11 miles.

**Start at** – Windmill End; Grid Ref: SO 953881.

**OS Landranger Map** – 139, Birmingham.

**Public Transport** – Details of local bus and rail services, Centro Hotline (0121 200 2700).

**Society** – Lapal Canal Trust, P.O. Box 5236, Halesowen, West Midlands B63 3NN.

The Dudley No2 Canal was opened in 1798 between Blowers Green at the south end of Dudley Tunnel and Selly Oak on the Worcester & Birmingham Canal. It included the 3,795-yard Lapal Tunnel, the fourth longest in England, which was closed when a short section collapsed in 1917. This walk contrasts the navigable section to Coombeswood Basin with the much abused remainder which is now the subject of an ambitious restoration scheme by the Lapal Canal Trust.

The walk starts at Windmill End, at the southern end of Netherton Tunnel, near the Dry Dock public house and the site of several IWA National Waterway Festivals. Leaving the junction, the canal is overshadowed by Cobb's Engine House which used to pump water from the coal mines. The route contours along the steep side of the Rowley Hills, the highest part of the Black Country. There are many signs of former industry, with the remains of side arms and the foundations of old buildings, but the acres of derelict land and pit banks have now been cloaked with gorse and bracken.

Most of the bridges have been rebuilt as a result of mining subsidence and many still carry cast-iron nameplates. All along, there are panoramic views across the Black Country to the pretty Clent Hills beyond.

At Wrights Bridge, moorings have been provided for the Wharf Tavern. This is the central scene of an excellent children's book, *Ghost In The Water,* by Edward Chitham. Suddenly, the canal disappears into the impossibly small looking black hole which is Gosty Hill Tunnel. The layby to the left used to have a boat house for a tunnel tug.

Unfortunately, the tunnel does not have a towpath, so head straight up Station Road past The Boat pub and past a tunnel ventilator improbably situated in the front garden of a council house. At the top of the hill, near the Lighthouse pub, cross straight over the main road. Steps lead back down to the towing path, descending into a deep, eerie and silent canyon between derelict factories. This is the site of the former Stewarts & Lloyds tube works, manufacturers of metal pipes and probably the last major industrial user of the BCN.

Beyond the factory site, the towing path is barred at Coombeswood Basin, which is used for moorings and is the limit of navigation. This need for security regrettably necessitates a $1/2$ mile diversion for the walker.

Leave the towpath and drop to the bottom of Hereward Rise, turn left along Dudley Road and left at the roundabout up Mucklow Hill for a few hundred yards. To the left, a factory stands on the canal line. If a short diversion is made along the industrial estate road on its top side, the canal can be seen in water back to the moorings. Now cross Mucklow Hill, taking care for it is a very busy road.

The canal is in water once more as it forms part of Leasowes Park and crosses a massive embankment. A miniature railway runs along the far canal bank. Restoration and re-lining of this part of the canal is planned by Lapal Canal Trust. At the far end of the embankment are the remains of a stop-gate and narrows beneath a footbridge. Then a length has been infilled and landscaped through a modern housing estate.

At Manor Way, a busy dual carriageway crosses the canal at water level. The route then forms the lower car park of the Black Horse pub and beyond can be seen infilled, contouring left across the fields, a different coloured green strip.

The towpath is not a public footpath, but a convenient well waymarked alternative exists a short distance down Manor Way. This follows below the canal route, passing through the former fishpools of Halesowen Abbey. It is unfortunate that there is little evidence of Lapal Tunnel. Approaching Lapal Lane, the canal cutting has been filled up to ground level but some brickwork, remains of old cottages at the tunnel entrance, can be seen in a field on the left.

Turn right, up Lapal Lane, then left over the M5. At the end of the road cross directly down the narrow lane into Woodgate Valley Country Park, keeping left of the Hole Farm Trekking Centre and following down the Bournebrook. It is interesting to note that the tunnel crosses the 'Backbone of England': Bournebrook water drains eventually to the Humber while Halesowen water drains to the Severn.

Follow the Bournebrook for over a mile; at the second canal-style brick arch bridge cross the stream, and follow the right hand bank until a large, unmistakable modern school can be seen on the right hand skyline. Climb up and pass along the right hand boundary of the school, down into the next valley, cross the road and take the track to the left of the houses. Then turn left along the nearest bank of the stream. At the Barnes Hill dual carriageway, cross the pelican crossing (SP 016829).

The eastern portal of Lapal Tunnel lies buried in the grassland near the crossing. The canal line can be confirmed behind the concrete palings at the far end of the grass, where the cutting is used as a stacking yard for reinforced concrete sections. Divert round the road to the left, in front of the Stone House pub and turn right down Somery Road to a canal bridge. Turn left onto the canal and note the substantial ruins of Weoley Castle behind the railings. (The castle is open to the public at certain times.)

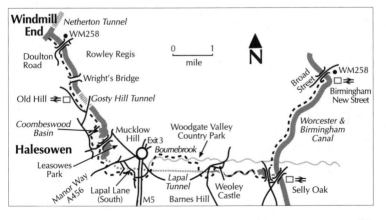

Although the rest of the canal passes through built up suburbs, there has been no encroachment by developers. The canal line remains, though filled in to various degrees and perhaps looking more like an abandoned railway. It now forms a well used walkway leading into Selly Oak Park where the empty channel reappears, crossed by an original brick arch bridge and a comparatively modern concrete structure carrying the busy Harbourne Lane.

From this point, the last two hundred yards are fenced off. A diversion can be made to the right, passing Homebase and Halfords on the Battery Park retail estate. At the traffic lights, cross straight over and take the small lane called The Dingle to the left side of the garage. This leads down to the towpath of the Worcester & Birmingham Canal. Turn left. The site of the junction with the Dudley No2 (Lapal) Canal is marked with a plaque, just before the railway bridge

The idea is now to walk along the W&B towpath to Gas Street Basin, three miles away (or hitch a lift on a passing boat as I did!). At Gas Street, leave the towpath through the gate, turn right and then right on to Broad Street. A 258 bus will take you to Doulton Road, Rowley Regis. Alight at the canal bridge and it is a short walk back along the towing path to Windmill End.

*The extensively redeveloped canals of Birmingham are busy with trip boats – such as this one seen outside the International Convention Centre – and have some startling contrasts to offer the walker.*

# 43 BCN

## Birmingham to Smethwick

*by Patrick Thorn*

**WALK TALK**

**Distance** – Gas Street to Bromford Lane, 5 miles.

**Start at** – Gas Street Basin; Grid Ref: SP 062867.

**OS Landranger Map** – 139, Birmingham.

**Public Transport** – Rail: Sandwell & Dudley to Birmingham New Street.

**Car Parking** – 4 hour meters in Gas Street. Longer term parking near Theatre.

Until ten years ago, one of the few entrances to Birmingham's hidden canal system was through Gas Street's 'hole in the wall'; now there are numerous points of entry but it is still worth going through the original 'hole' to start this walk round Gas Street Basin. Linger on the bridge which now crosses the stop lock and if you know what the view from this entrance used to be prepare to gasp!

Walk along the Worcester Bar past the James Brindley pub to view the splendid new bridge where you can imagine numerous working boats going in and out of Old Wharf. Proceed beside the 24 storey Hyatt Hotel through Broad Street Bridge and prepare to gasp again. The International Convention Centre is well integrated with the canal and in the summer several narrowboats work from its wharf taking passengers round two of Brindley's loops. Opposite the Convention Centre is an upmarket shopping centre and all the way to Farmers Bridge there are new establishments where you can eat and drink. Note Farmers Bridge and another

Horseley bridge nearby, which are both dated 1827, and were built by Horseley Iron Works in Tipton. During this walk we shall see a number of dated Horseley bridges indicating the progress of engineer Thomas Telford's improvement scheme along the canal. Now follow the sign to Wolverhampton and, soon after you leave the National Indoor Arena behind, the canal becomes a series of straight lines. I suggest that you keep to the right hand towpath until the end of the walk.

If you cross the bridge just past the canal crossroads you will see that it was cast by 'Thomas Astbury & Co, Smethwick'. Astbury's foundry was on the Engine Arm: Frederick Watkins worked for Astbury who was Arthur Keen's father in law. In the 1850s, Astbury set them up in business making nuts and bolts; they soon moved to the London Works alongside the Cape Ann. Their rivals Nettlefold & Chamberlain were on the opposite and of the Arm but it was not until 1902 that the rivals amalgamated to form GKN which was a canal-using industry well into the 20th century. Continuing on the right hand towpath to where the Soho Loop rejoins the Main Line you will soon see the entrance to two tunnels under towpath and feeder – the first led to Nettlefold's Basin and the second is the Cape Arm. The headquarters of GKN's international business left here about 12 years ago and moved to Redditch.

You are about to cross an unnamed cast iron bridge over the loop which went past Soho Foundry. We shall see the far end of that loop soon after we have walked under the bridge which carries Intercity trains between Birmingham and Wolverhampton. Once under the railway, the buildings on the right are all part of the Soho Foundry.

Matthew Boulton chose this site because it was on the canal. Boulton & Watt moved on to this site in 1795 because they had to start making all the components of their steam engines instead of using subcontractors. The opening under a small cast iron bridge was the other end of the Brindley loop off which was a basin for the foundry. In 1895 Avery's bought the foundry which they enlarged and have occupied ever since; they have achieved an international reputation for weighing machines of all sizes.

After the next bridge Cornwall Works is on the right. Tangye's came here in 1862; their world wide reputation depended on hydraulic jacks, pumps and steam engines. The eventual launching of Brunel's Great Eastern was done with Tangye's hydraulic presses and that set them on the road to success. The brickwork of their wall shows where the bridge carried the towpath over the entrance to their basin. Tangye's have now moved back to Birmingham.

After that remarkable concentration of world famous industries, all at some stage canal dependent, we now arrive at Smethwick Junction. It is worth

forking right and going up to Smethwick Locks before rejoining Telford's new line under the Engine Arm Aqueduct: this aqueduct is unique and may be a Horseley bridge. Continue on the right towpath as the cutting gets deeper until we reach Smethwick pumphouse which was opened in 1892 to return water to the higher (Wolverhampton) level.

The next four features come at regular intervals before the end of our walk. First as we emerge from a concrete tunnel, we go under Telford's Galton Bridge – a magnificent Horseley bridge dated 1829. Second are Chance's glass works and Stewart Aqueduct where the Old Line crosses the New, surmounted by the main line railway and the M5. Next we come to our last two Horseley bridges where the original Brindley line has descended Spon Lane Locks. Here you need to cross over to the left hand towpath in order to reach Bromford Lane Bridge, where our walk ends. Leave the canal at the bridge and turn left to Sandwell & Dudley station. As you return to New Street you will spot from the train many of the features seen while on foot. It is like running a film fast in reverse.

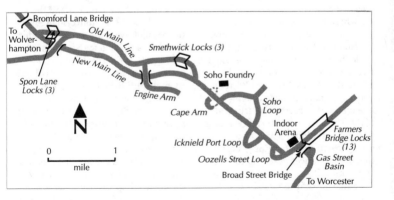

# 44 STOURBRIDGE AND STAFFS & WORCS CANALS

## Stourbridge to Kinver

*by Chris Dyche*

**WALK TALK**

**Distance** – Canal Street, Stourbridge to Kinver Lock, 5½ miles.

**Start at** – Canal Street, Stourbridge; Grid Ref: SP 898848.

**OS Landranger Maps** – 138, Kidderminster & Wye Forest and 139, Birmingham.

**Public Transport** – Stourbridge is served by rail from Leamington, Stratford-on-Avon, Birmingham, Worcester and Hereford and local buses. Canal Street is 10 minutes walk from Stourbridge Town railway and bus station. Return from Kinver to Stourbridge by West Midlands Travel Service 242 (0121 422 3401).

**Trip Boats** – Public trips from Stourbridge.

Our walk starts in Canal Street, Stourbridge, an area of industry on the fringe of the Black Country. In a walk of a little over five miles we soon leave behind the urban scene, and pass through some of the most pleasant countryside to be found anywhere on our canal system.

Canal Street marks the terminus of the Stourbridge Town Arm, and our walk starts by going down this cobbled street. On the right, immediately before the restored Bonded Warehouse, you may glimpse a small wharf and crane: this marks the actual end of the Town Arm. To the left is a large two storey building which also incorporates a weigh bridge. This was the original offices of the Stourbridge Navigation Company and is now the headquarters of the Stourbridge Navigation Trust. These buildings form part of a small conservation area administered by the trust.

In the next hundred yards we pass coils of steel and busy factory doorways (beware of vehicles!) before emerging onto the towpath in an area known as Joyner's Wharf. The small brick-built pier on the edge of the towpath is Stourbridge Pier! It was built originally for loading ash from the adjacent foundry into empty boats.

A small cast-iron bridge is crossed, once the entrance to the Foster Raistrick (later Bradley's) steel works, where the early locomotives *Stourbridge Lion* and *Agenoria* were built in 1829. The *Stourbridge Lion* was the very first steam locomotive to run in the United States of America.

A weir is crossed by means of unusual cast-iron foot plating, and shortly afterwards the canal passes through a 'mini lake' known locally as The Wide. There then follows a mile of quiet urban waterway passing a mixture of Victorian and modern housing interspersed with a few factories which date back to the canal's origin. After passing beneath the new Longboat Lane Bridge we reach Wordsley Junction and the main line of the Stourbridge Canal.

With the Junction Pool and the bottom lock of the Stourbridge Sixteen to our right, we cross a roving bridge, turn left, and head for Stourton. The canal crosses the river Stour, and leaves its urban environment behind. At Bells Mill Bridge we enter an area of beauty and tranquillity.

The river Stour runs below us to the right; in the background the roar of the water at Bells Mill can be heard. Trees arch the canal before giving way on the left to a sweeping field topped with woodland. For the next ½ mile the canal clings to a sandstone shelf, the river Stour running below us and fields rolling to the horizon. To the left, woodland comes to the waters' edge, trees mingling with those on the towpath side to form an arch.

As this wooded section is left we pass the picturesque Middle Bridge and then wend our way through quiet farmland for a mile until reaching the top lock of the Stourton Four. We now have houses again, lining the offside of the short pound between Locks 1 and 2. Their watersides are immaculate, enhancing the area and a credit to their owners. At Lock 2, the towpath changes sides by means of an attractive iron split bridge, with gap in the middle to allow for the passage of tow ropes.

Immediately, we plunge below the A449 Kidderminster–Wolverhampton road, and emerge into quite a different environment. An avenue of trees leads us through Locks 3 and 4 and down onto the Staffs & Worcs Canal at Stourton Junction. This area is beautiful and peaceful, an ideal spot to break the walk for a rest and picnic.

The Staffs & Worcs is joined via a roving bridge. Note here the impressive sign post on our right erected by the S&W Canal Society. Turning left we almost immediately arrive at Stewponey Lock and wharf. The wharf and its house was for many years a British Waterways' maintenance yard. The area has now been extensively renovated and the house converted into flats. Note also the excellently restored round toll

house adjacent to the lock and the circular weir, the design of which is a feature of the Staffordshire & Worcestershire Canal.

Leaving Stewponey, we walk for about ½ mile before reaching the short Dunsley Tunnel; only 23 yards long, mainly unlined, and one of the earliest tunnels on the canal system. It's narrow, as the paint on the walls shows! You may also note that the harder rock strata have been supported on brick piers, the softer materials having been eroded away.

A very attractive stretch follows. The canal sweeps around a long left hand curve with beech trees lining the towpath on the right, and field and woodland completing the picture to the left. Here the trackbed of the Kinver Light Railway runs parallel to the towpath and, although closed for over 50 years, is easily followed.

In a few minutes we pass cottages on the towpath side and arrive at Hyde Lock, with its neat garden and mown grass. To the right is woodland; this was once the site of a large iron works, one of the oldest in the Stour Valley, which closed around 1890.

We soon arrive at Kinver Lock and the end of our walk. Here, the main Kinver–Stourbridge road crosses the canal, with the Vine public house on our left. Turn right, and a few minutes walk will take us into the centre of Kinver.

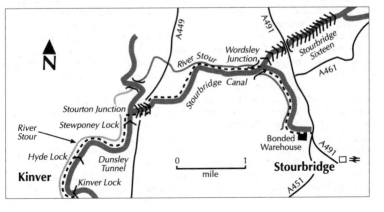

# 45 ASHBY CANAL

## Shackerstone to Shenton

*by John Cormack*

**WALK TALK**
**Distance** – Shackerstone station to
Shenton station, 5¼ miles.
**Start at** – Shackerstone Turn Bridge
(52); Grid Ref: SP 376067.
**OS Landranger Map** – 140,
Leicester & Coventry.
**Guide** – *Waterways World Guide to
the Coventry, Oxford & Ashby
Canals.*
**Public Transport** – Limited train
service on Battlefield Line on
Saturdays and Sundays, March to
November (01827 880754).
**Car Parking** – Shackerstone or
Shenton station.
**Bosworth Visitor Centre** – 01455
290429.

The northern end of the Ashby
Canal must surely be one of the
most rural waterways remaining in
the Midlands, passing through
peaceful and pastoral farming
country for most of its length –
indeed most of the canal is in a
designated Conservation Area. What
this walk lacks in industrial heritage
it more than makes up for by having
a preserved steam railway
connecting at each end, as well as
virtually overlooking an historic
English battlefield.

The lock-free Ashby Canal was
originally built in the 1790s to serve
coalfields and limeworks which have
long since died, in and around
Ashby-de-la-Zouch, from which town
the canal takes its name. Far-sighted
promoters had planned that the
canal formed a through route
between the Coventry Canal near
Bedworth in the south and the river
Trent at Burton in the north.
However this was not to be because

of problems on the proposed northern
section which would have required
expensive locks and reservoirs. Thus
the canal ended at Moira although
mining subsidence means that the
canal now terminates abruptly and
somewhat inaccessibly in a farming
area, just north of the village of
Snarestone, some nine miles south of
the original terminus.

This walk starts 3½ miles south of
Snarestone at the small village of
Shackerstone which seems to reflect
the pre-industrial atmosphere of the
canal, making an ideal point for
peaceful and uncrowded moorings.
To the west of the village the canal
flanks Gopsall Park, the house where
Handel is said to have composed his
famous oratorio *The Messiah*,
although sadly the house was pulled
down many years ago. The original
Ashby & Nuneaton Joint Railway
station at Shackerstone Junction is
alongside the canal at this point, on
the opposite bank. It has been
restored by the Shackerstone
Railway Society who conveniently
run steam trains to and from the far
end of the walk at Shenton, under
the brand name of 'The Battlefield
Line'.

Shortly after leaving turnover
bridge 52 on the edge of the village
the canal passes over a small stream
by way of a brick aqueduct, after
which can be seen milepost 18.12
(another musical connotation if one
thinks of the famous overture by
Tchaikovsky!) indicating eighteen
miles to Bedworth and twelve to the
original terminus at Moira. The
canal winds through pleasant
farmland and skirts to the east of the
village of Congerstone. A
considerable number of wrens are to
be seen on this stretch, nesting in the
abundant hedgerows bordering the
canal. In season, the waterway is
noted for several types of dragonfly,

as well as kingfisher. Human fishermen are able to enjoy the excellent coarse fish on offer.

There are two winding holes on this stretch, one immediately prior to Bridge 42 at Bosworth Wharf. This must have been a scene of great activity in its heyday, serving the small town of Market Bosworth, about one mile distant, for in the 18th century the town was of some importance in the area. The adjacent 'Battlefield Line' railway station is being restored to its former glory but regrettably there is no access to or from the trains for the time being.

The walk continues towards Shenton which lies to the west of the canal, crossing over a minor road by a splendid high brick aqueduct. The village is clustered around the old Hall, parts of which date from 1629.

A number of good overnight moorings have been specially provided on the opposite bank for boaters to visit the site of the famous Battle of Bosworth. The battle was fought on 22nd August 1485, changing the course of English history with Richard III killed by Henry Tudor who subsequently became Henry VII.

On leaving the well-preserved towpath and crossing over Wadfields Bridge (number 35) it is but a few hundred yards to a newly restored Shenton station, the southern terminus of the 'Battlefield Line' where an information centre and toilets are available. The bulk of the battlefield area is on the other side of the railway, reached by footpaths, which are all well signposted.

A Battlefield Visitor Centre, housed in a group of old red brick farm buildings, explains what happened on that fateful day over 500 years ago. It is open daily from 1st April to 31st October. Trails, open all year, lead through a wood and there are explanatory plaques en route explaining the salient points of the battle between the armies. There is also a convenient café and picnic area to sample at the Visitor Centre before catching the train for the short trip back to Shackerstone.

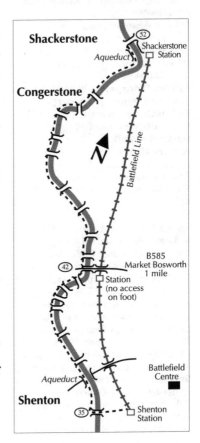

# 46 COVENTRY CANAL

## Foleshill Road to Bedworth

*by David Sewell*

**WALK TALK**
**Distance** – Foleshill Road to Marton Junction, 6 miles.
**Start at** – Foleshill Road; Grid Ref: SP 348829.
**OS Landranger Map** – 140, Leicester & Coventry.
**Guide** – *Waterways World Guide to the Coventry, Ashby & Oxford (North) Canals.*
**Public Transport** – West Midlands Transport route 20, Coventry–Bedworth, covers most of this walk.
**Car Parking** – Roadside at either terminal of walk.
**Arbury Hall** – With the remains of the private system of canals, the hall and grounds are open on summer Sundays and Bank Holidays (01203 382804).

As a lad it was almost a lifelong ambition to walk the length of the Coventry Canal to Bedworth. I attended a school in Coventry in the late '40s and round three walls of the assembly hall was a 50-yard-long mural of the canal. Artistic licence was used in that there was a snow-filled night at the Bishop Street Basin and a bright summer's day at the other end. It was also filled with boats, although commercial carrying finished in 1939 with the exception of refuse boats from Courtaulds at Foleshill. Later explorations on a cycle revealed a more dismal situation than that on the bright coloured mural.

In later days when I read about the canal I found it contrary, declining to extend from its profitable Coventry–Bedworth section, dismissing Brindley as its engineer, and having parts of its waterway built by two other companies.

I started my walk at Bridge 8 on the Foleshill Road by the Wheatsheaf, now re-named 'Carney's' to give appeal to the younger patrons. The towpath is on the right hand side of the canal which traverses in a wide arc back to the main road. This area was once a large gas works complex and past some modern housing is a board with a map pointing out all the good things the area has to offer.

The waterway bends sharply to the left; on the opposite bank is a pub and a row of houses which are on a lower level than the canal. After the next bend to the right, the motorway can be seen crossing the canal, although it has been heard for some time. What was interesting to me was that the hedge on this part was made up of crab apple trees. Some of its tart fruit, untempting to birds and small boys, still hung from the trees on the late November day that I passed. After the motorway and the next bridge is a lonely pub sign for the Greyhound Inn some yards distant. This is in fact Hawkesbury Junction, known as Sutton Stop, named after the family of toll clerks who collected here, this being the junction of the Oxford and Coventry canals. The bridge over the junction has a span of 50ft and was erected in 1837 at a cost of £630.

The Greyhound pub has changed little. It has a good selection of real ales, provides meals and boasts a collection of men's neck ties. Next to the pub is a row of cottages. These are about 200 years old and, like the Greyhound, are Grade 2 listed buildings. It is believed the first residents of the cottages were miners and their families, as the Victoria

Colliery was in the area. On the opposite side of the canal is the pump house. The first engine in the building was bought second hand from one of the local coal mines and was named 'Lady Godiva' and would raise water to the canal from a local stream. This proved inadequate and a 114ft shaft was sunk and an extra

engine was installed. The pumps fell into disuse during World War Two and the 'new' engine was scrapped. In 1963 Lady Godiva was moved to Dartmouth in Devon, the birthplace of its engineer, Thomas Newcomen.

The area is now a conservation area. It is also the start of a path called 'The Sowe Valley' which follows the river Sowe to Stonebridge Meadow, a nature reserve south of Coventry.

There are moorings on the towpath side and after this the canal swings to the left. At the end was the Newdigate Colliery Arm, but the main route turns right under a bridge and carries on through a wooded cutting, this area being known as Coal Pit Field. After Bridge 14 the condition of the towpath is not so good. Sometimes it is necessary to follow a path in the trees on the right. On the other side of this bank is a fast flowing stream. Before the final bridge is a boatyard known as Charity Dock. Willow Wren boats were overhauled here in the 1960s. At the next bridge leave the canal and turn left to the centre of Bedworth for the bus to Longford. However, a few yards on is Marston Junction with the Ashby Canal which is worth examination.

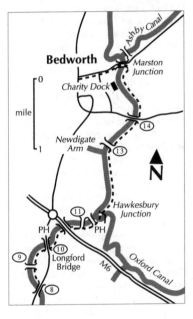

# 47 WORCESTER & BIRMINGHAM CANAL

## Tardebigge to Stoke Works

*by 'Walshy'*

**WALK TALK**
**Distance** – Tardebigge Tunnel to
Stoke Works, 4 miles.
**Start at** – Alcester Road,
Tardebigge; Grid Ref: SO 997693.
**OS Landranger Maps** – 139,
Birmingham and 150 Worcester &
the Malverns.
**Public Transport** – Local train
service Birmingham–Redditch every
30 minutes. Midland Red Bus 143,
Birmingham–Redditch (via
Bromsgrove) every 30 minutes; 141,
Stoke Works–Bromsgrove every
hour. No Sunday service. Further
information 0345 125436.

Leaving the Alcester Road a path
leads to the canal by the
southern exit from Tardebigge
Tunnel. A British Waterways
maintenance yard is to the right on
New Wharf. The crews of the tugs
once used to pull horse boats through
the tunnel were housed in a shed on
New Wharf. Whilst the shed has long
been replaced by houses the site is
still known as Tug Row.

Immediately to the left can be seen
St Bartholomew's Church, high on a
hill. In Saxon times the term
Tardebigge meant 'Big Tower' or
'Tower on a Hill', the parish taking
its name from the situation of the
church. A path leaves the towpath,
rising to the church and its sweeping
views over Worcestershire.

Lock 58 is Tardebigge Top Lock,
the first in the flight of thirty which
will allow a boat to descend 217ft in
2¼ miles. On the offside of the canal
is the spot where Tom Rolt moored
his narrowboat *Cressy*. Rolt's book
*Narrow Boat* chronicles the voyages
of *Cressy* before the Second World

War. A plaque on this site
commemorates the meeting between
Rolt and Robert Aickman which led
to the formation of the Inland
Waterways Association.

Leaving Lock 58 the pound is some
three quarters of a mile long before
the next lock is reached. To the left of
Lock 57 is the Engine House. This
originally housed a modified Watt
beam engine to pump water from
Tardebigge Reservoir back to the
summit level. A side arm was
excavated to allow coal to be carried
to the Engine House. This was
known as Jacobs Cut. 1911 saw the
last delivery of coal, the pump itself
being dismantled during the First
World War and shipped to Wales.
The Engine House has now been
converted to a nightclub which
sometimes opens at weekends.

In the pound below Lock 55 lie the
remains of a number of old
narrowboats, both wooden and steel.
These boats were sunk in years gone
by to protect the banks of the canal.

At Lock 53 is Reservoir Lock
Cottage where Pat Warner spent her
childhood years, which she retold so
delightfully in her book *Lock Keeper's
Daughter*. Between Locks 52 and 50
it is worth leaving the towpath for a
while and climbing up onto the
embankment that runs alongside the
reservoir. On the reservoir great
crested grebes, heron, kingfishers
and flocks of Canadian geese are
often seen, with swans as occasional
visitors. On hot summer days carp
can be seen basking near the surface
of the reservoir. The sweeping views
across the open countryside include
the Malvern Hills lying to the south
and the Clent Hills to the west. The
white sails of a windmill can be seen
in the grounds of the Avoncroft
Museum of Buildings just outside
Bromsgrove, some two miles to the
west of the canal.

As we rejoin the towpath the canal continues its gentle descent. Beyond Lock 43 on the left is Halfway House which was formerly a pub, well used by boaters and farmers alike. The last pint was pulled in 1959 and it is now a private residence.

At Lock 33 there is a footbridge allowing walkers using a nearby footpath to cross the canal. By the side of the canal between Locks 32 and 31 there is a lock cottage which has been renovated and is now owned by the Landmark Trust. This property can be rented by those seeking a holiday cottage that is definitely off the beaten track.

The canal now bends sharply to the left as we reach Tardebigge Bottom Lock (29). We now reach an area of the canal known down throughout the years as 'the foot of the thirty'. Just on around the bend lies the Queens Head pub, a popular pub with restaurant and carvery facilities. The Queens Head was formerly the Blacksmith's Arms with a forge standing on this site until the 1960s.

Having descended the Tardebigge flight we now reach Stoke Top Lock (28), the first of the six locks that make up the Stoke flight. The pace of the descent has now become much more gentle and the surrounding land is flatter. Just below Lock 27 there is a row of three pretty terraced cottages at the canalside. A further three closely grouped locks are passed before Stoke Prior is reached. A line of privately owned narrowboats are moored on the offside of the canal announcing your arrival at the busy Black Prince boatyard with its winding hole. We now reach Stoke Bottom Lock (23) and our descent is complete.

The canal bends to the left and leads to Stoke Works. Once a salt works, it is now the site of a large chemical works. The towpath rises over a now disused entrance to what was once Stoke Works basin. Along this section a thriving rabbit population claims the towpath as its own. Just before Bridge 42 our destination is reached. A path leads up from the towpath near to the Boat & Railway pub. After a well earned drink there is a bus stop opposite the pub for buses that will take you back to Bromsgrove.

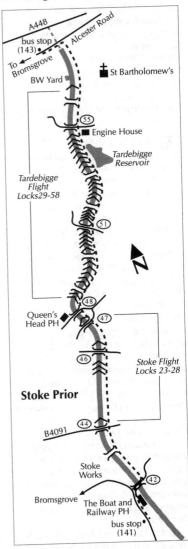

# 48 STRATFORD AND GRAND UNION CANALS

## Lapworth Circular

*by Carol Lawrence*

**WALK TALK**
**Distance** – 6¼ miles.
**Start at** – Car Park on Brome Hall
Lane; Grid Ref: SP 186712.
**OS Landranger Maps** – 139,
Birmingham and 151, Stratford-
upon-Avon.
**Public Transport** – Lapworth
Station (Birmingham Snow Hill to
Leamington Spa & London
Marylebone).
**Car Parking** – In Brome Hall Lane,
Lapworth.

When first published in March
1986 the introduction to this
walk warned that the area would
soon be desecrated by the M40. In
1988 ownership of the southern
Stratford Canal passed from the
National Trust to British
Waterways, and the configuration of
waterways at Lapworth was altered
in 1995. So I went to see what
changes the walker would notice.

A path from the car park leads to
the towpath at Lock 19. Turn right to
the original black and white iron
roving bridge. The deck is split to
allow towing ropes to pass
unhindered – meaning cheap
construction, as they did not need
towpaths beneath. A carved finger
post shows three routes: Lock 20 to
the left leads to the Grand Union
Canal. This walk stays to the right of
the canal, passing between the local
BW office and Lock 21.

Two cottages overlook the basin;
the first is now on an island, the
second, just below the new Lapworth
link, is one of three typical barrel
roof cottages, unique to this
waterway. There are three more on
this route.

Ignore the rebuilt footbridge below
Lock 21; the new towpath follows the
curved side of the basin. This path
passes along the offside of Lock 22.
Cross the new foot bridge which is in
'split' bridge style, but unfortunately
the deck is not split!

Locks are regularly and widely
spaced. Single top and bottom gates
are the norm here as another
economy measure.

Approaching Lock 25, traffic on the
M40 can be seen ahead, but is still
inaudible. Split bridge 39 carries a
bridleway and boasts two original
diamond-shaped weight limit signs
erected by the Great Western
Railway Co.

Below Lock 26 is a small wooded
area muffling the sound of the
motorway beyond. Mooring rings are
set in the towpath under its bridge,
as Lock 27, Lapworth Bottom Lock,
is just beyond. The M40 is much
more invasive now as it rises to pass
over the canal. But the canal soon
turns away, and the cottage below
Lock 28 displays a wide range of
painted canal ware for sale.

By Lock 29 the traffic noise has
virtually disappeared. The
meandering canal enters a wooded
length, filled with birdsong, then a
dismantled railway bridge marks the
outskirts of Lowsonford. Lock 30 is
unusual as, although the gates are
normal 7ft width, the National Trust
rebuilt the nearside wall to make
passage through Bridge 40 easier, so
the chamber is 8ft wide.

To visit the village, and the Fleur
de Lys pub, leave the towpath by the
stile. Otherwise leave the canal by
the gate below Bridge 41.

Turn right and follow the lane up
the hill for about a mile. Take the
footpath/bridleway signposted
opposite the white farmhouse, follow
the hedge to the fence, then turn
right to the motorway bridge.
Underfoot conditions indicate this is
a cattle transit route. Cross the

bridge, turn left under the railway, and go through the left hand gateway. Follow the right hand hedge to cross a stream, leaving the field through the metal gate. Horses' hooves will have done their worst to the surface here so be prepared in wet weather. The track climbs and eventually, at the top of the hill, beyond the five-barred gate, is a bridge over the Grand Union. Turn left down the path.

Immediately, this can be seen as a very different canal; not only is it wide, but the bank edges were piled in concrete as part of the 1930s' improvements. The bridge, number 62, is a monster compared with the 'economy' versions for bridleways on the Stratford. The canal is in a wooded cutting and the towpath, though wide, is wet, muddy and poorly surfaced.

Beyond the cutting the towpath is good as the canal curves round the hillside to where Dicks Lane crosses at Bridge 63, by the Tom O' the Wood pub.

The twin of the Lapworth fingerpost is opposite Kingswood Junction. Turn left. Under the railway, the new link forges ahead between the cottages. To the right, Lock 20 gives direct access to the northern Stratford. Use any of the footpaths to return to the car park.

I found little evidence remaining of National Trust ownership: apart from the plaque on the top balance beam of Lock 21, their logo is embossed on the concrete wall below Lock 30. Although locally intrusive, the M40 doesn't affect this route much, crossing it once, and then leaving it behind.

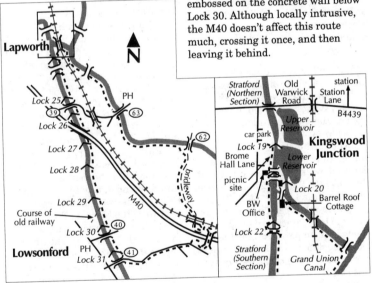

# 49 STRATFORD CANAL

## Lapworth to Wilmcote

*by David Sewell*

### WALK TALK

**Distance** – (1a), 2½ miles; (1b), 6 miles; (2a), 12 miles; (2b) 12 miles; (2c), 13 miles.

**Start at** – Hatton Station Bridge; Grid Ref: SP 224664.

**OS Landranger Maps** – 139, Birmingham and 151, Stratford-upon-Avon.

**Guide** – *Waterways World Guide to the Grand Union Canal (North)*; *Stratford-upon-Avon & Warwick Canals* by Geoff Elwin & Cathleen King.

**Public Transport** – Hourly train service Birmingham–Leaminton calls at Lapworth. Wilmcote/Brearley to Hatton is part of Stratford–Leamington service. No trains on Sundays.

This walk takes the rambler through what was the Forest of Arden, now all but vanished. There are only names left to remind us, such as Hampton-in-Arden and Henley-in-Arden.

If you start on the towpath by Hatton railway station it will be a down hill walk. Hatton is situated at the top of the flight of 21 locks which raise the Grand Union 147ft. These locks were rebuilt and widened in the 1930s to take larger boats and to create local employment. Further along the date can be seen on several stones at the edge of the waterway in this area.

Head north along the towpath to Shrewley Tunnel which is 433 yards long. In the cutting the towpath rises, crosses a lane then enters its own small tunnel to reach the towpath on the other side. To the left you can see and hear the main Birmingham–Paddington railway line. Keep on past Rowington, where there is a Manor House, an interesting church

and a pub with the unusual name of Tom O' the Wood.

At the waterway junction turn left. However, if you continue and go over the next bridge, the footpath leads to the National Trust's moated Manor House of Baddesley Clinton.

But back to the waterway junction where the Kingswood Junction Canal joins the Grand Union with the Stratford-upon-Avon Canal. This important piece of canal is only 220 yards long and when opened in May 1802 reduced the mileage of Black Country coals bound for London.

The next junction is with the Stratford Canal at Lapworth and is a very busy place. Windward House in the village was once owned by the Van Wart Kell family. A nephew of the family, Washington Irving, wrote Rip Van Winkle whilst staying at his uncle's Birmingham home. The canal is often busy, as it is on both the 'Warwickshire Ring' and the 'Avon Ring'. The northern Stratford Canal leads off to the right, with its locks, waterfalls and pools. On one of my walks here I found freshwater mussels. Further up this towpath is the National Trust's property of Packwood House.

To the left is the southern Stratford Canal, now administered by British Waterways, having been in the care of the National Trust for 25 years after restoration. Turn left onto the towpath by Lock 23. The canal follows the stream, which is the boundary of Lapworth Parish. At Lock 25 is Dicks Lane Public Wharf and bridge. Here is a winding hole where long boats can turn, a much modernised Stratford Canal lock keeper's cottage with its distinctive roof, and a split bridge which enables the towrope of boats to pass through the middle of the bridge. In the fields on the other side of the waterway was a Roman tile kiln complex; tiles are still sometimes found in the area.

At Lock 28 a stream enters the canal. Next to this is the remains of the bridge which carried the railway branch line from Rowington Junction to Henley-in-Arden, long since closed. After this is Lowsonford with its pub, the Fleur de Lys, once famous for its home-made steak and kidney pies.

Carry on to the next road bridge, which carries the B4095. Should you wish to shorten your walk, turn left here (2a) and the lanes will take you to Hatton via Claverdon. There is a station at Claverdon which will save you the last mile if you are tired. To the right at the bridge is the Old Crabbe Mill, a pub which provides meals. Further on from this is Henley-in-Arden, with its pubs and shops and a train or bus in to Stratford or Birmingham.

For the next 1½ miles no roads will be crossed until Wootton Wawen. Here there is lots of interest: a boat hiring base, the Navigation pub and the aqueduct which carries the canal over the main A34. The path on this and the next aqueduct are alongside the trough which carries the water.

After crossing the aqueduct the canal bends to the left and the towpath changes sides at the first bridge. Soon the 200 yard long Edstone or Bearley Aqueduct is reached, carrying the canal over both railway and road. The canal was taken over by the railway company in 1856, which used the aqueduct to water its steam locomotives. A pipe with a valve was fitted in the aqueduct and locomotives would stop underneath for their tanks to be filled. There are now only trains on the Birmingham– Stratford line. The Alcester Branch, which also ran underneath, has long been closed.

At the next bridge leave the towpath and take the public footpath on the left until the lane is reached, turn right under the railway bridge (2b) and take the first on the right for Bearley station for the train back to Hatton.

For a longer walk (2c) and another mile with extra interest, carry on along the towpath through attractive countryside to the next road bridge at Wilmcote. To the left is Wilmcote railway station and to the right Mary Arden's House. This was the home of Shakespeare's mother and it is now administered by the Shakespeare Birthplace Trust. It is believed that the kitchen of the house gave Shakespeare the idea for the kitchen scene in *The Merry Wives of Windsor*. There are pubs and shops in the village.

Souvenirs are available from the gift shops of the houses mentioned.

Stout walking shoes will be needed for this walk. In some parts the towpath can be overgrown, so ensure that your arms are protected because of tall nettles and brambles. The towpath is a treaury of wild plants, including alder, meadow sweet, great willow herb, figwort, orange balsam, ash, burdock, goosegrass, elderberry and white campion. Herons have been seen on this stretch and locals feed various wildfowl on the canal.

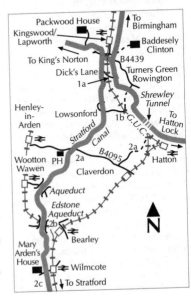

117

# 50 NORFOLK BROADS: RIVER WAVENEY

## Beccles to Geldeston

*by Barry Green*

### WALK TALK

**Distance** – Beccles to Geldeston, 5 miles. Return via Shipmeadow Lock, 4 miles.

**Start at** – St Michael's Church, Beccles; Grid Ref: TM 421904.

**OS Landranger Map** – 134, Norwich & The Broads. OS Tourist Map 11, The Broads; Footpath Map of Beccles by Wilfred George and other local guides obtainable from the Broads Authority Information Centre at Beccles Quay (01502 713196).

**Public Transport** – Trains to Beccles station on the Lowestoft to Ipswich line, 2 hourly in each direction.

Beccles bus station in the old market place is served by several different companies on a variety of routes, including some through Geldeston, Norfolk Bus Information – Freephone 0500 626116.

**Car Parking** – Town centre (pay and display). Beccles Quay and Waveney Meadow Picnic Area off Puddingmoor (free).

The historic town and one time fishing port of Beccles stands on a bluff on the right bank of the river Waveney, dominated by the tower of the Church of St Michael's, which is the starting point of our walk. From the terrace at the west end of the church (or better still from the top of the tower), there is a fine view over the river and adjacent marshes which, 2,000 years ago, lay under the shallow salt waters of the great estuary of Gariensis, towards Geldeston on the rising ground at the other side of the flood plain.

A flight of steps takes us down from the terrace to the street known as Puddingmoor, onto which we turn right and soon come to the old market place. Here, before proceeding down Northgate, it is worth making a short detour down 'The Score', a narrow way leading to the river, which was once used for the movement of fish and other goods between boats and the market.

Along Northgate there are opportunities to explore similar links with the river down Cambridge Score, Railway Score and Tannery Score, before crossing over Bridge Street into Fen Lane. Here the old maltings have been sensitively converted into flats and the bars and restaurants of the Loaves & Fishes free house.

At the junction of Fen Lane with Quayside we bear right past the Broads Authority Information Centre and the general stores, which serve the busy yacht station. Crossing the footbridge over the end of the mooring basin we turn left along the quay heading to reach the river bank. On the opposite bank, just below the 19th century town bridge, the old sawmill chimney stands high over the timber yard of Darby Bros, where the company has traded since 1845. This historic landmark has been threatened with demolition by plans to redevelop the site for housing.

Just downstream again are the basins and yards of Aston Boats and H.E. Hipperson, hire companies.

From the yacht station we follow the riverbank downstream to cross the Waveney on the Beccles bypass road bridge (opened in 1982) and then follow the footpath on the opposite bank of the river back upstream, skirting round the boatyard basin to reach Gillingham Dam Road. Here we turn left and follow the road for a short distance to Darby Bros' yard, where we cross the road and bear right to reach the bank of the river again.

The hard standing for timber and boat trailers hereabouts soon peters out but the footpath remains well defined. On the abutment of the dismantled bridge that once carried the Waveney Valley Railway over the river is the first of the discrete direction signs, pointing the way and proclaiming that the Country Landowners Association welcomes caring walkers.

Flanked by a profusion of willow herb, this quiet pathway, so different from the busy streets on the other side of the water, provides excellent views of the Beccles river frontage. Just past our starting point, the hire base of Arrow Boats and the private yard of Waveney Valley Boats off Puddingmoor are invariably crowded with a miscellany of craft.

At the sharp bend in the river, known as Short's Corner, we turn our backs on Beccles to follow the bank of the meandering river across the marshes towards Geldeston. With little traffic on the river and nothing but quietly grazing cattle on the open marshes, the next three miles provide a taste of the tranquil solitude of broadland at its best.

The profusion and variety of wild flora and fauna, surely sufficient to assuage the appetite of the keenest biologist, provides endless pretext to pause for a closer look.

At the junction of the river with Geldeston Dyke the footpath leaves the river to follow the line of the cut towards the village. Just short of the village the utilitarian concrete bridge, which once carried the Waveney Valley Railway over the dyke, has been bypassed with a cut to provide unrestricted navigation headroom. The multiplicity of crudely painted warnings of 'low bridge', 'danger under water' and advice to 'use the cut' on the already far from attractive bridge exemplify traditional broadland tattiness at its worst – a reminder of the magnitude of the task faced by the Broads Authority in its duty to 'enhance the natural beauty of the Broads'.

Beyond the bridge, quiet well patronised moorings lead to the premises of Rowan Craft Ltd, and on to the village street. Here the 16th century Wherry Inn, with its garden and children's room, where the available refreshments include food and Adnam's real ale, is a convenient place to wait for one of the occasional buses bound for Beccles.

The more energetic may prefer to continue their walk for a further four miles, along the lanes to Shipmeadow Lock and from thence back to Beccles via the well defined footpaths across the marshes on the south side of the river.

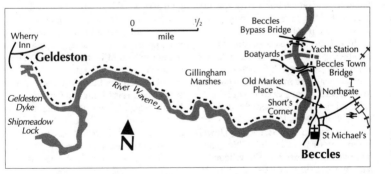

# 51 WELL CREEK

## Upwell and Outwell Circular

*by Barry Green*

**WALK TALK**

**Distance** – 7¹/₂ miles.

**Start at** – St Peter's Church, Upwell; Grid Ref: TF 505027.

**OS Landranger Map** – 143, Ely & Wisbech.

**Guide** – *Nene–Ouse Navigation Link* (Fenland district Council).

*Well Creek – The Continuing Story of a Waterway* (Well Creek Trust, 29 Old Market, Wisbech).

**Public Transport** – Occasional bus service to and from Downham Market and Wisbech.

**Information Centres** – Downham Market Town Hall (01366 387440) and Wisbech Library (01945 583263).

The villages of Upwell and Outwell form one continuous ribbon development astride the old river Nene and Well Creek. They originate from the ancient settlement and port of 'Wella', the seaward end of which became known as 'Out-Wella' and the inland end 'Up-Wella'.

Our walk forms a circuit along roads close to both banks of the navigation. It is possible to start and finish at any point, but an appropriate place is Bridge 11 by St Peter's Church in Upwell.

Here, there is the opportunity to imbibe the wondrous mulled beverage offered by the Norfolk Punch Health Inn. Beyond the inn stands Welle Manor Hall, a rare example of a fortified medival prebendary manor house. Down New Road is the site of the terminus of the Wisbech & Upwell Tramway (dismantled in 1968). The tramway is featured on the village sign by the bridge. St Peter's, like St Clement's in Outwell, is a large and impressive Fenland Church, indicative of the one time prosperity

of the area. Both are of mainly perpendicular architecture with some early English in the towers and built of Barnack stone and Ragstone – brought by water from quarries near Stamford, conveniently situated between the Nene and the Welland.

Leaving the church we take the minor road on the east bank of the old Nene in the dirction of March. After about a mile we cross the river via a footbridge (14) just before the road parts company with the old Nene to follow the course of the old Croft River. The latter is now little more than a ditch but at one time it carried the waters of the upper Great Ouse to join those of the Nene at Upwell.

From the footbridge we continue to follow the old Nene for half a mile to Marmont Priory sluice/lock, built under the Middle Level Act of 1844 to increase the draught of the navigation through Upwell and Outwell. The lock was lengthened in 1997 to allow passage of full length narrowboats.

Having examined the lock we retrace our steps towards Upwell, but stay on the north west bank of the river to follow the navigation through to Outwell. Fine old buildings face each other across the water in the manner of a Dutch village, and conveniently situated mooring stages give access to the banks for visiting craft. There are several opportunities to pause for refreshments along the way; perhaps the most appropriate being the 'Old Mill', the meeting place of the Well Creek Trust.

In Outwell the navigation does a U-turn around St Clement's Church into Well Creek, at what used to be a junction with the Wisbech Canal. The canal was built in the 1790s along the course of the old Well Stream (which had become silted up from the 13th century on), the object being to improve the trading importance of Wisbech in relation to Lynn. However, with no water supply other than from 'putting the tide in' at spring high tides, the canal was sometimes hardly navigable. Its viability was further threatened by the opening in the 1880s of the Wisbech & Upwell Tramway, which was constructed parallel to the canal for most of its length. The tramway brought Outwell a new role as a transhipment centre between the tramway and Fenland lighter, but the canal was formally abandoned in 1926 and subsequently filled in.

However, thanks to the Well Creek Trust, the Creek was restored to navigation in 1975 and a pleasant public open space created round the basin at the old junction. Most of the line of the canal and tramway is still discernible beside the Outwell–Wisbech road and some hundred yards up the road, where a right of way still crosses an old bridge, the coping stones of what was Outwell Lock can still be seen in what is now a back garden.

We cross Bridge 9 to St Clement's Church and continue our walk along the minor road on the south bank of Well Creek. The origins of this ancient waterway, partly man made

on the basis of a natural stream, are obscure. In the 13th century, the estuary at Wisbech became silted up, and the water of the major rivers began to flow eastwards along Well Creek towards King's Lynn. Whether the Creek was dug around this time for drainage or whether it was already in existence as a much older (perhaps Roman) navigation is not certain. By the 14th century, Well Creek was a major trade route between the port of Lynn and the Midlands.

After about one and a half miles we come to Mullicourt aqueduct and sluice, built in 1848 by Ransome & Rapier of Ipswich and unusual in the it enables the then new Middle Level Drain to flow under the much older Well Creek.

Keen walkers may continue along the 'Well Creek Nature Trail' to Nordelph (2 miles) or even to Salters Lode (4 miles), returning to Upwell by one of the few buses. Lesser mortals should retrace their steps to Outwell Church and follow the minor road along the east bank of the Old Nene back to the starting point.

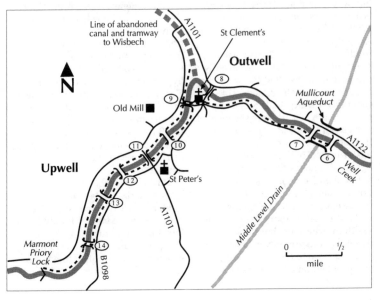

121

# 52 LITTLE OUSE

## Thetford to Brandon

*by Barry Green*

**WALK TALK**

**Distance** – Thetford to Brandon, 9 miles (Santon Downham 6 miles).
**Start at** – Thetford Town Bridge; Grid Ref: TL 868831.
**OS Landranger Map** – 144, Thetford & Breckland. Forestry Commission Guide Map (Thetford Forest Park).
**Public Transport** – Rail: 2 hourly service between Brandon and Thetford. Bus: 2 hourly service along B1107 – very occasionally via Santon Downham (01603 613613).
**Information** – Ancient House, 21 White Hart Street, Thetford (01842 752599). Forestry Commission, Santon Downham IP27 0TJ (01842 810271).

The heathland around Thetford, with its abundance of flints, was settled by early man as far back as the stone age, and the Little Ouse river must have been an important highway in and out of the area long before its first navigation Act of 1669–70. Following the construction of eight staunches between the confluence with the Great Ouse and Thetford, the navigation eventually prospered, but by 1890 the staunches were in poor repair and by 1914 commercial traffic had ceased. For narrowboats and cruisers the head of navigation is now at or just above Brandon Lock, but the river upstream to Thetford is still used by light craft and its course can be followed on foot along the bank through one of the loveliest riverscapes in eastern England.

We start our walk in the centre of Thetford, where the bus station and free car parks are conveniently situated close to the river. A fine watermill stands across the former head of the navigation, downstream of which the attractive iron Town Bridge bears the Thetford coat of arms on one side and the date 1829 on the other.

At one time the land either side of the river above Town Bridge was crowded with industrial buildings which were served by lighters carrying to and from the adjacent wharves. One of the users of the navigation was James Fison, who founded an agricultural import/export business here in 1809, which developed into a major national industry as the Fisons Chemical Company.

Most of the old buildings were demolished in the 1960s when the old town was overwhelmed by a grandiose expansion to accommodate London overspill, but the river frontage is tactfully landscaped, with an unusual tripodal footbridge linking the two banks of the river with Batten Island.

Crossing Bridge Street we take the paved path along the south bank of the river, opposite which the Charles Burrell, museum is housed in the old paintshop of the works that once produced steam boats as well as the famous traction engines.

We proceed under the old (inner) bypass bridge into open parkland. Here, as we walk on the north side of the river, are the ruins of the 12th century priory of St Mary's, for which the Barnack stone used in its construction must have been brought by river from the famous quarries near Stamford.

The bridge of the new (outer) A11 bypass marks the beginning of Thetford Forest which, at 20,000 hectares, is the largest lowland pine forest in the country.

The footpath along the old haling way is generally well defined, if occasionally somewhat rough, and usually dry underfoot. Walking conditions are best between late autumn and spring, when the vegetation has died back. A mile or so into the forest, the site of Middle Staunch is now occupied by a steel sluice but, a mile beyond that, little remains of Turfpool Staunch other than crumbling walls in the riverbank.

A further half mile brings us to an industrial site which from 1853 to 1925 was occupied by 'Fisons Manure and Vitriol works'. Raw materials such as bones, guano and sulphur were brought here by water from King's Lynn and the finished products were sent out by the same means.

Half a mile further on a footbridge over the river marks the site of Croxton Staunch of which there is now little to be seen other than the abutment walls and a few timbers in the bed of the river. The path now becomes less distinct, but conditions

soon improve again after crossing the bed of a small stream (usually dry) that joins the river at Two Mile Bottom.

At Stanton Downham road bridge there is the opportunity for a short detour to the village where the Forestry Commission District headquarters includes an information centre and public toilets, and where there is a small but well stocked post office/stores.

Continuing along the riverbank to Brandon the footpath ends in a small new housing development which connects with the A1065. Those wishing to complete the walk with a visit to Brandon Lock can bear right over the road to a track which follows the river for about ¼ mile downstream.

For public transport back to Thetford the railway station is within sight and the bus stop is in Brandon town centre on the Newmarket road.

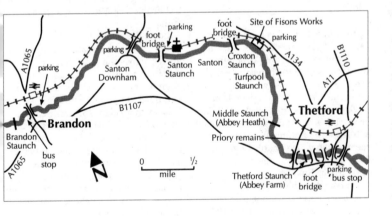

123

# 53 RIVER LARK

## Bury St Edmunds to Lackford

*by Barry Green*

**WALK TALK**

**Distance** – Fornham Wharf to Lackford Bridge, 5½ miles.

**Start at** – Fornham Wharf; Grid Ref: TL 849665.

**OS Landranger Map** – 155, Bury St Edmunds & Sudbury.

**Guide** – Booklet *The Lark Navigation* by D.E. Weston.

**Public Transport** – Occasional buses along A1101 which parallels the river. Details from County Connections, Suffolk County Council, Ipswich IP4 1LZ (01473 265676).

**Information** – Tourist Information Centre, 6 Angel Hill, Bury St Edmunds IP33 1LY (01284 764667). The Visitor Centre, West Stow Country Park IP28 6HE (01284 728718).

The history of navigation of the river Lark dates back at least as far as the early Saxons. Stone from Barnack used in the construction of the 11th century abbey of Bury St Edmunds came by river. The legal navigation dates from an Act of 1699 on the basis of which several artificial cuts, locks and staunches were constructed which enabled lighters from King's Lynn to reach the outskirts of Bury. Subsequently various restorations and improvements were made over the years, the latest as recently as 1948 in a scheme that was never completed.

Today the locks above West Stow are gateless and only small portageable craft can navigate. However, most of the towpath between here and Bury is walkable, much of it having been incorporated into the Lark Valley Path (LVP).

Our walk begins on the outskirts of Bury at the site of Fornham Wharf.

This is located on the east side of the A1101 road some 500 yards north of its junction with the A134, behind the former Dunnell's Maltings of 1851, now a home furnishings store. The basin that was the terminus of the navigation (until 1890 when it was extended by ¾ mile to St Saviour's Wharf), has been filled in and is used as a car park.

To find the start of the LVP we walk back to the A1101, turn right onto it and, just past the nearby garage, turn right again onto the public footpath which runs along the towpath of the old Fornham Cut.

At the junction of the Cut with the river we turn left onto the towpath of the main line, which initially runs past the unattractive backyards of industrial scenery of the Lark Valley Country Club golf course. Here a modern bridge which gives access to the club house marks the site of Lock 2 (Fornham St Martin) which is in ruins.

Beyond the club house two attractive wooden footbridges provide access across the river, but we continue along the west bank to the chamber of Lock 3 (Causeway), which is immediately upstream of Causeway Bridge (13) that carries the B1106 road over the navigation.

Crossing the road we continue to follow the path along the west bank. Thick alder carr now covers the opposite bank and there is an atmosphere of quiet seclusion. At the site of Lock 4 (Ducksluice) we cross a modern bridge over the chamber. The footpath now follows the east bank to Hengrave Bridge (14) which carries a minor road.

Here the LVP diverts away from the river to follow a pleasant, but relatively tortuous, route through Culford village and park to get to Flempton Bridge (15). For walkers wishing to stay with the river the towpath is on the west bank, but it is not maintained. Going is easy to the ruins of Lock 5 (Hensgrave), but for the remainder of the distance past Lock 6 (Chimney Mill) and Lock 7 (Flempton) to Flempton Bridge, conditions vary – easy in winter months when the vegetation has died back but possibly difficult when summer growth is lush. For those wishing to bypass this section the nearby minor road which runs roughly parallel with the river past Chimney Mill to West Stow and Flempton Bridge is a shorter alternative route. (The chamber of Chimney Mill Lock is in excellent condition, having been rebuilt in 1948.)

From Flempton Bridge the LVP follows the towpath along the north bank of the river past the remains of Staunch 2 (West Stow or Boyton), which has a modern accommodation bridge over it, to a small sewage treatment works on the southern edge of the King's Forest. Shortly after the treatment works the LVP turns sharp right into a forest ride, on a short detour to avoid disturbance to the Larkford Wildfowl Reserve established in flooded gravel workings south of the river. The detour also bypasses Lock 8 (Fulling Mill).

The route of the LVP through the conifers is tortuous but it is well signed, and the 1887 pumphouse and chimney of a former sewage works to which it leads are unmistakeable. The pumphouse marks the western boundary of the 125 acre West Stow Country Park. Nearby, a bird hide on the north bank overlooks the river and the wildfowl refuge beyond.

The LVP rejoins the river at Staunch 3 (Lackford or Dullingham). A short distance further along the towpath two small hills can be seen to the right. One is the site of Anglo-Saxon and pre-historic settlement and the other is a landscaped 20th century rubbish tip! A path between the two leads to a reconstruction of an Anglo-Saxon village and a fine visitors' centre, which provides excellent information on the fascinating history of the area.

Continuing along the towpath we pass a cluster of old fruit trees amongst the alder carr, once part of the garden of the lock keeper's cottage that was demolished in 1979. A short distance further on is the site of the unusual Lock 9 (Cherry Ground) which was crescent shaped.

For most of the remaining distance to Lackford Bridge (16) the path runs along a narrow strip of land between the north bank of the river and a pleasantly landscaped flooded gravel pit. Arriving at the bridge, which carries the A1101 road over the river, walkers can find a suitable place to hail a bus to Bury.

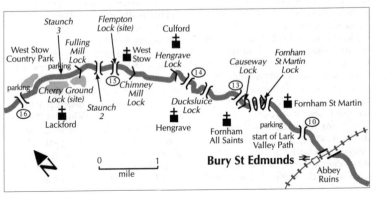

# 54 RIVER AVON

## Stratford-upon-Avon to Marlcliff

*by David Bolton*

### WALK TALK

**Distance** – Stratford-upon-Avon to Marlcliff, 9 miles; Welford, 4 miles.
**Start at** – Stratford Canal Basin; Grid Ref: SP 204549.
**OS Landranger Maps** – 150, Worcester & The Malverns and 151, Stratford.
**Guide** – Stratford District Council free leaflet (Church Street CV37 6HX).
**Public Transport** — Trains to Stratford from Birmingham (via Hatton) or from Leamington Spa (through to London). Midland Red South buses connect with Stagecoach along the route (01788 535555).

As no official towing path ever existed for the Avon navigation, there are all too few stretches of this famous and lovely river easily and officially accessible to walkers. All the more credit, therefore, to Stratford District Council for its efforts in the 1980s at a cost of £6,000 (grant aided by the Countryside Commission) in formally establishing a fascinating, varied route of nine miles between Stratford itself and Bidford-on-Avon.

Sadly, despite all this official backing, there remains a half mile of walking along a fairly busy, though country, road; also much of the waymarked route is along rough, at times extremely muddy, land. The path can be tackled in sections, but there are few places where you will not need stout footwear.

Starting from Bancroft Basin in the heart of Stratford, the intersection between canal and river, you cross the old tramway bridge and walk along the riverside opposite the fine waterfront between the Royal Shakespeare Theatre and Holy Trinity Church which contains Shakespeare's tomb.

Pause to study the unusual top lock of the Upper Avon Navigation Trust with its commemorative plaques to the re-opening in 1974; then by the next bridge a wooden sign denotes the official start of the route.

By the second lock the riverside is left by climbing steps up the steep wooded hill; this turning is not clearly marked so do not repeat my mistake the first time of struggling along the tortuous slippery, fisherman's path.

From above the river, there are attractive views across the racecourse opposite and back to Stratford town, pinpointed by Holy Trinity's spire, as well as across open rolling farmland.

Another former railway bridge is reached; once the Stratford–Cheltenham line it has been converted into a cycle track. It affords the chance of taking a short round walk back into Stratford along the other bank on a public right of way.

For those striding on to Bidford, pass under the railway bridge and turn immediately left, soon afterwards crossing a somewhat rickety footbridge over the river Stour, surging above a weir and around an S-bend.

Along a somewhat flat exposed section, the path is a field away from the river but the beautiful group of trees around Luddington Lock can be seen in the distance before reaching the charming quiet village of Weston.

The river makes a great circuit away to the north as the path takes a short cut through the pretty village of Welford, crossing a busy minor road by the Bell Inn (occasional buses back to Stratford). Boat Lane, leading back to the river by Welford Lock, is a supreme example of a Warwickshire black-and-white thatched house.

The path now follows the line of the river more closely through a series of grazing meadows until, sadly, turning up to the road which has to be taken for ¹/₂ mile into Barton. This is a tiny village of quaint stone buildings perched on the edge of the river and the path returns to the waterside immediately opposite the lock and weir.

Cutting a corner, there is a fine view of Bidford Church standing among stately riverside homes. The ancient narrow bridge of many pointed arches is reached, offering a good choice of refreshment in the smart little town, and transport to Stratford.

It is worth continuing, however, on the same side of the river for another 20 minutes since it is the easiest strolling of the entire walk, offering a good view of Bidford's pleasant waterfront and a scene of much boating activity in the season.

Finally, the walk ends officially at Marlcliff where the river curls right under a steep hillside. The right of way, in fact, continues further along the bank and up Marlcliff Hill but, by now, you will already have had an excellent sample of the Avon's appealing mix of black-and-white historic villages.

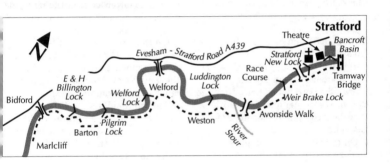

# 55 GRAND UNION CANAL

## Blisworth to Northampton

*by Dennis Needham*

**WALK TALK**
**Distance** – Blisworth Mill to Northampton, 6 miles.
**Start at** – Blisworth Mill Bridge (51); Grid Ref: SP 724534.
**OS Landranger Map** – 152, Northampton & Milton Keynes.
**Guide** – *Waterways World Guide to the Grand Union Canal (North)*.
**Public Transport** – Stagecoach bus service 38 picks up from the stop on bridge 51 (01604 620077).
**Car Parking** – Side streets in Blisworth, very close to the canal.

Join the canal by Blisworth Mill at Bridge 51 and head north. In the days of the Grand Junction Canal Company – and beyond – this was a busy spot. The company once operated a warehouse here. Now the Blisworth Tunnel hire fleet, with their brightly painted boats, are based here.

On the right, a row of quite modern houses push their gardens down to the canal. Candle Bridge (50) takes a minor road over the canal and the village immediately falls behind. The towing path is good, as it will remain for the duration of this walk.

After passing under the electric railway, Gayton Junction hoves into view. There is also a busy new road ahead. This is the A43 Northampton to Oxford road, which once passed through the middle of Blisworth. Now, it has been linked to the M1 at Rothersthorpe services. Much of it is built on the course of an old railway, the abutments of whose bridge remain alongside the canal, close to where it joined the main line.

Bridge 48 is a roving one. It also offers a short choice of route. Which you take depends on your priorities. To follow the towing path, cross to the left bank. Pass the junction and walk to the next bridge. Here, cross again and return to the junction down the other side, turn left and at the first (Arm End) Northampton Arm bridge, cross to the right bank.

If you eschew the first roving bridge, walk to the road and turn right. After only a few yards, the walk returns to the towpath at the aforementioned Northampton Arm bridge. The former is further, but offers a good view of the junction and the buildings of the BW yard, where they once operated an extensive hire fleet. The latter looks at the ugly side of the BW yard and cuts ¼ mile from the walk; take your pick.

On the left is a huge off-line marina, also the base of another hire fleet; so much more desirable than the long linear moorings that mar so much of our canal network.

Beyond Sandlanding Bridge, the canal curves to the right and reveals the first lock on this walk. The first dozen in the Rothersthorpe flight are quite close together as the terrain falls away dramatically into the valley of the river Nene. Opened in 1815, with 17 locks in the 5 miles to Northampton, it gave the town a connection with the industrial Midlands. Prior to this, the Nene, which was made navigable 50 years earlier, was the town's only link with the great world outside, via the North Sea. Trade continued along the canal and its main line, not finishing until the late 1960s.

A decade ago, this was a completely rural backwater, only occasionally used by pleasure boats. The towing path was overgrown and unkempt, the pounds shallow. Now, hedges are carefully laid, pounds are dredged, and a programme of shrub planting alongside the locks has been undertaken. But, a decade ago, there was no A43 . . . Also to be seen on this flight are Oxford-style lift bridges. Although chained open now, they still add an aesthetic dimension that will soon be destroyed as the walk reaches the M1 motorway.

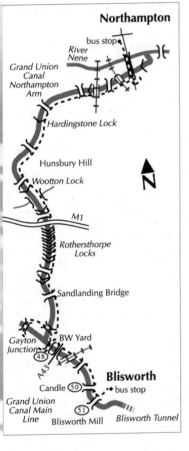

By lock 7, the road is close again. The boundary posts between the two are still the old railway ones. At the M1 crossing, a more graphic illustration of improved architectural techniques would be hard to find. On either side of the motorway are tastefully designed rustic brick bridges carrying the new A43 link. Between is the most grotesque concrete cavern, designed and built in the 1950s, carrying the main road.

After another couple of locks, the canal takes a long sweeping right turn around the base of Hunsbury Hill. The river Nene comes charging in from the left before taking its own left turn just before the canal, to run more or less in company to the town.

Past Lock 16, another electric railway passes overhead with a whole new retail park on the left. Ahead, a huge chimney and modern factory is the centre for Carlsberg lager production in this country. Once, the town's brewer was Phipps until they were taken over by Watneys. Then came the Red Barrel fiasco, and that brewery was demolished.

Just under the next – new – road bridge, a path leads away to the right. Take this, cross back over the river and canal. Turn right at the far side, to walk alongside the left bank of the Nene. The way is soon blocked by another river. Turn left, walking alongside. Ignore the right turn which leads over this river, and continue to the road. Here, turn left, and left again at the huge traffic island. The return bus stop is a few yards along here, close to the gas works.

129

# 56 GRAND UNION CANAL

## Tring Summit

*by David Cragg*

**WALK TALK**

**Distance** –Cheddington station to Tring station, 6 miles.

**Start at** – Cheddington station; Grid Ref: SP 922186.

**OS Landranger Map** – 165, Aylesbury & Leighton Buzzard.

**Guide** – *Waterways World Guide to Grand Union Canal (South)*.

**Public Transport** – Local trains between Milton Keynes and London Euston offer an hourly service between Cheddington and Tring.

**Car Parking** – At either station.

This walk commences at Cheddington station and ends at Tring station. There are regular trains between the start and end points, and since both stations have car parks you can leave your car at which ever end of the walk you wish. The walk is through the countryside on the north side of the Chiltern Hills with the Grand Union Canal climbing up to its summit level near Tring from the valley of the river Ouzel.

Leaving Cheddington station we go east to join the B488, then follow the road south for just over ½ mile to the canal bridge. Join the towpath and walk south towards the hills. We will be following the towpath all the way to Tring cutting with an optional side excursion.

Just round the bend from the bridge you will find the first lock of the walk. This is one of the three Seabrook Locks which are spread out over the next half mile. By the middle lock is a pumphouse in a good state of repair. This once housed one of the 'Northern Engines' – steam engines used to back-pump water past each lock or group of locks between Stoke Hammond and Tring.

The three locks at Seabrook were served by the engine in this pumphouse. The system is now being restored with new pumps.

Beyond the locks a swing bridge is overshadowed by the railway above. At the next road bridge is the Duke of Wellington pub, which also sells sandwiches.

Continuing on the walk, the canal bends away from the railway. Two locks (complete with pumphouse) continue the climb towards the summit. From the locks there is a good view of the railway which reaches its own summit level in Tring cutting overlooked by Pitstone Cement Works. To the north-west Mentmore House can be seen across the fields.

A short way on we come to one of the sights of the walk. We have reached Marsworth where generations of boaters have moored and as a prelude to this most interesting section comes a thatched house in near perfect setting. A short distance beyond the towpath changes sides. On the west bank is the BW Canal Manager's office adjacent to the entrance to the Aylesbury Arm.

As you approach the next bridge you may notice that the towpath arch is rather large. Back in the 19th century the wide locks of the canal were duplicated with narrow locks in an effort to save water. The narrow locks have long since been infilled but the towpath bridge is evidence of the position of the narrow lock entrance.

At the bridge the towpath changes sides once again. The flow of traffic is controlled by lights and every care should be taken when you cross the road.

Continuing our walk along the canal towpath we have reached the bottom lock of the Marsworth Flight. To the right of the canal is Startop's

End Reservoir and further up the flight comes Marsworth Reservoir. There are walks all round the reservoir area and they are popular, as you will notice if you pass this way on a warm weekend.

From the next lock onwards the numbers of other walkers tend to thin out and you can begin to appreciate the flight. Notice how the canal twists and turns between locks never allowing you to see far ahead. This flight was disliked by the old boatmen because of its twists and still causes frustration today.

Halfway up the flight a house is overlooked by a large bank topped by the Wendover Arm. Further along, an overflow channel from the arm passes under the towpath. At the top of the flight is a dry dock and the bridge over the arm.

If you have a few minutes to spare take a short walk down the

Wendover Arm. Within a few yards of the junction the water begins to clear and you will see fish swimming along. The fish always seem to be at their most plentiful near the sewage works on this section. A short way along the arm the canal overlooks the house on the Marsworth Flight below you. Continue to the first bridge, beyond which is the site of Bushell Brothers' yard where wide boats were built for the Grand Union in the 1930s. The yard was (and most of it still is) between the flour mill and the bridge. Return to the junction with the main line.

Back on the main canal we soon reach the BW Bulbourne Depot where lock gates are built. There is a narrow gauge railway to move the (heavy) gates around and you may see some of the gates partly submerged in the canal alongside the depot.

Beyond the next bridge the canal widens before entering the Tring summit cutting. While this cutting is not as spectacular as some of those on the Shropshire Union Canal it does have its own charm and is some $1\frac{1}{2}$ miles long and up to 30ft deep. At one point a pipe pours water into the canal from the massive parallel cutting built for the railway. The canal cutting is a haven for big fish which can sometimes be seen in the shallows on the far bank.

At the second bridge in the cutting (number 135) we leave the canal and walk east along Station Road to Tring station. This is the end of the walk but, if you would, take a last look at the mighty railway cutting ($2\frac{1}{2}$ miles long and 50ft deep) which runs north-west from the station and remember that both this and the canal cutting were built by men with picks and shovels and no modern machinery.

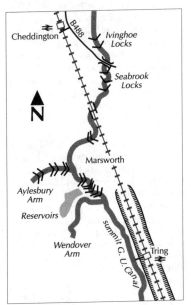

131

# 57 SWANSEA CANAL

## Clydach to Ynysmeudwy

*by Patrick Moss and Julia Edwards*

**WALK TALK**

**Distance** – Clydach to Ynysmeudwy, 5½ miles.

**Start at** – Clydach; Grid Ref: SN 689013.

**OS Landranger Maps** – 159, Swansea & Gower, 160, Brecon Beacons and 170, Vale of Glamorgan.

**Public Transport** – South Wales Transport bus 120. Hourly service Swansea–Clydach–Pontardawe–Ynysmeudwy–Ystalyfera (01792 580580).

**Car Parking** – On-street at Clydach.

Starting from Clydach, find the aqueduct which can be seen to the left of Clydach market, once the Public Hall. Cross the iron and stone footbridge over the canal to the towpath. In this attractive area are stone benches, in keeping with the timeless setting around them, and particularly welcome if this is the end, rather than the start, of your walk.

Take a moment to examine the aqueduct. It is in a style unique to the Swansea Canal, incorporating over-flows which empty directly into the Clydach river below. The canal goes no further towards Swansea and thus the overflows are always running.

Heading north, the scenery is industrial, and the canal overgrown in places, the considerable flow keeping a narrow channel clear. At the first bridge the walker must climb to and cross the main road. Immediately on the far side is Lock 6. Skeletal bottom gates and a winching mechanism remain to operate them, the bridge being too close to allow balance beams. The deep, well-preserved, chamber is of English narrow lock dimensions, unlike locks on other Welsh canals.

The next few hundred yards of

canal are in good condition, but come to an abrupt halt at a council yard. Climb the path and follow it between high walls round the yard. Lock 7 was once on this length and the thunderous roar of water falling into the culvert heralds the restart of the canal. This next length, up to the locks at Trebanos, has been restored for local leisure use. The canal is in cutting up to the bridge under the main road after which Coed-Gwilym park is alongside, where a small exhibition commemorates the canal's history and reopening. A stone monument incorporates one of the Great Western Railway bridge plates, the canal having been sold to the GWR in 1873, for double its construction price.

From here to Trebanos the canal is very scenic, with the river to one side and the other side often wooded. The main Clydach–Pontardawe road is almost alongside, but its presence is unnoticed. The two locks at Trebanos are in an attractive setting, and are shallow, perhaps half the fall of the one in Clydach. A brick bridge crosses the canal between them, completing the genteel scene. Above the locks the canal is once again shallow, weeded and fast-flowing.

On the outskirts of Pontardawe the canal is infilled. Follow the path along the edge of playing fields before passing a large Somerfield Store. At the far end of the car park an underpass takes you under the new road and leads straight to Pontardawe Aqueduct. Similar to the one in Clydach, this is less scenic but more frequently visited, as it lies on the main pedestrian route from the superstore to the town centre.

Immediately beyond the aqueduct is a low bridge practically in the centre of Pontardawe. Cross the road and continue along the canal past the imposing Eglwys Sant Pedr (St Peter's Church) and to an even lower bridge which seems almost to touch the water. There are benches on the towpath here, a suitable halfway resting point. Beyond the bridge the canal is briefly industrial before once again entering attractive countryside. From here a trip boat operates during the summer months. You will pass its predecessor, a scaled-down Swansea Canal boat, as you emerge into the countryside.

The walk continues through the pleasantly wooded valley, incorporating two original canal bridges. The second is very skewed, and has a paddle start mounted in the towpath next to it, which presumably once drained the canal, although there is no trace of a run-off channel. Nearby is a GWR mile post identical to their railway distance markers. Shortly beyond here, the old Cilybebyll Branch ran across the valley floor. The dry bed is easily discernible, despite the trees in it. This branch was the only source of trade this far up the canal this century, although the Swansea Canal carried twice the tonnage of the neighbouring Neath Canal and remained profitable longer than any other south Wales canal.

Continuing north, a flight of two locks is reached. The first lock has

been heavily repaired in blue engineering brick. The upper is as built, with one top paddle, seemingly designed for dwarves, still in place. Both are in remarkably good condition after over one hundred years of disuse. The short length beyond here is picturesque with another stone bridge, reinforced with lengths of old railway track, leading to a tiny aqueduct over the Nant Ddu (Black Stream). Beyond is another flattened bridge and the hamlet of Ynysmeudwy. Go up the hill for car parking, bus stop and pub, noting the pub sign which depicts (inaccurately) the canal at work.

Another half a mile of canal remains intact, although this is a nature reserve and thus there is a much greater sense of exploration. Cross the road in Ynysmeudwy, and find the towpath again behind the brick shelter. This leads to a lock and two solid stone-built bridges which seem lost in the undergrowth. Finally, the path emerges next to the main road near the village of Godre'r-graig, where a lock wall forms an unusual rockery in a garden. The only other surviving feature of the canal is the massive three-arch aqueduct at Ystalyfera, further up the valley and accessible by car or bus.

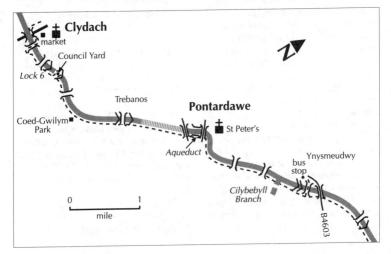

# 58 THAMES & SEVERN CANAL

## Thames Head and the Golden Valley

*by Tony Davis*

### WALK TALK

**Distance** – Kemble station to Stroud station, 13½ miles.

**Start at** – Kemble station; Grid Ref: ST 985975.

**OS Landranger Maps** – 162, Gloucester & Forest of Dean and 163, Cheltenham & Cirencester.

**Guides** – The Cotswold Canals Trust publish 2 booklets of *Walks Around the Cotswold Canals* at £2.95 each + 50p postage from Abberley House, Park Street Cirencester GL7 2BX.

**Public Transport** – Train service is easiest. About hourly, but timings irregular. About 2 hourly on Sundays.

**Car Parking** – At either station; but train access is easy, from London and South Wales, change Swindon; or the Midlands, change Gloucester.

A superb day's stroll in three parts, with a pub between each. This is a 13½ mile walk over the Cotswold escarpment from Kemble to Stroud, or vice versa, the return journey being made by train. The Kemble to Stroud direction is marginally preferable, as it will then be mostly downhill. Let the train take the strain back!

Start from Kemble station in the direction of the old line to Cirencester, turn left, then turn right off a minor road, and you are out of the village on a footpath across a field leading to the infant Thames. After ¼ mile turn left to follow its course across a field. Cross the Fosse Way and the source is about ½ mile further, marked by a plaque. At some times of the year this is quite dry, at others just muddy, but seldom will you find much water along this upper length of our major river.

The line of the old Thames & Severn Canal can now be discerned just on the right following the contours, and the footpath carries on to join it and becomes the towpath. In high summer this can be overgrown, but persevere because it gets easier in the stretch leading up to the Coates Portal of Sapperton Tunnel where you will see the channel lined in concrete, with water in it, this having been done in an attempt to cure leaks in the bed. Just beyond a railway bridge you will come across one of the old roundhouses on the left hand side, quite remote from any other habitation.

Just as you approach the imposing, and beautifully restored, portal of the tunnel, the Tunnel House Inn comes into view on the left hand side. You will only have completed 3 miles, but if it is lunchtime, you will find that they do excellent snacks and it is a good spot for refreshment, set well away from any roads. It was used firstly as a lodging for the tunnel diggers, then for boat crews.

The next stretch takes you over the Cotswold escarpment on footpaths, and one stretch of road, to the Daneway Portal. This part roughly follows the line of the tunnel, whose presence and line can be judged by the spoil heaps from the original diggings. A pleasant path through Hailey Wood is followed over two fields; cross a main road and turn left onto a minor one, to arrive in Sapperton Village, pleasantly laid out at the top of the Golden Valley, of which you will now gain your first glimpse.

Turning right on the road to the village centre, the start of the footpath is a little hard to find, but make for the church, and then double back on yourself down a field aiming for where you think the canal ought to be. You will soon come upon the tunnel mouth, where you can rejoin the towpath and within a short distance arrive at the Daneway Arms, convenient for a drink and another rest as you will by then have covered a further 3 miles.

Admire the beautiful castle-like Daneway Portal of Sapperton Tunnel, recently rescued from its overgrown state by the Cotswold Canals Trust and restored at a cost of £25,000.

The final stretch is delightful, as you slowly descend the Golden Valley, following a well kept towpath, and passing lock after derelict lock, but with many a pound resplendently full of water between. This is a well-wooded stretch, with some delightful houses and cottages, and gently downhill all the way of course.

The railway follows closely, but higher up the valley side, and a main road joins at Chalford. Just here can be seen another roundhouse. The towpath can continue to be followed

very easily to Brimscombe, once a thriving canal port, with warehouses and a basin, much now having been lost. This was the last length to be abandoned, and again much is in water.

From here to Stroud some dredging and lock repair work has been carried out, and you will pass Wallbridge, the interchange basin between the Stroudwater and the Thames & Severn Canal. The last few hundred yards into Stroud are therefore along the banks of the Stroudwater Canal, and the railway station will then be found close by.

Be warned that between Brimscombe and Stroud the canal and towpath have been blocked in places, and you must divert several times, but it is usually not too difficult to find how to regain the line of the waterway.

From Daneway you will have walked a further 7½ miles, and if you have time to walk through the town you will find other places of refreshment before the train journey back, from which you will have a view down to the canal from the steep valley side.

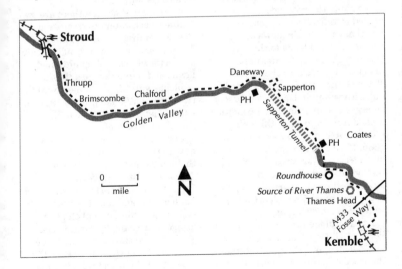

# 59 RIVER THAMES AND OXFORD CANAL

## Oxford Circular

*by Colin Ward*

**WALK TALK**
**Distance** – 5 miles.
**Start at** – Oxford station; Grid Ref: SP 505063.
**OS Landranger Map** – 164, Oxford.
**Guide** – *Waterways World Guide to the Oxford Canal.*
**Public Transport** – Oxford station on the London (Paddington) to Birmingham Line. Frequent City Line buses (01865 785400) connect the ends of the walk at the city centre and Wolvercote.
**Car Parking** – Oxford station (pay) or Wolvecote (free).

This circular walk is unique in that it could also be followed by boat, but you'll see just as much, if not more, on foot.

Oxford railway station is conveniently situated close to both the city's waterways, so from the station follow the main road to the right then right again to join the Thames at Osney Bridge. About 200 yards along the riverside path an arched iron footbridge marks the junction with the Sheepwash Channel, which leads to the Oxford Canal. Continuing straight ahead, along the main channel of the Thames, the path is quite wooded, but with water on both sides. It soon emerges to cross the river by another arched iron footbridge, this one erected, according to its plaque, in 1865. Here also are two boatyards and a sailing club, all at the site of the former Medley Lock and weir, although the only remaining sign is one which proclaims 'Weir Cottage' on a riverside dwelling.

Further along are moorings for the Perch at Binsey, a partly thatched pub reached by a short path through the woods. In the next riverside field

cattle are often grazing, while across the river is the huge flat expanse of Port Meadow with, beyond it, a view of the famous spires of Oxford. Although Port Meadow has been designated as a Site of Special Scientific Interest it is still much used by walkers and horse riders and the hooves of galloping horses would appear to do more damage to the Meadow than the activities of the riverside boatyard.

Just beyond the immaculate Godstow Lock is the ruined Godstow Nunnery, where in the 12th century Rosamund Clifford, mistress of Henry II, had been educated and was later buried. Her name is recalled today by the locally based restaurant boat *Rosamund the Fair*. On the lockside there are some useful information boards, although the map on one of them is a bit mystifying until one realises that North is at the bottom! At Godstow Bridge the route leaves the river for the half-mile walk through the village of Lower Wolvercote to the Oxford Canal.

*En route* to the canal there are two Thames backwaters to be crossed. Beside the first is the well-known Trout Inn, beside the second a picnic area with tables, well maintained lawns and a free car park. In the roadside wall there is a memorial to two airmen killed nearby in 1912, in what must have been one of Britain's first flying accidents.

Beyond the village the canal is next to the main railway line; take the non-footpath side of the road and descend the steps to Wolvercote Lock. The faint-hearted may stay on the footpath and take the road to the right to join the canal at the next bridge. If arriving by car this is a good place to start the walk, there being plenty of space to park, while if one is halfway round the walk the

Plough is a good place to pause for a pint and a bite to eat. It's real ale, and seafood is a speciality. Back on the towing path, and heading for home now, the Oxford to Bicester railway line crosses at an acute angle, and beyond here is a long line of permanently-moored residential boats.

There follows a traditional Oxford Canal lift bridge, wooden construction and rolling on its toothed iron pivot, then the well-known mechanised lift bridge which connects two parts of a canalside factory. After the pleasant gardens of Victorian houses industry returns in the shape of a foundry, whose fierce yellow flames would be more typical of the Birmingham Canal Navigations than the southern end of the Oxford.

Soon the end of the canal appears, with Isis Lock straight ahead and the original terminus of the canal, now the truncated Hythe Bridge Arm, branching off to the left. This arm had been disused for many years when in the early 1980s members of the Oxford Branch of the Inland Waterways Association restored it to navigation. Keep to the path on the right of Isis Lock, through the forest of cow parsley and round the corner to the Sheepwash Channel and the once infamous railway swing bridge. This was too low for boats to pass beneath and it was necessary to arrange for railway staff to come and swing it, but since March 1984 the low level ex-London & North Western Railway tracks have been out of use and the bridge is now permanently open to water traffic. The turning gear with its square spindle is still there but looks a bit meaty for an Oxford Canal windlass! Then it's heads down to pass beneath the main ex-Great Western Railway lines just outside Oxford station, and there's the Thames again. Retrace the outward route, back to the station and the train home.

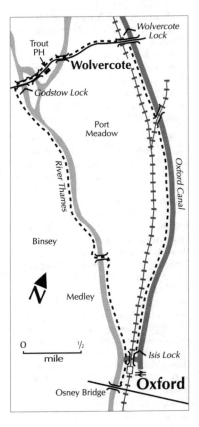

# 60 RIVER THAMES

## Molesey to Walton

*by Louise Mathurin*

**WALK TALK**
**Distance** – Molesey Lock to Walton Bridge, 5 miles.
**Start at** – Molesey Lock; Grid Ref: TO 152686.
**OS Landranger Map** – 176, West London, or *Stanford's Map of the Thames*.
**Public Transport** – Frequent buses from Walton-on-Thames to Hampton Court, service 131.
**Car Parking** – At Molesey Lock, limited space available; if starting walk from Walton Bridge, plenty.

The walk to Walton Bridge starts at Molesey Lock, just upstream from Hampton Court Bridge, where there is parking space for a few cars.

One of the most unusual sights on this river of infinite variety is just above the lock: a genuine Swiss chalet, and so cosmopolitan is the river in the lower reaches that it does not really look out of place. Tagg's island is adjacent. Long ago it had a slightly naughty night-clubbish reputation, but now it is the mooring for some houseboats, which are an excellent advertisement for this type of living. There are some double deckers among these floating palaces and, to add to the domesticity, several have resident cats complete with their own cat-doors.

Some very unattractive, expensive houses have been built on the old racecourse, Hurst Park. A desirable site for a home, no doubt, but aesthetically leaving a lot to be desired, though they seem to be mellowing slightly with the passing years.

On the north (Middlesex) Bank of the river can be seen a small domed temple, called after the actor David Garrick who once lived here. The small Garrick's Ait, and Platt's Ait, a little further upstream, are two tiny islands of little interest.

Riverside homes line the Middlesex Bank most of the way to Walton Bridge, and being so near to London and Kingston-upon-Thames makes them much sought after. Living by the river has become fashionable over the years and therefore prices have risen disproportionately. In my youth the people who lived by the water's edge were considered a little eccentric to say the least!

Some of the reservoirs of the (former) Metropolitan Water Board at Apps Court Station are sited on the left here, and the river bank is edged with trees and bushes, mainly types of willow.

Once, some years ago the boatyard just below Sunbury Locks was the home of the Vjera fleet which, when owned by Horace Clark & Sons in the 1950s, were arguably the smartest hire boats on the Thames. They were painted a pale grey, but now the yard has changed hands and it is no longer possible to hire a cruiser from here.

One of the old College Barges which used to be moored at Oxford now has a new home just by the lock, and is being restored. It is a good thing that some of these historic vessels have been salvaged and will not be lost for ever.

There are two locks at Sunbury, the old and the new, the former rarely if ever used now. There are two lock keeper's houses here also. The old one, built in 1912, is just upstream from the lock. The second one was built about 40 years later.

Just above the lock is the maintenance yard of the former Thames Conservancy, now the Environment Agency. It is a typical working yard, rather untidy, but very interesting to the enthusiast.

By the towpath is the Weir Hotel, a pleasant port of call if it is open! A little further on is the Sports and Leisure Centre. The road past leads to a small shopping centre which is really part of Walton-on-Thames, but is like an isolated village. Continue along the towpath, past the Swan Hotel and the Anglers Inn. A fairly steep road leads down to the very edge of the river, and would present a hazard for unwary imbibers!

A completely new marina has been created from what was an overgrown pond when I was a child, and is fed by a little stream called the Engine River. There is also a chandlery which I remember as a rather shabby boathouse.

There have been several bridges over the Thames at Walton, where Julius Caesar is said to have crossed, and certainly old stakes have been found there dating from his time. The present bridge was put

there in the 1950s, and is one of the ugliest ever, surpassing its predecessor which had many critics, though I was not one of them. Many visitors over the years have thought the present bridge a temporary structure, and that they were the subject of local leg-pulls when told it was not. A far cry from the beautiful ancient structure once painted by Canaletto!

The local council has made a great effort with the land here, the historical Coway (or Cowey) Stakes (or Sale); so ancient is it that the name cannot be agreed. Once just a rough rutted track, it has now been tarmaced, rails erected so cars cannot be driven accidentally or deliberately into the river, and car parks have been constructed.

Those with time and energy to spare can walk on to Weybridge, but we go over the bridge into Walton itself, where there are plenty of places for refreshment while waiting for the frequent bus service to Hampton Court to collect the car.

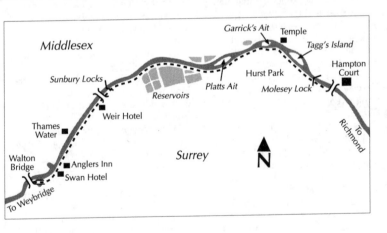

# 61 KENNET & AVON NAVIGATION

## Limpley Stoke to Bath

*by John Cormack*

**WALK TALK**

**Distance** – Limpley Stoke to river Avon, 6½ miles.

**Start at** – Limpley Stoke Bridge; Grid Ref: ST 784613.

**OS Landranger Map** – 172, Bristol & Bath.

**Public Transport** – Train, Bath to Freshford with short walk to Limpley Stoke, about 2 hourly, or Badgerline Bus 265, Bath to Limpley Stoke hourly.

**Car Parking** – Limpley Stoke village.

**Society** – Kennet & Avon Canal Trust, 01380 721279

The unspoilt Avon Valley in 'Somerset and Avon border country' is the setting for this attractive walk along the tranquil western extremity of the restored Kennet & Avon Canal. The lush valley gets steeper and narrower for the first part of the walk, with thick woods on both sides as the river and canal, together with a railway line, are squeezed together, the latter thankfully not destroying the peace of the pleasant setting which is reminiscent of parts of the Cromford Canal in Derbyshire.

The towpath is joined at Limpley Stoke Bridge with views across the valley as the canal approaches the impressive Dundas Aqueduct switching the waterway to the western side of the valley after crossing the river and railway line. The large three-arch stone edifice was built in 1804, and fully restored to use 180 years later. It is deservedly one of the best known features of the canal, serving as a fitting monument to the engineer John Rennie. To see it at its finest, it is well worth making a slight detour off the towpath to view it from the river bank below.

Dundas Wharf is on the other side of the aqueduct – all that remains is a small stone building and an old iron hand-worked crane standing guard over the water. The wharf saw busy times years ago as it was the junction with the Somerset Coal Canal which provided a means of transport for around thirty collieries. Inevitably, competition from the railways meant its demise and the canal was abandoned in 1904. However, the first ¼ mile was restored in the mid 1980s and is used by a boatyard and for moorings. Access is gained via a disused narrow stop lock, now crossed by a lift bridge.

Continuing, there is a turnover bridge almost immediately and the K&A enters a wooded section, hugging the contours of the valley side, affording views across the countryside prior to arriving at Claverton and its famous pumping station situated on the river below. Not much to look at externally, there is a giant undershot waterwheel concealed inside, some 23ft wide and 18ft in diameter, which drives a pump lifting up to 100,000 gallons an hour from the river to the canal some 46ft above. The waterwheel pump is the only one of its kind on British canals, and was designed by John Rennie and operable from 1813. It has been fully restored with viewing on specific 'pumping' weekends. New electric pumps now do the normal day-to-day work.

Open countryside continues, with views of the magnificent Warleigh Manor, now a college, on the opposite side of the valley. Just prior to Holcombe swing bridge there is an attractive canal cottage which offers welcome light refreshments during the summer months. The canal hugs the valley side at this point and then turns west towards Bath before passing through the picturesque village of Bathampton complete with canalside school, and welcoming hostelry. On the opposite bank there is a mix of old canal buildings and modern houses using the cream-coloured Bath stone, the latter sympathetically designed to blend in well with the original dwellings.

The waterway continues on a straight stretch with the glory of Bath's Georgian buildings seen on the skyline, before entering a short tunnel with a fine Adam-style portal, followed by two cast-iron bridges dating from 1800 on the edge of the city's famous Sydney Gardens. A further tunnel carries a road and houses over the canal, among them Cleveland House which was once the old canal company's headquarters. For a short distance the towpath continues on the opposite bank, passing a boatyard and old wharf buildings which have been converted into private houses. The towpath ends abruptly at Sydney Wharf Bridge but can be rejoined on the opposite bank after crossing the busy road.

Back gardens of large Georgian houses flank the canal together with two old grain warehouses, the latter converted to office accommodation, before Lock 13 is encountered – the first one to be seen on this walk. This is the top lock of the Widcombe flight of six, dropping the canal down to join the Avon just below the famous Pulteney Bridge. Locks 8 and 9 have been merged as part of a road-building scheme, making one lock with an awesome fall of over 19ft. Finally, at Bath Lower Lock number seven (the seemingly 'missing' six locks are actually situated on the Avon in the Bristol direction) the canal joins the river, almost opposite Bath railway station which is reached by a convenient footbridge over the river. The bus station is a short distance beyond. The city has much to offer walkers, not least the Roman Museum containing the 18th century pump room and bath, the Royal Crescent and the Abbey.

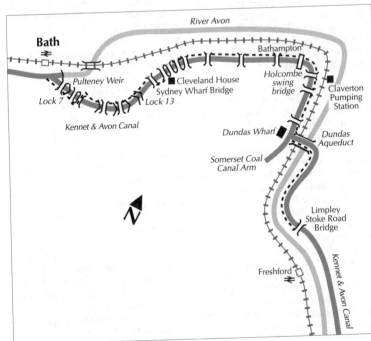

# 62 KENNET & AVON NAVIGATION

## Seend to Devizes

*by Dennis Needham*

**WALK TALK**

**Distance** – Seend Cleeve to Devizes 4 miles – but see return transport details.

**Start at** – Seend Cleeve Wharf; Grid Ref: ST 937614.

**OS Landranger Map** – 173, Swindon & Devizes.

**Public Transport** – Plenty of variety, but little continuity. One service operates on the 3rd Saturday of every month! Badgerline Service 272, Devizes to Bath, calls at the end of Seend Cleeve Lane, about ½ mile from the canal. The Seend Shuttle operates infrequently from Devizes to the Barge, or Badgerline Service 77 runs to Trowbridge along the A361, calling at Seend Cleeve, about ½ mile from the canal. The whole is co-ordinated by Wiltshire Bus (0345 090899) who are very helpful.

**Car Parking** – Roadside space at Seend Cleeve, either side of canal.

**Society** – Kennet & Avon Canal Trust, 01380 721279

A 'must' on any towpath walker's schedule, the Caen Hill flight of locks on the Kennet & Avon Canal is arguably the most stunning on the whole system. The sixteen in tight formation, each with an acre of side pond, storm up the hill in quite spectacular fashion. This is not a long walk, but the exact distance will be decided by which bus you manage to get back. Full details in Walk Talk above.

At Seend Cleeve Wharf the towpath heads east towards Devizes and the first of 32 locks that punctuate progress. This will see the walk finish nearly 260ft higher than the start, another unusual feature of this Waterside Walk. Strange though it may appear to today's eyes, there was an ironworks by this wharf until the start of this century, but finding any trace is not easy today.

The going is good, with a fine firm towing path throughout. The view now is pastoral, rural Wiltshire at its finest. Just over half a mile into the walk, having passed two other locks in the Seend flight, is the second swing bridge and the site of an old coal wharf. Sells Green is on the left, a pretty little village with an excellent pub, The Three Magpies, just up the lane on the main road. An undistinguished aqueduct over Summerham Brook keeps the line moving eastward, but there is nothing very exciting for the next mile or so.

But this is only the calm before the metaphorical storm. Already, the town of Devizes can be picked out on top of the hill, and the first of the Devizes flight of locks arrives. This is at Lower Foxhangers and the new brick building across the way houses pumps which return lockage water up the flight, a £1m scheme that came to fruition in 1996.

The towing path changes sides before the first lock, whilst at the next road bridge the flight starts in earnest. Admire the house just to the right. Once owned by the K&A Company, it was provided for the canal engineer, but was eventually sold and turned into a laundry which drained waste water into the canal making a very soapy pound. It is now privately owned.

Construction of the Caen Hill flight caused a long delay in the original opening of the canal. Boats could use the section to the west by 1801, but it was not until 28th December 1810 that work here was finished and the through route completed. From 1804, in an effort to keep traffic moving, a horse drawn tramway was provided to bypass the flight, freight being trans-shipped at the top and bottom. It was only fitting that when the whole canal was re-opened in 1990 Her Majesty The Queen should perform the ceremony at these locks.

The next thousand yards or so provides that rarity on a Waterside Walk: an uphill section. The locks on this wonderful flight are so close together that there is hardly a respite in the slope. But unless your legs really aren't up to it, please don't be tempted to walk it downhill. Appreciation of the drama of this flight will be much attenuated if you do.

Soon, the locks start to collect names, commemorating the efforts of various worthies without whom the canal would undoubtedly still be unnavigable. The water restrictions concentrate boat movements, so you need to time it carefully if you want to see the locks in use. This is a considerable change from the days when gas lighting was installed on the flight to allow night working. Any locking after dark incurred an extra 1/- (5p) charge. This was to help defray the cost of gas used: supplied by the canal company of course.

The main road passes overhead by Lock 47, at Prison Bridge, and again below the top lock. Here, the towpath moves to the left for a short distance. You should also be getting the steamy sweet smell of a brewery by now. It's across the way just above the top lock, backing onto the canal. Wadworth's has a fine (and justified) reputation locally, and it's not difficult to find one of their establishments.

Now into the start of the Long Pound. It is fifteen miles from here to the next flight of four locks at Wootton Rivers and the summit pound. The canal has now risen to well over 400ft above sea level.

At the next bridge, leave the canal, cross over the bridge and turn left into Couch Lane. Walk down to the main road, straight across into Snuff Street, which leads to Market Square and the bus stops. But before you leave the waterside, spend a little time at Devizes Wharf. Handsomely restored, there are two of the original buildings still standing. One has been converted into a theatre. But perhaps one of the finest buildings on the canal is the old granary. Built in 1810, it is now occupied by the K&A Canal Trust. They have a fine exhibition and shop.

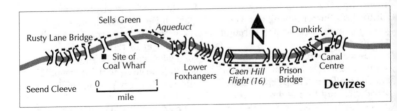

# 63 KENNET & AVON NAVIGATION

## Kintbury to Great Bedwyn

*by Ruth Parry*

**WALK TALK**

**Distance** – Kintbury to Hungerford, 4 miles; Hungerford to Great Bedwyn, 6 miles.

**Start at** – Kintbury Lock; Grid Ref: SU 385671.

**OS Landranger Map** –174, Newbury & Wantage.

**Public Transport** – A regular rail service runs between Great Bedwyn and Kintbury.

**Car Parking** – At Kintbury Lock.

**Society** – Kennet & Avon Canal Trust, 01380 721279.

**Trip Boats** – *The Rose of Hungerford* is operated by the Kennet & Avon Canal Trust (01488 683389). Horse drawn cruises are operated on *Kennet Valley* (01635 44154).

**Crofton Beam Engines** – 01672 851639.

The Kennet & Avon Navigation passes through tranquil countryside with abundant wildlife. Here one may observe Coots in plenty and the shy Little Grebe. Butterflies flutter among the wild flowers, and lizards scurry through the grass.

The canal between Kintbury and Great Bedwyn is justifiably popular among walkers. The towpath is in excellent condition and most locks have benches where you can sit and look at the scenery or boats.

This walk begins at Kintbury where the railway station is next to the lock and a British Waterways public car park is alongside the towpath. From the car park turn right along the towpath, away from the lock.

The Gothic vicarage is passed; its grounds, complete with magnificent

copper beech tree, reach down to the canal. Brunsden Lock and Wire Lock are in pleasant wooded surroundings where you can see wild violets and primroses in springtime. Soon after Wire Lock the towpath enters water meadows with the canal on one side and the river Kennet close by on the other. Dun Mill Lock is on the edge of Hungerford Common where cattle roam freely.

The access to Hungerford station is over the small footbridge by the sanitary station. The town of Hungerford, which has a range of facilities and shops, is best accessed from the town bridge by Hungerford Wharf where the A338 crosses the canal.

Leaving Hungerford, the towpath enters a Nature Reserve with a network of waymarked paths and information boards. The Nature Reserve stretches from the swing bridge by the church to Cobbler's Lock, with its pretty lock cottage.

After Cobbler's Lock the canal enters a more remote and wild area where you may need to push through stinging nettles for a short distance. Picketfield Lock and the three Froxfield locks, overlooked by Oakhill Down, come in quick succession. The charm of the well kept lock at Little Bedwyn is somewhat marred by the railway which is so close that the towpath vibrates at every passage of a 125mph train.

Leaving Little Bedwyn the canal takes a straight course through farmland to Potters Lock and Burnt Mill Lock. Burnt Mill Lock is a favourite gathering place for the cattle which use the balance beam on the opposite side to the towpath as a scratching post, sometimes pushing so hard that they open the gate. Soon the outskirts of Great Bedwyn are seen.

Great Bedwyn wharf is the nearest point to the station, but it is worth continuing along the canal to Church Lock then taking the footpath through the churchyard and back to the village as this road goes past the Great Bedwyn stone museum. Here you can see the fossilised footprint of a dinosaur and press a button to work a large and ancient-looking fountain. There are numerous unusual carved stones with inscriptions both amusing and sad.

Along the canal, Crofton pumping station is only two miles distant. It has two 19th century beam engines, one of which is the oldest of its kind in the world. It is open weekends and Bank Holidays, daily from Easter to the end of September (except Tuesdays) 10.30am to 5pm. The engines are in steam on selected weekends throughout the summer. Unfortunately to see Crofton you would have to walk both ways, returning to Great Bedwyn.

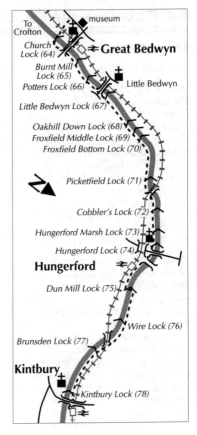

museum
To Crofton
Church Lock (64)
*Great Bedwyn*
*Burnt Mill Lock (65)*
*Potters Lock (66)*
Little Bedwyn
*Little Bedwyn Lock (67)*
*Oakhill Down Lock (68)*
*Froxfield Middle Lock (69)*
*Froxfield Bottom Lock (70)*
*Picketfield Lock (71)*
*Cobbler's Lock (72)*
*Hungerford Marsh Lock (73)*
*Hungerford Lock (74)*
**Hungerford**
*Dun Mill Lock (75)*
*Wire Lock (76)*
*Brunsden Lock (77)*
**Kintbury**
*Kintbury Lock (78)*

# 64 BASINGSTOKE CANAL

## Odiham to The Hatch

*by Dennis Needham*

**WALK TALK**

**Distance** – Odiham to The Hatch, 6 Miles.

**Start at** – The Water Witch, Odiham; Grid Ref: SU 747518.

**OS Landranger Map** – 186, Aldershot & Guildford.

**Public Transport** – Basingstoke to Camberley bus service 200 (not Sundays) operated by Stagecoach Hampshire. Details on 01256 464501.

**Car Parking** – The Water Witch.

This walk takes in the current navigable limit of the Basingstoke Canal, with the perhaps-to-be-restored section. This rolling story is updated regularly in *Waterways World*.

Join the canal from the car park at Colt Hill Bridge, north east of Odiham, turning right. This was once a wharf, and very busy with boats. The Water Witch pub, originally known as The New Inn, replaced The Cricketers. Today, that building is a private house, but the gable wall still carries evidence of its past, advertising 'Crowley & Co Ltd, Alton Ales and Stout and Foreign Spirits'.

The length to Lodge Copse Bridge is generally straight. After that, the course becomes somewhat convoluted. By the bridge in Warnborough, a flight of steps leads to a road. On the right is a filling station offering basic sustenance, and a pub, The Swan, with more substantial food and a good pint.

A lift bridge takes a minor road over the water. This was a swing bridge until 1954 when it was replaced. Approaching the end of the navigable section, right alongside the towing path, are the remains of Odiham Castle. Also known as King John's Castle, it was from here that the king left for Runnymede to set his seal on Magna Carta in June 1215. What is left is listed as an Ancient Monument.

By the castle is a very pretty clear chalk stream arriving from the right into the canal, which widens appreciably at this point. This is a winding hole and marks the western limit of navigation. Ahead is Greywell Tunnel. 1,230 yards long, it was built between 1788 and 1792. The tunnel collapsed in 1932 and, as trade was already moribund, no attempt was made to repair it.

Approaching the mouth, there was once a lock. This was a later addition, to provide a better depth of water from here to the head of navigation in Basingstoke. It was subsequently removed.

Even with the restoration climate existing today, Greywell is a non-starter. The tunnel is of ecological importance with the largest known bat roost in Britain. Due to its constant temperature, lack of draught and damp atmosphere, it is a perfect location and up to 12,000 of these little beasties take advantage of it each year.

Walk up the path and turn left to cross over the mouth of the tunnel. This leads to a road and a junction. Turn right, noting that there is a pub, The Fox & Goose, on the left. Some 40 yards along on the left is a Public Footpath sign. Follow this track gently uphill, swinging to the right as it does so. Then there are two junctions in quick succession. Ignore the first left, a crush, and take the second, a stile.

Walk across this field, keeping close to the left hand fence, towards a house on the skyline. The path then meets another arriving from the left. Turn right across the field, aiming for a large oak tree. Past that tree, start bearing slightly left as the well worn path goes over a crest and down towards another oak tree and into woodland. A metal gate then bars the path, with a wooden gate a couple of yards to the right. Pass through here and down the path.

Some of these turns have had a hand painted white 'Tunnel' sign indicating the way, and the most important one is about half a mile along this path. It is broken, and points right, to a much lesser track. This is a Permissive Footpath, courtesy of the Greywell Hill Estate. Down here is the other end of the tunnel, currently in the process of being excavated. Much of the masonry that was buried for years is now revealed, although there is little evidence of water.

The canal then moves in rapid succession from 'under restoration' to 'disappeared completely' to 'shallow ditch holding water except in high summer'. Eastrop Bridge soars high over the canal as the walk is in a shallow cutting. Across a footbridge, the line turns sharp left, with an old arm to the right. This was the

Brickworks Arm, which served the Hampshire Brick & Tile Company, a *fin de siècle* establishment which provided much of the canal's traffic until 1908.

The towpath condition is variable along this section, but there are ambitious plans to upgrade the whole length of it to a very high standard. Soon, waters end. Walk along what was the canal bed to a road, bear right, effectively continuing to walk in the same direction. Follow this road as far as the motorway, and immediately after, turn left. At the end, a bus stop will be found across the main A30, right outside a garage.

On this road section, there is an option of a couple of left turns which give access to the line followed by the canal. The first one leads to Little Tunnel Bridge, a listed structure.

For the return, alight at the first stop beyond the centre of Odiham and walk back a few yards to turn right into a narrow lane. There is no name to this, but a signpost indicates that the Vine Church, Basingstoke Canal and Water Witch pub are down the road.

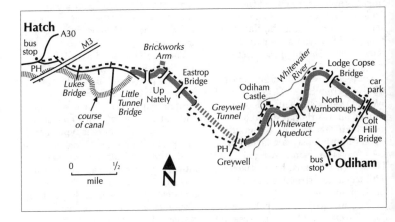

# 65 RIVER WEY

## Guildford to Godalming

*by Louise Mathurin*

**WALK TALK**

**Distance** – Guildford High Street to Godalming Bridge, 4½ miles.

**Start at** – Guildford High Street Bridge; Grid Ref: TQ 995494.

**OS Landranger Map** – 186, Aldershot & Guildford, and *Imray's Map of the Wey* is excellent.

**Guide** – The Inland Waterways Association's guide to the Wey is a very handy size and quite informative.

**Public Transport** – Local trains between Godalming and Guildford usually every half hour. Bus service (271, 272, 292 or 267) approximately every 20 minutes.

**Car Parking** – At each end (quite costly at Guildford).

The beautiful city of Guildford is the county town of Surrey, and one of the most attractive of inland waterways, the river Wey Navigation, runs through it. Prior to 1964 it was privately owned, but Mr Harry Stevens, who owned the part from Guildford to Weybridge, donated his section to the National Trust and four years later the remainder of the navigable section was given.

There is a treadmill crane on the wharf by High Street Bridge which is over 200 years old. This has been re-erected on its original site and is the main feature of the city's riverside walk. Slightly upstream is Mill Mead Lock, past the Yvonne Arnaud Theatre, which must be the theatre with the most attractive setting in the British Isles.

The popular riverside pub, the Jolly Farmer, can be seen across the river, and a footbridge leads over. At the site of St Catherine's Ferry a cliff of sand falls down to the water's edge, and this is the only part where walking is a little difficult. It is a very popular spot for swimming and picnics. The ruin of St Catherine's Chapel is at the top of the hill and is quite easy to reach.

St Catherine's Lock is set in open fields, unlike most of the Wey locks which are surrounded by willows and alders, so typical of the scenery. If there is time, it is possible to deviate slightly to visit Losely House, a beautiful mansion built about 1650. It is open to the public during the summer months and the delicious ice-cream which bears its name is worth sampling!

The railway bridge which crosses a little further on carries the Guildford to Redhill line. The next bend brings Broadford Bridge into view. This is not a particularly attractive bridge, with headroom of only 6ft. The Parrot Inn is a couple of minutes' walk up the road. There is a small factory by the bridge, and a short distance further on is the entrance to the Wey & Arun Canal, which is in the process of restoration. At the moment it is navigable for a couple of hundred yards, to the road bridge and Stonebridge Wharf, where there are moorings.

There are more industrial buildings near Unstead Lock, but they are fairly well hidden by trees.

Past Unstead Lock is a long straight cut with reed-fringed banks, and water meadows lying on either side. The scenery here is typical of this part of Surrey, with rich pasture lands and hayfields, and wooded hills. There is such tranquillity amid this rural scene it is hard to remember that one is in the world of jet planes and nuclear power stations. Understandably, this is a favourite picnic spot.

The few riverside houses blend in with the landscape, as does the delightful Trowers Bridge, a mellow red-brick structure with a flat centre span and semi-circular arches. Past the bridge on the right the open water meadows lead almost all the way to Godalming. The opposite bank is crowded with alders and other trees.

Farncombe Boat House is situated on the left just below Catteshall Lock. It offers a good selection of hire boats, including rowing boats and canoes as well as narrowboats of various sizes. A short walk from the bridge leads to the main road and shops.

Once past the bridge and Catteshall Lock, the scenery continues as before, flat water meadows on one hand and tree-lined banks on the opposite side. Just before Godalming itself is a very sharp bend (it is possible to cut across the field here, if one wishes, and not follow the towpath) and moored here at Godalming Wharf can be found the horse-drawn trip boat, *Iona,* which once operated from Norbury Junction on the Shropshire Union. Some knitwear manufacturers have a factory here.

Godalming Bridge is an attractive structure, as can be expected from this lovely old country town where there are many interesting buildings to be seen. There is also a pleasant riverside walk through well-kept public gardens, just above the bridge.

There are many places in Godalming where one can get refreshments, before catching one of the frequent buses back to Guildford, or, if preferred, there is a very good train service.

This is a short walk, but as the countryside is so beautiful, and there are one or two good stopping places for liquid refreshments, it is possible to take half a day or more over it. If one is feeling very energetic, there is no reason why the return journey should not be walked – things often look so different on the way back.

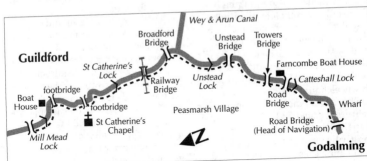

# 66 BUDE CANAL

## Out and Back or Circular

*by Gerry Hollington*

**WALK TALK**

**Distance** – Bude (Lower Wharf) via Canal to Helebridge Wharf, 2 miles; Helebridge Wharf via Coast to Bude (Lower Wharf), 4 miles.
**Start at** – Falcon Bridge, Bude; Grid Ref: SS 207062.
**OS Landranger Map** – 190, Bude & Clovelly.
**Car Parking** – Bude, The Crescent and Lower Wharf and Helebridge Wharf.
**Refreshments** – Pubs and cafés in the Lower Wharf area, Bude.
**Museum** – The Old Forge, Bude Lower Wharf. Open daily in summer, admission 50p adults, 25p children and OAPs (01288 353576).

As a complete change from strenuous cliff-top walking in Cornwall, a stroll along the Bude Canal gives you a chance to take a leisurely journey through history. And, with a good tarmac path nearly all the way, this is a walk which can be enjoyed equally by disabled people in wheelchairs.

The Bude Canal was a remarkable venture, opened 1823–5 and serving a sparsely populated rural area mostly by means of a narrow tub-boat canal; these boats were fitted with wheels which enabled them to traverse the six inclined planes between the different levels of the waterway. Only the lowest two miles were broader, to accommodate barges, and it is these which survive virtually intact today. The tub-boat canal was abandoned in 1891, the broad section in 1960.

The place to start is by Falcon Bridge in Bude. From here, a short walk seawards brings you to the Sea Lock where the canal meets the Atlantic. This lock (which is still in use) measures 116ft by 29ft 6in; it has massive, wooden balance beams, and gates (manually operated) with 'traditional' rack and pinion paddles.

Turning inland along the north-east bank of the basin above the lock, you can see the rails of the 2ft gauge railway by which trucks of sea sand (used to improve the soil and the main *raison d'être* for the canal's construction) were transferred from ships at the lower level of the river Neet to boats on the canal.

Nearby, situated in The Old Forge, is the Bude-Stratton Museum. It is well worth a visit for its old photographs of the canal in its heyday, plus old newspaper cuttings, maps and boat-builders' tools, a half-size model of a tub-boat and a model of one of the inclined planes. And, close to the museum, Mr Sampson's Boat House offers rowing boats and canoes for hire.

Continuing to walk inland along the Lower Wharf you must cross the main road at the Falcon Bridge. The present bridge dates from the 1950s and severely restricts headroom; it replaced a swing bridge. The tarmac path proceeds along the canal's north-east bank and, on the opposite side, you can see an old lifeboat house (built in 1863) and one surviving former warehouse (Granary Court).

The canal soon reaches pleasant, open countryside and, about a quarter of a mile from Falcon Bridge, passes the Bude Marshes Nature Reserve, lying between the canal and the river. At one mile from Bude, you need to look carefully to spot a cast-iron milepost, lurking in the grass on the edge of the path. Shortly afterwards, there is a low, concrete bridge and the towpath crosses to the opposite bank of the canal.

Passing an attractive, partly thatched, farmhouse, you must make your way through a gate before reaching Rodd's Bridge Lock, the first disused barge lock, measuring 63ft by 14ft 7in. Its masonry is in good order and the upper rack and pinion ground paddles are still used to regulate water levels, but it has lost its gates, the upper pair being replaced by a concrete dam. Also in a similar condition a little further along the canal is Whalesborough Lock. This lock now has the benefit of a new bywash channel, constructed by the Waterway Recovery Group in 1996.

The canal then enters a wooded stretch and undergrowth begins to intrude between the towpath and the water's edge. On reaching a flat, concrete farm bridge, the path passes through two gates. The canal soon broadens out into a wide channel, on the far side of which an overflow weir lets water spill into the river Neet. River and canal share the same course for the next few yards until, after crossing a new footbridge over the river Neet, the modern bridge carrying the A39 road is reached and the tranquillity of the waterway is rudely interrupted.

You should cross this busy road with great care and continue along the footpath ahead. This brings you to a stone bridge over the now dry bed of the canal. On the east side of the lane is a grassed picnic area and car park, occupying the canal wharf; the canal alongside is still in water. It was here, at Helebridge, that goods were transhipped from barges to the smaller tub-boats for their journey up an inclined plane to the next level of the canal. At the far end of the wharf, there is a low stone building which once acted as the barge repair workshop and is now used as a museum store. A Bude Canal interpretation board, with a map and details of the canal, is attached to one of the windows. On the opposite side of the basin, there is the house where George Casebourne (the canal engineer, 1832–1876) lived.

Having reached this point, you have a choice. You may retrace your steps to Bude (and would have to with a wheelchair), or you can return via a longer route, signposted at the river Neet footbridge, which takes you to Widemouth and the coast. Whatever you do, remember that Helebridge marks only the start of the fascinating remains of the Bude Canal's tub boat network. A car-borne voyage of discovery inland to Holsworthy, the Tamar Lakes and Launceston awaits intrepid canal explorers.

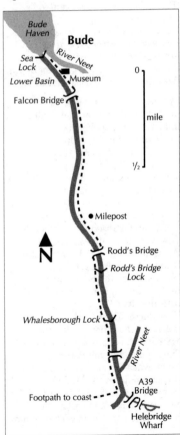

# 67 BRIDGWATER & TAUNTON CANAL

## Bridgwater Circular

*by Gerry Hollington*

**WALK TALK**

**Distance** – 4½ miles.

**Start at** – Bridgwater Docks; Grid Ref: ST 298376.

**OS Landranger Map** – 182, Weston-super-Mare & Bridgwater.

**Public Transport** – The docks are ½ mile from the bus station, 1 mile from the railway station.

**Car Parking** – Ample adjacent to Bridgwater Docks (signposted off A38).

**Refreshments** – Admiral's Quay (PH) at Docks, or town centre services nearby.

**Further Reading** – *Bridgwater Docks & The River Parrett* (Brian Murless); *By Waterway to Taunton* (Tony Haskell). *The Canals of South West England* (Charles Hadfield).

This is a circular walk which combines ancient and modern: industrial archaeology being rejuvenated for the 2000s. Ware's Warehouse epitomises this: it was derelict until just a few years ago but now houses a pub, offices and flats. It forms the centrepiece of the revitalised Bridgwater Docks and is an appropriate starting place.

Although subsequently extended, this Warehouse dates from the Docks' opening in 1841, when the Bridgwater & Taunton Canal was extended into the busy port of Bridgwater from its earlier junction with the river Parrett upstream at Huntworth. The Warehouse overlooks the inner, or non-tidal, basin; on the opposite side used to be The Mump: a prominent mound which was very simply where much of the spoil from the Docks' excavation was tipped, but which has now been removed to allow the construction of housing. There's new housing too next to Ware's Warehouse, in the form of imaginatively designed houses and flats.

Walking around the edge of the Basin past this housing brings you to Newtown Lock, the stop lock where the Bridgwater & Taunton Canal enters the Docks. The lock has been restored and a swing footbridge installed to replace a fixed road bridge. Alongside the lock stands Bowerings Mill, an old but still operating animal feed mill.

Leaving the Mill behind, the canal towpath branches off from the road and enters a shallow cutting, which is crossed by a considerably extended (in 1931) road bridge, complete with deeply scored iron rubbing strips on the arch's corners. Through another bridge and into a deepening cutting, the chatter of birds and chirping of grasshoppers becomes more noticeable than the seemingly distant traffic – and yet the town centre is just a stone's throw away. As the canal grows narrower, you enter the Albert Street cutting, with high, sheer stone walls, a tunnel-like road bridge and, on the far side of this, massive wooden buttresses above your head.

After passing under another bridge, the canal emerges to give views of the Quantocks to the right. On the left, the YMCA has moorings and a slipway and makes good use of the canal. Next door, a new Safeway food store has moorings for shoppers arriving by boat. The broad, well-surfaced path is well-used by walkers and should be followed past three road bridges until the canal draws alongside the river Parrett, the two waterways being separated only by a thin neck of land. Hamp Weir allows canal water to spill into the river and, on the towpath side, you pass close to a flooded clay pit, a reminder of Bridgwater's once flourishing brick industry.

Continuing through another bridge, the canal gradually enters more rural surroundings. A concrete pill box on the far side of the canal stands close to the point, on the outside of the bend, where the original (1827–41) line of the canal headed straight for the Parrett at Huntworth. The Crossway Swing Bridge was the first on the canal to be restored, replacing an older structure which was immobile and blocked canal traffic.

Cross the canal at this point and keep left on the footpath between rows of cottages and close to the site of the original canal basin until you reach the river Parrett. To your right is Somerset Bridge, carrying the railway and constructed in 1904 to replace an earlier, unsuccessful Brunel effort. Steps and a pedestrian walkway take you to the other bank of the river, which can be followed northwards, back towards Bridgwater. This is primarily an industrial area, and hardly scenic. The river, too, is not enhanced by its steep, muddy banks; at low tide, you may see in the mud on the opposite side the skeletal remains of what appears to be a wooden barge.

The footpath joins a busy road which in turn reaches the main A38, which crosses the Parrett by Blake Bridge, opened in 1958. Go straight ahead, alongside the river, to the elegant Town Bridge. This dates from 1883 and replaced a Coalbrookdale designed structure of 1797. Crossing the river by this bridge, you can appreciate the fine buildings on both banks, giving the town an almost East Anglian character.

West Quay is particularly attractive, and a stroll along this brings you to Chandon Bridge (built in 1988) and, next to it, the old Telescopic Bridge. This unusual structure is now fixed and preserved as a footbridge, but it was completed in 1871 to carry a railway over the river and its central section could be slid out of the way of ships. Continuing northwards along the flood bank returns you to the Docks at the entrance locks. Both the larger ship lock and the smaller barge lock are now sealed off from the river, although the barge lock was restored in the hope of giving the Docks a new role as a marina for sea-going vessels. Notice, on the far side of the river, the one bottle kiln which survives from the brickworks' days.

Turning left, the outer, or tidal, basin is surrounded by sluice mechanisms which were used to flush the all-pervading Parrett mud back out into the river. And spanning the passage between the two basins is a restored bascule bridge, which still operates as originally designed although it has been altered several times since 1841. Returning to Ware's Warehouse, there is a plaque on the quayside recording the official re-opening of the restored canal in June 1994.

# 68 TAVISTOCK CANAL

## Tavistock to Lumburn

*by Gerry Hollington*

**WALK TALK**

**Distance** – Tavistock to Lumburn, 3 miles.

**Start at** – Abbey Bridge, Tavistock; Grid Ref: SX 482744.

**OS Landranger Map** – 201, Plymouth & Launceston.

**Public Transport** – Lumburn is served by buses 79 and 185 to Tavistock, operated by Western National (01752 222666).

**Car Parking** – Canal Street, Tavistock.

**Further Reading** – *The Canals of South West England* (Charles Hadfield). *The Tavistock Canal* (Carolyn Hedges).

There can be few canals which were built not just for boats but with water power in mind and even fewer which still act as a source of power. The Tavistock is one such canal: its swiftly flowing waters originally propelled water wheels and today turn hydro-electric turbines.

The abundant source of this water is the river Tavy, from which water is led via sluices just downstream from Tavistock's Abbey Bridge, where this walk starts. The box containing the mechanism stands at the edge of the riverside footpath. The water for the canal immediately disappears under the path and high stone wall, surfacing in the grounds of the Bedford Hotel. To join the canal, continue along this path and turn right through an opening in the wall into the Canal Street public car park – the canal marks the boundary of its opposite side. At this point it is partly hidden by trees and bushes but, turning to the left, an attractive collection of wharf buildings is reached (at the car park

entrance/exit). This part of the canal towpath has been turned into 'Drakes Walk', with a series of interpretation boards.

The canal flows under one of the former canal company buildings (now a Guide Hall), while others are grouped around a cobbled quay. One bears a plaque in memory of John Taylor (1779–1863), the local engineer who designed the canal (it was opened amid great ceremony in 1817). A detour via the road to the Meadowlands Leisure Pool is necessary in order to rejoin the canal at the side of the pool building, just before reaching a low footbridge over the canal. Immediately noticeable is the clarity of the water and its pronounced flow (the canal falls about 4ft in its 4½ miles). This stretch through Jessops Hay looks more like a municipal boating lake (but without the boats) as it passes between neatly manicured lawns and gardens.

Having passed a low modern footbridge and an overflow weir, the canal leaves the park under a stone road bridge, on which a plaque proclaims 'Rebuilt 1903', some 30 years after the canal's closure. After crossing the road, an interpretation board describes the nearby Drake's Statue, unveiled in 1883 and standing in the centre of the roundabout, and the Fitzford Cottages on the far side of the canal, built by the seventh Duke of Bedford.

From this point, vistas of green hillside appear. After curving around school grounds, the canal begins to take on its more characteristic nature: clinging to the hillside and passing through woodland. Just beyond a wooden gate across the path, there is a range of stone farm buildings. Its central, two-storey part has two openings on to the canalside, presumably to facilitate the carriage of agricultural produce. At the far end, a low flat metal bridge spans the cut and the canal opens out to give views to both sides; over the fields on the opposite side can be seen the remains of the disused Tavistock/Bere Alston railway line.

A short distance further along, the canal enters a shallow cutting and is crossed by an arched stone bridge which looks as though it could date from the canal's construction. Close by is another interpretation board, referring to the nearby site of Crowndale Farm, the alleged birthplace of Sir Francis Drake. Beyond this, the canal follows the hillside through more woodland, fortunately screening it from the waste disposal site down in the valley bottom. As it approaches the farm at Shillamill, the canal turns to the right and into the Lumburn Valley, narrowing as it does so to cross an iron aqueduct over a small stream. The towpath passes through a metal gate and gives a marvellous view of the magnificent, disused, Shillamill railway viaduct, soaring on stone arches high above canal and valley.

The sound of rushing water in the Lumburn becomes apparent as the canal continues its parallel, tree-lined course. After a towpath stile, the canal's width is constricted by a stone-sided 'lock', itself crossed by a simple, flat footbridge. Whether a lock ever existed at this point is a matter of conjecture: the evidence on the ground shows a curved recess for a gate (on the towpath side just upstream of the bridge).

Just beyond this point, the canal turns sharp left to aim for the far side of the Lumburn valley. It makes this crossing by means of an impressive, 60ft high embankment, constructed from the spoil excavated from the canal's 2,540-yard Morwell Down Tunnel. Undergrowth

obscures the aqueduct arch through which the river Lumburn pierces the base of the embankment. The twin towpaths are linked at the far end by a low accommodation bridge, beyond which the 'main line' turns left, but this part is private, with no public access.

However, this sharp bend also marks the junction with the Millhill Branch, just two miles long, opened in 1819 and closed in the 1830s. By crossing the bridge, the towpath along the Branch's north side can easily be followed. Although dammed off, the first few yards of the Branch contain water which leaks in from the main line but, above an earthen dam, the bed is dry but discernible. Continuing towards the main road at Lumburn, the canal gradually peters out, until the course of the final few yards to the road is marked only by the trackway along its line. The main road offers a return bus to Tavistock.

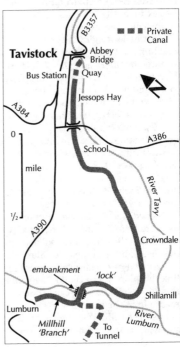

# 69 EXETER SHIP CANAL

## Exeter to Starcross

*by Tony Davis*

**WALK TALK**
**Distance** – Exeter Quay to Starcross station, 7½ miles.
**Start at** – Exeter Quay; Grid Ref: SX 923917.
**OS Landranger Map** –192, Exeter & Sidmouth.
**Public Transport** – Train from Starcross to Exeter St Thomas. Irregular but fairly frequent service 7 days a week.
**Car Parking** – Roads or car parks near St Thomas station.

This is a walk with enough of interest to occupy a whole day if you wish; with a museum at the far end; a stroll along the towpath of an ancient but still operative canal, then alongside a river estuary; and with pubs well recommended for both food and drink at the one-quarter and two-thirds points on the walk.

Start by looking round the buildings of Exeter Quay, many restored by the Exeter Canal & Quay Development Trust over the last few years and now housing traditional crafts and various commercial and recreational activities. This is a thriving area coupled with environmental improvements of all sorts. During the enhancement work the oldest warehouse building in England was uncovered and the original Tudor dock was found. The most attractive building is the renovated Custom House, built of local bricks and slate in 1680, at a time when the canal was widened and improved and the quayside enlarged. A ferry and new pedestrian footbridge link the Quay to the Canal Basin and this can be visited either now or on return from the walk.

Start the walk from the quayside, going downstream alongside the river to Trews Weir, originally constructed in 1560. Just past this, cross to the other side on a pedestrian suspension bridge built by the city council in 1935. Continue across the flood relief channel to join the canal towpath just south of the side lock into the river. Look back to see the quay and basin complex; the merchants' houses behind; and the cathedral on top of the hill. Continue along the canal towpath to the first bridge then cross to the opposite side and keep to this side until the end of the walk.

After another quarter of a mile, you will come to Double Locks, beside which is the Double Locks Hotel, a convenient refreshment stop to sit and contemplate the very long history and development of this unique waterway. The original canal dates from 1564, the city council obtaining an Act of Parliament to build it in order to circumvent the interference to the Port of Exeter occasioned by the Courtenay family, who first built a weir across the river – Countess Weir – then a quay below it at Topsham to take the trade! Widening took place after a further Act of Parliament in 1675, Exeter by then having been made a royal port by Charles II. Further works took place around 1725. It had thus been built, and twice improved, some 50 years before the canal age is reckoned to have begun elsewhere in the country!

Walking southwards from Double Locks one passes the old Exeter bypass, where two lift bridges carry the dual carriageway road over the canal; then under the new high level M5 bridge. Just around the next corner is the Exeter sewage works and, like as not, you will see tied up there the sludge boat which forms the last regular commercial traffic on the canal. Then past the side lock – now disused – into the river opposite Topsham. Here also a pedestrian swing bridge leads to a landing place on the river bank, whence plies a foot ferry across the estuary.

The final mile and a quarter southwards consists of yet another improvement scheme, this one from 1825, to extend the canal to Turf, a deeper part of the Exe estuary and to deepen the channel to 15ft, thus really making it into a ship canal and giving it a final length of five miles. Beside the sea lock at Turf sits the Turf Hotel, approachable only on foot and occupying a quite splendid, isolated location. Apart from other walkers, your companions here are likely to be bird watchers, as the next mile of towpath along the estuary itself is a favoured spot to watch wading birds on the mudflats, avocets, oystercatchers and the like, making a Site of Special Scientific Interest and an estuary of international importance.

This brings us to Powderham church and, as no further progress can be made along the shoreline, the first choice is to continue walking along the secondary road, between the estuary on one side and Powderham Castle and deer park on the other, regaining the greensward a quarter of a mile short of Starcross station, where you walk straight on to the platform. In summer when the park is open, the possibility exists to detour through the parkland itself. Should you then have to wait for a train at Starcross, then there is a chance to visit the Railway Museum by the station, situated in one of ten engine houses built at 3 mile intervals between Exeter and Totnes for I.K. Brunel's South Devon Atmospheric Railway. This improbable sounding venture did exist and all will be revealed by a visit to the museum. On your return to St Thomas station, a walk of just 5 minutes along the river will bring you back to Exeter Quay. As an alternative in summer only, a ferry from Starcross station across the estuary to Exmouth will allow you to return by train along the opposite

bank of the river, to Exeter Central station, with a walk down through the town to the quayside. The former Maritime Museum collection of craft from all over the world has now, sadly, been dispersed but the old warehouses and canal basin, otherwise known as the floating dock are still worth a visit.

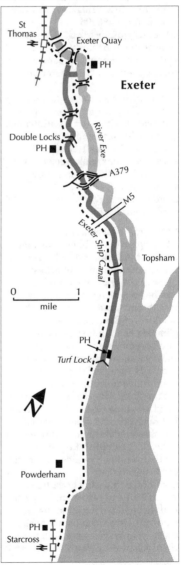

# 70 ITCHEN NAVIGATION

## Winchester to Eastleigh

*by David Foster*

**WALK TALK**

**Distance** – City Bridge, Winchester
to Eastleigh station, 7 miles.

**Start at** – City Bridge, Winchester:
Grid Ref: SU 486296.

**OS Landranger Map** – 185,
Winchester & Basingstoke.

**Public Transport** – Frequent train
services between Winchester and
Eastleigh.

**Car Parking** – *Monday to Saturday.*
Use the Park & Ride service from
Bar End (M3 junction 9 southbound,
junction 10 northbound). Buses drop
you at the Guildhall, close to the
start; after your walk ride back to
your car from Winchester railway
station. (01256 464501).
*Sunday.* Chesil Street car park, 100
yards from City Bridge.

This route largely follows the
towpath of the Itchen Navigation,
built in the 17th century to carry coal
from Southampton to Winchester.
Some of the original eleven locks can
still be seen along the way, now
mostly converted to weirs. On the
outskirts of Eastleigh there are
glimpses of an industrial landscape
briefly reminiscent of northern
waterways; but this quite backwater
is mainly rural walking, with a
comfortable lunchtime stop.

Start from City Bridge, a couple of
hundred yards east of the Guildhall
in Broadway, and close to one of
Winchester's best-known landmarks
– the King Alfred statue. Strike
south down the riverside path beside
the Louisiana pub; cross the river in
front of the imposing brick-built
Wharf Mill and turn right into Wharf
Hill. Keep left along an unmade
road, until a wooden footpath sign
points your way down a path to the
right; follow it to Wharf Bridge, and

re-cross the waterway.

Here was Blackbridge Wharf, head
of the 10½ mile navigation which
linked Winchester to the tidal
portion of the Itchen at Woodmill,
near Southampton. The waterway
was authorised by Act of Parliament
in 1665 and should have been
completed by 1671, though
construction actually dragged on
until about 1710. The Act had
granted the promoters an operating
monopoly, but they seem to have had
little sense of commercial reality.
There were persistent complaints
about 'exorbitant rates' and poor
service, resulting in several further
Acts to widen competition and
regulate traffic.

Turn south at Wharf Bridge, cross
the navigation at Tun Bridge, and
follow the towpath as it squeezes
between the waterway and the
rounded bulk of St Catherine's Hill.
In the 1930s, the new Winchester
bypass was shoe-horned into this
narrow gap, already shared by the
Navigation, the Didcot to
Southampton railway, and the old
Twyford road. For all its faults, the
controversial new motorway over
Twyford Down has allowed this
corridor to be restored as a peaceful
haven for wildlife, walkers and
cyclists. Just beyond the nature
reserve access at Plague Pits valley,
look out for the remains of Catherine
Hill Lock, half hidden in the trees to
your right.

Soon the path dives under an old
brick railway bridge and comes
alongside the M3 motorway. The
navigation has been culverted here,
and walkers follow a pedestrian
route towards Twyford, sharing the
road bridge under the motorway.
Beyond the bridge sanity is restored
as you turn right onto the Itchen
Navigation footpath, opposite the
Hockley Golf Club. Pass the shallow

Compton Lock, and soon you come to Shawford village where the canalside Bridge Hotel makes a pleasant stop; alternatively you can shorten the walk here, and catch a train back to Winchester.

Leave Shawford with the navigation on your left; half a mile further on, near some farm buildings, cross the cut and pick up a farm track, once again signposted as the Itchen Way. The track crosses the waterway just below the derelict College Mead Lock, and you rejoin the towpath at the start of a charming rural section. Look out for the unique wickerwork fishing lodge on the far bank, and pass the fast-flowing section below Brambridge Lock where trout leap out of the water on their way upstream. If you feel peckish again, there's an attractive tea shop in the garden centre, just up the road towards Brambridge.

Beyond the road the towpath continues along the narrow bank separating the navigation on the right, from the river on the left. Soon the river swings away, the railway draws ever closer across the water to the right, and you come to Allbrook Lock. In fact the railway is so close here that, before it was opened in 1839, the railway company rebuilt the lock with a substantial brick chamber. It now houses a 'staircase weir' in place of the original gates.

The navigation, never strongly commercial, outlasted opening of the railway by a mere thirty years. Traffic had always been predominantly one-way, and towards the end income trickled in from a variety of sources; Winchester College, for instance, paid an annual £20 for scholars' bathing rights! The last coal barge unloaded at Blackbridge Wharf in 1869.

Beyond the Allbrook road the navigation turns hard right and

loops under the railway for half a mile. Once more east of the line, the extensive railway sidings at Eastleigh close in across the water; soon the path swings sharp right, and crosses the waterway on the site of Withymead Lock.

With the navigation now on your left, it's plain sailing to Bishopstoke Lock, just north of the B3037. Turn right at the road for the last half mile to Eastleigh station, and trains back to Winchester.

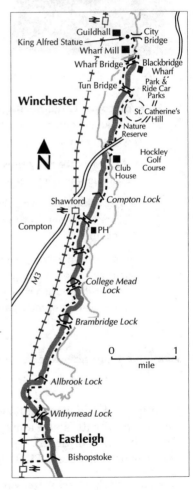

# Waterways
### World

## the *NUMBER ONE* inland waterway magazine

- **enjoy the waterways** – explore a different waterway each month with cruising reports, waterside walks, hire boat reviews, continental cruising

- **discover canal heritage** – waterway histories tell of the boats, people and companies that built and worked the canal system

- **follow waterway news** – in reports which tell you all that is happening on canals and rivers

- **get afloat** – *Waterways World* has more boats for sale or hire every month than any other inland waterway magazine

- **practical advice** – for boat owners and aspiring boat owners *Waterways World* has new and used narrow boat and cruiser reviews, engine developments, the latest equipment, and much more

•

**Available from newsagents, boatyards and on subscription**

•

*Waterways World* also publishes guidebooks to individual canals, canal videos and a map of the inland waterways of Great Britain. For details telephone the WW Reader Services hotline 01283 742970, or write to:

Reader Services, Waterways World, The Well House, High Street, Burton-on-Trent, Staffordshire DE14 1JQ